Michael C

What are we at?
MINISTRY AND PRIESTHOOD
FOR THE THIRD MILLENIUM

THE COLUMBA PRESS
DUBLIN 1992

First edition, 1992, published by
THE COLUMBA PRESS
93 The Rise, Mount Merrion, Blackrock, Co Dublin

ISBN 1 85607 049 2

Cover by Bill Bolger
Origination by The Columba Press
Printed in Ireland by
Colour Books Ltd., Dublin

Contents

*I dedicate this book to
Mom and Dad,
my nephews and nieces,
and the children of Ireland.*

Preface

Father Mick Casey is a very tall person. Perhaps it is that physical characteristic which encourages him to look around and try to see the signs of the times, to reflect and to analyse. This book is a collection of his carefully thought-out reflections on twenty-five years of priestly experience in Dublin. It is not a survey of what is going on in Dublin or elsewhere. It is a story from practice, one person's view, subjective but yet full of reflections on values and indeed on fundamental issues.

When Mick Casey asked me to write a preface for his book on Ministry and Priesthood for the Third Millenium, my initial reaction was to doubt whether a mere Dub could add anything to what a Kerryman has said! I was conscious also of the fact that this book is the result of editing down a much longer text. Yet, perhaps the old lady in Sean McDermott Street had the answer when she told the six-foot-six tall Kerry priest, 'If you fell you'd be half ways home!' What Mick has written takes us half way, points us, invites us, but it doesn't answer all the questions. We are the ones who have to look at the signposts he gives us and make our own decisions if we are to reach home, the answers to the questions.

Anyone who knows Father Mick Casey will agree that words come tumbling out of him like the water of a river tumbling down a mountainside after heavy Spring rain! If one did not know him well, one might assume that the words were mere sounds, symptomatic of the modern torrent emanating from the communications media. This book, on the contrary, is the result of two years of intensive and extensive reflection and analysis of the experience of twenty-five years in Dublin parishes.

The book is enriched, and the contrasts are stimulating, when he includes reflection on pastoral strategies in Latin America and worldwide. We can only benfit by reflecting on what is happening elsewhere.

A book like this can be entertaining, amusing, interesting in its perspectives. It can also be annoying, frustrating and provocative when it questions our long-established assumptions. Mick Casey does not claim to hold out a clear pastoral strategy for the future of the Church in Dublin or indeed in Ireland. He does, however, invite his readers to reflect, to analyse, to question and, I would suggest, above all to look for the priorities in priesthood and in pastoral practice for the future.

This book should challenge us, the readers, theologically, intellectually and emotionally. But above all, it should challenge us to action.

Bishop Des Williams
Auxiliary Bishop of Dublin

Author's Note

I owe many people thanks for their support and encouragement during the research and writing stages of this book. Thanks to all the Caseys, the Hynes and the Spillane cousins, especially Sean and Mary for the 'Study' room. Thanks to the Social Science Research Centre in UCD. Thanks to my critical but supportive research committee: Bishop Des Williams, Noreen O'Shea, Conor Ward, Margaret Quinn, and diocesan colleagues Joe Kelly and Brian Power. Thanks to Des Williams for writing the Preface and thanks to the Dublin Archdiocese for financing the research project and for facilitating every stage of its development. Thanks to Cathy Brennan, typist, Val Bresnihan, research on the Irish monastic Church, Ann Grogan, SSRC, Martin Brennan, transcriber, and Joe Drumgoole, my genial and generous parish priest. Thanks to my USA 'support group': the Casey cousins in New York, the Spillanes in San Francisco, the Klaukes in Chicago, the Flemings in Maryland, the Cunninghams in Pittsburgh, Frs Phil Murnion, New York and Tom Sweetser and Brendan O'Sullivan in Chicago. Finally, thanks to three very creative and committed people, Conor Ward, Mary Whelan and Seán O Boyle who helped me plan the project initially, shape and develop it in between and, finally, see it published.

Mick Casey
11th February 1992
Feast of Our Lady of Lourdes

SECTION I

The Sean McDermott Street Experience

CHAPTER 1

Sean McDermott Street

I: THE PEOPLE

My first day

It was a nice Autumn day. The third of September 1978. I remember it well. It was the first time that I had walked down Sean McDermott Street. All 6' 6' of me. It was going to be my first real meeting with inner city Dublin people in their own place. 'Are you the new priest?' shouted an elderly little woman in her Moore Street accent as she came towards me. 'Yes, Ma'am,' says I, in my broad, rural Kerryese. 'You are very welcome and may you be happy here always,' says she shaking my hand warmly. Then, looking me up and down from head to toe she said, 'If you fell you'd be halfways home!'

That's my first memory of Sean McDermott Street. The Sean McDermott Street that was then the black spot, especially the media black spot, of Dublin. Sean McDermott Street, the home of the infamous 'Bugsy Malones', the notorious teenage gang who had overrun the area and the north inner city of Dublin. 'I'm sorry for you coming to our parish, father,' says the old lady, 'It's no place for a priest. No respect for priests or polis. No respect for property or person. God be with the old days, father.' This was a refrain I would hear time and again for the next few years.

As we moved down the street towards the church, Maggie – that was her name – kept introducing me to everybody. 'Look at the size of him,' she'd say, 'Nelson's Pillar is back!' And all the time, 'He's from Kerry,' a remark which brought out some unprintable comments from the men, and one or two anti-country ones like

11

the one I heard recently: 'O, Jaysus, we've had enough culchies in Dublin! We've had Mick O'Dwyer and Brendan Bowyer, Daniel O'Connell and Daniel O'Donnell...!"

A flotilla of prams

At the front of the convent we met a flotilla of prams with their 'pilots' on the way back from Moore Street and Henry Street. They looked tired. 'He's from Kerry,' says my self-appointed PR person. 'From Kerry? Jaysus, father, why don't you send back that bunch of culchie cops? They're chasing us all day!' – a reference to the fact that some of these traders are still illegal despite 'owning' the streets of Dublin since Molly Malone wheeled her wheelbarrow. The pram, I noted, had replaced its country cousin, the wheelbarrow, as the great multi-purpose, human-propelled, vehicle of transport. Henry Ford had his Model T but the 'Molly Malones' have prams. And they would do more miles to the gallon!

On this first trip down Sean McDermott Street I was fooled for the first time by a Dubliner. It would not be the first or last time that a poor innocent Kerryman was fooled in Dublin. Kerry and Dublin have always been great rivals in Gaelic football and especially since 1975 and 1976 when these two outstanding teams met. In 1978, Dublin were on the way down and Kerry were on the way up. So I was surprised when one of the men I met said, 'Father, I'll put on a bet with you on Sunday.' 'Sure,' says I, being sure of winning, 'What's the bet?' 'Well, if Dublin win you buy me a pint at Kelly's (the local) and if Kerry win I'll put two quid in the poor box.' 'You're on,' says I happily. Kerry won easily but, of course, there was no way of verifying the bet was paid! I didn't realise I had been fooled till two weeks later!

'Lourdes' Parish

Now after my long, slow, informative, sociable, and enjoyable walk from the presbytery to the church (the first of many!), a distance of about three hundred yards, I finally got my first glimpse of the Church of Our Lady of Lourdes, Sean McDermott Street, the home of Matt Talbot, and the church that would become famous one year later as the church where the Pope didn't stop!

The last time that I had seen that church was on one of the first *Radharc** films on RTÉ. I remembered the church well because of the remark of a little local girl as she stood proudly outside her parish church, the Church of Our Lady of Lourdes. 'Our parish is Lourdes Parish and Lourdes in France is called after our parish!' A sense of parish, a sense of place, a sense of humour — characteristics of many inner city Dublin people as I was later to discover.

Apprehensive
Of course, I was apprehensive that first day I walked down Sean McDermott Street. The challenge, the totally different culture to my rural background, the gangs. Would I understand the accent, not to mind the mentality and culture of working-class people? There was also fear of the unknown. But the warmth, the humour, the welcoming kept coming through.

These were not the tough people, the cold-hearted people, that I had been reading about in the newspapers for the previous five years or heard reported on television. Here were the gangs of children with their huge smiles, their sparkling eyes, their fascinating faces ... some with traces of hardness or hurt or maybe suspicion. But they were wonderful children and they all reminded me of some of my more outgoing and roguish nephews and nieces. They all had character and wit and stories. They would have to. They were the children and grandchildren or cousins of the Moore Street traders, the Molly Malones, and the living and dead Brendan Behans of Dublin's inner city.

---

*Religious documentaries produced by a group of Dublin diocesan priests. Won many awards. Showed different faces of the Church in action all over the world and brought new theological awareness to many Irish people.

Problems or victims?

On that very first day in Sean McDermott Street, I formulated my first very important 'thesis': that the media had got it all wrong. And so also had outside society which gets its information and views and prejudices from the media in situations where it has no first-hand information itself. The media had mixed up the problem with the people, they had made the people into the problem. I decided, there and then, that I would spend a lot of my time in Sean McDermott Street as a priest separating the people from the problems. And this would have to be with the people themselves, as well as with the media and public at large. The little old woman had come to believe totally what she read in the papers, that the people of Sean McDermott Street were the problem and were hurting society and, also, damaging the image and life of the capital city. What rubbish! What a load of guilt to have to live with! Life was hard enough without that. I was angry for the first time in Sean McDermott Street. It is bad enough to have to suffer for the sins of rich people – to have to live in poverty and degrading housing conditions at the centre of a thriving and prosperous capital city and in the twenty-sixth richest country in the world. To have to suffer as a result of others' greed and privilege is bad enough. But also to have to bear the guilt people laid upon you by blaming you for being 'poor' and 'delinquent' and 'useless'. What a smart trick!

Alfie Byrne or Gulliver

The huge gang of children, which had swelled as the little old woman and myself progressed slowly, were now pulling out of my coat, my sleeves, my trousers, all wanting to get in a word, to tell me about the parish, or their pet dog, or cat, or goldfish, and the others would ridicule the speaker or his dog or his mother! They would come out with some great repartee so typical of city working-class Dublin culture. We could have been on Moore Street or in one of Behan's plays on the Abbey stage. But we were on a real street in Dublin with real people, who would have to live out their total lives on this street and in this area of downtrodden

Dublin. I was there now too – for better or for worse. Please God, for better.

I felt like Alfie Byrne, the famous Lord Mayor of Dublin, as we moved along, or maybe more correctly Gulliver, as the weight of pulling hands and bodies increased. And I thought, 'these children are not delinquents, these children are not callous, mean, cold-hearted. These children are warm, loving, innocent. They are just children hoping, dreaming – with their future in the hands of Irish society. They are not 'problems', they are not delinquents. They are victims – victims of birth, of poverty, of the sins of society … and then I heard a voice saying from within me, 'Watch that anger, Mick. Enjoy the present. Lavelle, Lemass, Brady, Murphy and yourself are a good new team of priests. Ye'll have a go at it! Give it a lash, as Mick Doyle, the Irish Rugby coach, would say.'

Recurring questions

Recurring questions started to simmer and make their presence felt on this very first 'field trip' in Sean McDermott Street: Are the people problems or victims? Is poverty a virtue or a vice? Where does the Church stand? What are the schools doing? What is the meaning of education in this area? Why is the area so poor? Why do the well-off do this to poor people? Do they realise what they are doing? What the f... am I doing here?! The last was the most recurring question during many of my eight years in Sean McDermott Street.

A people described

What are the chief characteristics of inner city Dublin people? Easy going? Laid back? Industrious? Callous? Caring? Cute? The people of almost every county in Ireland would be seen to have different dominant characteristics. Here is how our team of priests working in Sean McDermott Street described the people's main characteristics one year later:

The heart of Dublin

Peter Lemass, the leader of our parish team, wrote as follows in a parish fundraising brochure: 'If the parish of Our Lady of Lourdes, Sean McDermott Street, has its problems, it also has its strengths. The greatest of these is the quality of the people who live here. Living in the centre of Dublin, they are the very heart of the city. A few months ago, a group of the priests who work here, fed-up at the adverse publicity the area was getting, decided to list what we had found as the good qualities of the area.

Here is what we came up with:

Compassion: We have seen and ourselves experienced a marvellous fellow-feeling for people who suffer. The people in this area must be among the best funeral-goers in the world. And there is a real identity with and sympathy for the bereaved. Death is faced with honesty and courage, maybe because people know they can depend on the sympathy and support of neighbours. People in hospital are visited, the sick are prayed for. Old people are kept at home, even when there are not too many spare spaces in a flat. The granny is sent to St Mary's in the Park only when she is so ill that, even with the help of the district nurse, the family simply can't cope.

Neighbourliness: Outsiders remember Foley Street and Corporation Place for the starkness of the accommodation. Those who lived there remember the deep sense of extended family that existed there. 'You were never short of a bag of sugar or a few spoonfuls of tea,' the old timers will tell you. Much of that neighbourly tradition has survived. It is considered a disgrace if someone is taken to hospital alone in the ambulance. It is taken for granted that a neighbour will drop everything and comfort the invalid *en route*, and that another will mind the house while she is away. Because the families are big, there are cousins everywhere, so the natural family easily extends to the community. Most of the people who live in the area belong to families who have had a home here for decades. These families were good neighbours back in their grannies' time. They still are.

Generosity: You see it in the children, when they get money, or

16

sweets. They never hoard. It seems an invariable rule that what you have, you share. It is a lovely quality. At a party or a wedding you won't be allowed put your hand in your pocket. Families will double up to make way for a homeless child. Members of the Simon Community, who have a hostel here, find a more welcoming atmosphere in this area than anywhere else.

Celebration: The people in this area love to laugh, to sing, to dance, to listen to music. At the wedding the speeches are mercifully short, so that the table can be pushed away and the music, the real business of the evening, can begin.

And you won't get away with just letting the hired musicians play. Christy has to give his well-known favourite, and Biddy her speciality. Everyone will know the chorus and help her out, especially at one of the monthly socials for old folk or at weddings, christenings, Confirmation, First Communion. Dressing up is very important. If possible the children have a new outfit for Christmas, Easter, June, and Halloween. The parade of children at First Communion or Confirmation would do Carnaby Street proud.

Living in the here and now: This can have its difficult side, as when bride and groom come to the wedding breakfast without any clear idea of where they are going to live when the ceremony is over. But it can also be a marvellous strength. Today's tragedies are tomorrow's memories. Life moves on here. People don't have any time for morbid ruminations over past agonies. There may have been horrendous anguish at yesterday's funeral, but today there are mouths to feed, children to be dressed, and a house to be kept. Psychiatrists must wish some of their clients had the ability to put sorrows behind them that the people of the inner city have. But then inner city people have had a lot of practice at it.

Trust in God: The favourite prayer here is, 'Sacred Heart of Jesus, I place all my trust in thee.' That prayer is lived. There isn't the same trust in white-coated scientists, specialists, or experts that there might be elsewhere. There isn't the same trust in ten-year plans, or government interventions, or duplicated forms, that there is elsewhere. You might say that people here trust God because there is no one else to trust. That would be an exaggeration. Better, they trust God because they have experienced that when there is no one else.

Gospel Values

So there it is: compassion, neighbourliness, generosity, hospitality, celebration, living in the here and now, trust in God. It is not a bad list. When you compare it to the charter Jesus set his followers in the Sermon on the Mount, you find a remarkable number of similarities. Dubliners have got used to looking at the people of Sean McDermott Street with curiosity, or horror, or pity. Is it now time to look on them with admiration too?[1]

Peter Lemass's picture of the people of Sean McDermott Street could be seen as slightly romantic and over-idealistic. It may be, slightly. Nevertheless, these qualities do exist in great quantities among Dublin working class people.

II: THE PLACE

Sean McDermott Street is imprinted indelibly on my soul, as indelibly as the 'character' or 'mark' of baptism and ordination, or the 'mark' of an Irish Catholic upbringing. My sojourn, in this, the heartland of Dublin's north inner city, was one of the great experiences of my life, a moving and chastening experience, an eye- and heart-opener. It was an epic experience in every sense, one that challenged my life's meanings and propositions, one that also challenged many sociological and symbolic paradigms. It was an experience above all that went beneath the surface of institutional and propositional religion and living, to touch base at the core of religion, relationships, ministry, meaning and life. For a pagan or a priest such an experience must inevitably lead to adoration or alienation. Where did it lead me? And where did it lead the people of Sean McDermott Street?

Geographical location

Sean McDermott Street is located just round the corner from the Gresham Hotel at the top of Dublin's main street, O'Connell Street. On its west side is Mountjoy Square with its many Georgian houses, once the homes of Dublin's rich and well-to-do. On the east is the port and docks – the dockland which was the main provider of jobs, and therefore, family and community support for centuries.

On the northside is Croke Park, the national headquarters of the GAA; Clonliffe College, Dublin's Diocesan Seminary; Archbishop's House, and Dublin's famous landmark, The Five Lamps.

Sean McDermott Street itself is a small area, a half mile long by a half mile wide. History is all around it with the G.P.O., the Custom House, O'Connell Street (the Larkin, Parnell and O'Connell monuments), The Abbey Theatre, the Pro-Cathedral, the Gresham Hotel, Croke Park, Liberty Hall, Belvedere College, Mountjoy Prison, all within a mile radius of Matt Talbot's resting place, in Our Lady of Lourdes Church, Sean McDermott Street.

Monto and Strumpet City

The chief characteristic of Sean McDermott Street and the north inner city, besides its location, is that it has been the home of Dublin's northside working-class people for many generations. Like most inner city areas, it is poor and looks poor – despite the beautiful new houses built in the early 1980s. Before that it was a mass of mostly ugly, run-down tenement houses and flats located in Gardiner Street, Summerhill, Gloucester Diamond, The 'Monto', Foley Street, Rutland Street, Buckingham Street, Liberty House, Railway Street and Sean McDermott Street. It had changed little since the poverty days of the twenties, thirties and forties. A local joke, which was true in fact, was that no sets had to be made for the production for the film *Strumpet City* in the 1970s though it was about this area of Dublin around 1913. The area and tenements hadn't changed. 'We left our own behind,' said Billy Comiskey, a Labour Lord Mayor of Dublin and a great Dubliner.

He said this with great sadness when he opened a new park at Liberty House, Railway Street in 1981, because he was so aware of the anomaly and the shamefulness of such great poverty in the midst of so much wealth and prosperity right at the heart of our capital city in the prosperous Ireland of the 1970s and 80s. Big business had always been the cuckoo in the nest of the Dublin working-class. James Connolly and Jim Larkin would tell you that. Matt Talbot would. Molly Malone would. Sean O'Casey would. Today, the street traders and Tony Gregory would tell you the same. So would I and the rest of the priests' team.

A context for ministry
We are looking at the location, nature and history of the place (and its people) in order to throw light, later on, on the encounter between us, the team of priests, and the area (people and place). A way of life or an encounter can be changed radically depending on where it happens – on a busy street, in a desert, a war zone, a concentration camp, in prison, in a luxury hotel, in a rural or urban setting, in a rich or poor area. Depending on the location and circumstances, the encounter will be different, not necessarily better or worse.

As well as place or location, the history of a place and its people will also influence later encounters. In this case, the encounter of the people of Sean McDermott Street, being a poor but highly historic part of Dublin, with the representatives of a large, high-powered middle-class organisation called the Dublin Archdiocese, is most interesting, surprising in outcome and very enlightening.

Location and Culture
The Parish of Our Lady of Lourdes, situated in the north inner city of Dublin, *'is* the north inner city,' its inhabitants would say. With a great sense of pride and a great sense of place the old people would tell you that they and their ancestors have been here for a thousand years and more – before Brian Boru was a boy in short trousers! 'We're still here,' said Florrie Cunningham in a recent

RTÉ/Channel 4 documentary on Dublin and its inner city (1989). With a twinkle in her eye, and with great dignity, she reminded the viewers that she and her ancestor Molly Malone were an integral part of Dublin and, in a sense, 'owned' Dublin until the multinationals and the money moguls came to sweep away their heritage and way of life. 'We're still here,' was also a statement of defiance by a true Dubliner that they would not easily give up their city or their way of life as a person-first, non-commercial-orientated, caring people. Money moguls and multinationals may come and go, planners will plan, priests and police will pass through, the weather may change but the Liffey and ourselves will still be here, seemed to me to be the sentiments expressed by Florrie in that television documentary.

My experience is that whoever passes through this place, and lingers for a while, will never be the same again.

III: THE PRIESTS

The novel, *Strumpet City*, had shown three priests playing different roles in this area in 1913. Like them, the priest today in this area is challenged to preach and live the gospel of Christ and, with the people, to identify the pro-kingdom or gospel values and forces in the area. As in 1913, he must also fight against anything that de-humanises or denies the people a chance to live full human lives as individuals and as a community.

The priests of today experience success and failure, joy and sorrow, disillusionment and fulfilment just as the priests in *Strumpet City* did. Like them, the priests of today are the designated leaders of the parish or Christian community, and the people accept or reject them as their predecessors in *Strumpet City* did – but mostly accept them.

Our newly-appointed priests team, like any other team, was made up of individuals. Like the priests in *Strumpet City*, each member had his own history, upbringing, prejudices, assumptions and life experiences. All of these made each of us what he is and who he is. Who we are, what we are, where we are, all influence our perceptions, our interactions, our reactions and the living out of the roles we play in any given situation.

The finger of God
Here is a cameo picture of the five priests as we were in August 1978:

Mick Casey: 6′ 6′. Ordained 1965. A country person. Diploma in Social Science. Warm-hearted. Third parish appointment.

Having just finished a two years Masters degree in community development and pastoral planning at the University of Toronto in Canada, I headed north, not to Alaska, but to Nova Scotia. There, at the University of St Francis Xavier in Antigonish, I spent the next two weeks at a conference on the Cooperative Movement. The title was 'Beyond the Economic'. It dealt with the clash of the economic with the social needs of people, or profit versus people.

I made lots of friends at this conference, and of course we sang all the Irish songs at the final party – *Danny Boy, Galway Bay, Does Your Mother Come From Ireland?* and *Molly Malone*. Little did I know then that I would be getting to know every street she walked in a short few weeks. The Holy Spirit and Archbishop Dermot Ryan, who had an SOS out for me, knew it though!

Paul Lavelle: 5′ 7′. Educated at St Gerard's, Bray, and Castleknock College. A Dublin city person. A business manager. Late vocation. Ordained 1972. Sean McDermott Street was his first parish.

Paul Lavelle was relaxing on the campus of Notre Dame University in Indiana where he had spent the previous year studying urban living and pastoral ministry. He was feeling satisfied having been renewed by the year's sabbatical from his previous five years working in Sean McDermott Street, and was glad that he had asked Archbishop Ryan to allow him go and study and get a better understanding of ministry in an urban setting. He had availed of the rich experience and learning in the Institute for Pastoral and Social Ministry, Notre Dame, the institute which was to do the unique and famous study of parish in the USA, the largest and most in-depth study of parish ever done worldwide. He also felt that he had made some very valuable contacts in Chicago, especially with Mgr Jack Egan, the legendary priest of Chicago diocese, who had linked social action with spirituality and the gospel. He also liked the approach of Fr Leo Mahon, who is credited with being one of the founding influences of Basic Christian Communities. In Notre Dame he met Paul White, a final year accountancy student who was to come and work voluntarily in Sean McDermott Street for two years. Altogether, a very worthwhile sabbatical. Now Paul was glad to be returning to Sean McDermott Street with fresh ideas and renewed spirit.

Frank Brady SJ: A Jesuit. A free spirit. Loves his bicycle. Secondary school teacher. Country person. First parish appointment.

Frank Brady has been enjoying the flats in Sean McDermott Street during the summer. Peter McVerry, himself and the other Jesuits are glad of the change from teaching and academic life. The people are so warm-hearted. Summerhill is agog with children hanging out of balconies and bannisters on the stairs, the women hanging out the washing at the windows, and regailing people below with stories and laughter, and the men at the doorways talking horses and politics and cursing the 'Corpo' and the 'motorway' (which the Corporation is trying to build through the area).

But it's not all joy. The rats in the basement are getting bigger and bolder. Some of them have already shown that they do not agree with our capitalist class structure of upstairs, downstairs! The brazen ones are coming upstairs. The toilets on the stairways stink. The gangs are getting dangerous, the teenagers volatile, unpredictable and mean. Violence is boiling up inside. 'Too long a sacrifice turns the heart into stone.' Yeats was right.

Frank feels his flatmate, Peter McVerry, hit the nail on the head when he wrote for *Intercom*, November 1978: 'The environment here produces what I call a confinement of spirits. Confinement of spirit – to me it means you're hemmed in the whole time, not just

23

physically but psychologically and spiritually. Life is depressing here. That depression becomes part of you so that you don't even notice that you are depressed. The first time I came up those stairs I got a sort of a sinking feeling. The second time it's much less and the third time I was used to it.'

And Peter goes on: 'Do I see this as a scandal in the Christ community? Of course it is. The people here are victims of a society in an Ireland that provides a large measure of comfort and security for the majority.'[2]

'Dead on, Peter,' says Frank. But who outside gives a damn? The politicians preach, the Church sends pastorals, the priests pontificate, the Corpo prevaricates, and the media moguls make news and money washing the laundry of suffering humanity in public. And Frank thinks to himself, 'Is there anybody goin' with a titter o' compassion?'

Christopher Murphy CSSR: A Galwayman. An Irish-speaker. Very droll wit. Redemptorist retreat-giver in Scotland, Ireland, and England in the fifties and sixties.

Christy Murphy was in the parish now for more than a year. He was enjoying the change from the itinerant type of lifestyle of mission and retreat work. It was a chance to put down roots for a while. The wit of this community of Sean McDermott Street sharpened his own wit. He was very struck by the great warmth of the people. He did a lot of house-to-house visitation so he saw how much the elderly were hurt and frightened by the violence and the mindless vandalism of the Bugsy Malones. He saw a great need for more prayer, atonement and the help of Our Lady. He would concretise these ideas in practice by praying the rosary with families, consecrating their homes to the Sacred Heart an enrolling them in the Brown Scapular. Christy looked forward to Peter Lemass becoming Administrator. He liked his *Radharc* programmes and his retreats to priests. The parish needed prayer and Our Lady and the intercession of Matt Talbot.

Peter Lemass: 5' 6' and a bit. Great sense of humour. City person.

Founder member of *Radharc*. Diocesan Press officer. Ordained 1957. Writer. A modern day prophet.

Peter Lemass was apprehensive. Would he survive? Would he fail? He was putting himself on the line. Not just his reputation, which he didn't care too much about. Peter had been giving priests' retreats for the past few years where he challenged priests and bishops with the gospel imperatives and the lifestyle of the master, the Fisherman of Galillee. He had been criticising the Church and priests about their lifestyle and their lack of commitment to the elimination of poverty. As Diocesan Press Officer, he had been strong on the same message. Now his 'speechifying' was being put on the line.

Peter was also happy. He had won his ongoing battle with his great friend and protagonist, Archbishop Dermot Ryan, to allow him to work in the inner city. It was great to be going to work in the inner city. 'Dubs' would come up trumps if given half a chance. Peter was a 'Dub' and he loved the 'Dubs'. He loved their forthrightness and honesty and innate goodness and humanity. And he hated poverty.

Peter was a doer. He couldn't wait to get started. He had his team, and he liked it. Paul Lavelle, with a good knowledge and love of the people, and strong business background; Mick Casey, a bit over-idealistic but very enthusiastic and lots of community development skills; Frank Brady, with his heart in the right place, already forming a strong link with the other Jesuits, Michael Sweetman and Peter McVerry, in Summerhill; and finally, Christy Murphy, an older Redemptorist priest who would enjoy the maintenance aspect of the parish work and allow the others freedom to be 'missionary' and mobile.

Notes
1.   Peter Lemass, *Lourdes Parish*, Dublin 1979.
2.   Peter McVerry SJ, 'Our Fourth World in *Intercom*, Catholic Communications Institute of Ireland, Dublin, November 1978.

CHAPTER 2

Developing a Christian Response in a Deprived Community

When we, the five priests, were appointed in August 1978, our general intention was to run a good parish or, in theological terms, to make a Christian response to the situation. What shape that response would take could only emerge with time. We would have to get to know the situation and the people first.

1. Hard times

There was a lot happening in the inner city at the time. The local residents were blocking the streets because of the housing conditions and the de-tenanting plans of Dublin Corporation. The Bugsy Malone gang was running riot. This gang of young people, aged between fourteen and sixteen years, consisted of about five leaders, thirty to fifty active members, and about two hundred followers or admirers among the local teenage population of approximately two thousand. At this time, the gang was out of control, robbing local elderly people as well as cars, garages and, reputedly, banks. The Church was under siege, literally and metaphorically, with the parish priest's name scrawled on the walls of the Church as an enemy of the gangs. And all was on the national media on a daily basis. There was no need for a national film studio. It was all happening on location and for real in inner city Dublin.

These were very hard times for the people of Sean McDermott Street and the whole north inner city. And indeed for the priests. All were being viewed and judged by the national judges and jury. Everyone had a solution or at least a view, usually harsh. Everybody blamed the people. Some people said it was good enough for them. What more did they deserve? No control, no sense of responsibility. Wrecking schools, wrecking churches, wrecking public property. How the local people, especially the elderly and the parents cringed with every photo, every article, every condemnation. Nobody outside the area seemed to realise that the delinquent gangs were only 2% of the people, or less. Yet all the people of the area were being tarred with the same brush.

By the summer of the 1978, Sean McDermott Street was in many ways a bruised, battered and broken community. The community was on its knees, for the first time since the 1913 Lock-Out. 'What can you do when your own have turned against you?' the old people would lament.

No miracle workers
It was into that situation in Sean McDermott Street that the five of us priests were catapulted. And we were no miracle workers, no Robin Hoods, no Mother Teresas or Oscar Romeros or Martin Luther Kings. The 'priests team', as we saw ourselves, would have to address these hurting problems and their causes, since they were affecting the lives of everybody in the parish. What we would do we didn't yet know. We knew that some very good priests had gone before us in the parish, so that would be a bonus. We knew that the faith of the older Dublin people would be a bonus. We knew that there were some very active and committed local leaders. But we also knew that the Church in Dublin, as elsewhere, was beginning to arrive later and more out of breath – that the old Church structure and mentality was having difficulty coping with the new reality of 1970s and 80s Ireland.

The role of the Church
Peter McVerry SJ who, with some other Jesuits, had moved into the decrepit and decaying tenement flats in Summerhill and Sean McDermott Street in 1972, wrote:

'When we first came there was a strong sense of local community. No one, for example, would steal from anyone else in this area. But in the past six years, we have seen almost a complete breakdown in confidence and trust take place before our eyes.'[1]

In that article, written in August 1978, Peter McVerry outlined the dire poverty, the overcrowding, the substandard housing, the officially neglected and decaying centre of the city of Dublin. He also elucidated the results of the poverty and official neglect – depression, apathy, alienation, and internalised and externalised violence.

Peter concludes his sad but incisive and challenging article by making a call to the Church leadership, at diocesan and parish level, to tackle the apathy, poverty and alienation in a new and challenging way. Under the heading, *Let's tackle apathy*, Peter says: 'I don't want to see the Church as another pressure group trying to get better housing, better education, and employment. I don't think that that is the function of the Church, and in the long-term is often counter-productive. I would like to see the Church involved in creating a community which has the confidence to stand on its own two feet, the confidence to demand its own rights and to demand rights for others in the community.'[2]

Peter then outlines the steps of community-building:
(1) Awareness.
(2) People-building.
(3) Skills-training.
(4) Political and social action.

He continues: 'I would like to see the Church develop a pastoral plan for an area like this, based on the real needs of people. Such a plan, in my view, would concentrate on community develop-ment.'[3]

Peter concludes his article with the prophetic words: 'A team con-sisting of priests, nuns and lay people, who were deliberately try-ing to implement a community development programme, could begin to work wonders.'[4]

During the summer of 1978, Archbishop Dermot Ryan must have been thinking on the same lines – not working wonders, but set-ting up a team. He sent in the nucleus of such a team in August 1978 for ministry in Sean McDermott Street.

2. The early days

What the priests tried to do, and I emphasise *tried*, at the very beginning, can now be summarised on reflection, under the following nine headings. They were not as clear to us then as they are now:

(1) Openness/listening
We had an open-house presbytery; we tried to be a 'listening Church' as a pre-requisite to a good teaching or pastoral Church.

(2) Relating/dialoguing/confrontation
We went out to meet the 'area', to dialogue, to challenge, to confront and to be confronted.

(3) Needs assessment
(i)   We tried to assess of the needs of the people and the area;
(ii)   We also did an assessment of the parish structure and priorities in order to become a more effective instrument of evangelisation and pastoral care.

(4) Formulation of policy, priorities and plans
This was a major area of activity and energy-investment on our part. On the policy and priority level, we made a major shift from a *maintenance* Church, to a *mission* or *outreach* Church with all its mistakes, risks, failures, excitement, fulfilment. On a personal level, I made a lot of input at this policy and planning level with regard to models of evangelisation and models of parish; models of community development, models of alternative education.

(5) Implementation (What? Why? and How?)
We took initiatives at the Church and community level: integrating Church and community, spiritual and social, evangelisation and community development. In chapters 3 and 4, I will describe some of the major initiatives.

(6) Participation
We went for the maximum involvement. In community development and evangelisation terms, this is a slower and more mistake-prone process of achieving tasks but it is quicker in developing

people. We were trying to bring alive and make real, very fundamental goals of the gospel and community development.

(7) Community-building

We tried to identify and build upon the positive aspects of the
people, the community, the situation – to transform the image of
Sean McDermott Street both within and outside the community
and to rejuvenate the spirit and dignity of the people.

(8) Evaluation

We had an annual review and evaluation of the work for one or
two weeks in places like Kiltegan, Gort Muire, or Killnacrott. We
also began to build in mini-reviews or mini-evaluations at the
parish meetings, e.g. one month on liturgy, another on education
and training, another on youth needs.

(9) The local Church

We wanted the people of the parish to see themselves as the
Church because we knew that we, as priests, were just passing
through and that the local Church has to take, and be given, responsibility for being Church. We saw that we were also the
Church, full-time ministers of the Church, but we weren't altogether clear on the theology of Church and how exactly to work
out roles and relationships in practice. We also saw that there was
a difference between the local community (everybody living in
the area) and the local Church (people who were part of the
Church activities or wanted to be identified with the parish) but
again we were not very clear.

3. Our first meeting

While recognising how essential it would be to get the people's
own views of their needs and aspirations as individuals and as a
community, and how best we could serve them, we saw that it
would be important, initially, to come together as a group of
priests and see where each of the five of us was coming from with
regard to assumptions, theologies, skills, hopes and aspirations.

At our first meeting:

(i)   We shared our visions of the Church and parish and examined how the people and ourselves might make that a reality in the area.

(ii) We outlined our individual skills and aptitudes and discussed how they might contribute to the development of the parish based on a People of God model of Church.

Individual visions and priorities

Peter Lemass

Peter had two overall priorities with which we all concurred:

1. To build a caring and worshipping Christian community.
2. Uplift and dignity for the people.

His priorities to make these happen were:

a. A homely and open house, the presbytery.

Firstly, he set out to make it suitable for community living for us priests – to create togetherness and privacy. Secondly, he decided to make it an open house, with hospitality and openness a priority. Essential would be a good cook who would be open and welcoming. In fact Dolly, our housekeeper and a local woman, became one of the key people in developing a caring, hospitable and community spirit in the parish. The 'open house' played, I believe, a most significant part in the success of the parish. Everybody came to the house; everybody felt welcomed; and Dolly felt part of the team mission and ministry, not just in the meal ministry.

b. Prayer and the Bible

Peter gave a lead, with prayer as a very important emphasis. He had an oratory/prayer room built in the presbytery, done beautifully and simply by Sr Souziq, a French nun working with the Travellers in Ireland. Peter was a person of prayer and deep but simple spirituality and very Bible-centred – two vitally important areas to be retrieved and redeveloped in the role and life of the secular priest for today and tomorrow. Of course, some of us were too much into activity to make huge use of the oratory.

Paul Lavelle
Paul's priorities for the parish were:
1. Suffer with / *com-passio*
Being with the people in their suffering and struggles and getting involved with that.
2. Ministry and priesthood
'Working out the meaning of ministry and priesthood in Sean McDermott Street today.'
3. Administration and Communication
Getting efficient administration and communication going is '... the key to a lot of success. A parish office with a full-time secretary is a necessity,' said Paul. We all agreed. Where is the money to come from though? Eventually the money was procured and this allowed us to employ first Doreen and then Mary, who contributed greatly to the support of the team and the organisation of the parish.
4. Youth and unemployment
'The main targets were the Bugsy Malones and prisoners. Counter unemployment by starting projects.
5. Liturgy
Working at the liturgy, making it relevant, adopting it to a working-class milieu.

Mick Casey
1. Gospel alive
Bringing the gospel alive in the area and in the people's lives – taking the Church to the people and the streets, making justice live.
2. Community development
Looking at values and ideologies, structures and forces at work in the area; putting community development into practice. Using a 'development model' as a team. Making Vatican II operational – a 'People of God' model of Church; democracy – giving people charge of their own lives and destiny, or at least a say.
3. Planning
Steps: needs assessment; policy making; priorities; implementa-

tion; evaluation. I had seen the value of planning during my two years at the University of Toronto and I had studied some of its theory and practice.

4. Education

'For liberation' – today's jargon! Making it happen, or letting it happen in formal and especially in informal situations. Education is wider than schooling. Community education through projects, sport, personal development programmes. Use of Freire model – in other words more than '4 x 2' – between the four walls of the school and the two covers of a book.

5. Liturgy

Linking liturgy and life, worship and service.

Frank Brady SJ

Frank had been living in Summerhill prior to the formation of the team and was appointed parish chaplain to form a link between the Jesuits and the parish. His priorities were:

1. Respect culture

To respect, understand and build on the culture of the area. The annual outdoor Stations of the Cross on Good Friday were initiated by Frank from the custom of the people carrying the coffin from the house to the Church by groups of men in procession.

2. Being with the people

The value of spending a lot of time with the people – in their homes, around the flats to get to know them, to know their needs, their suffering and so that they can really get to know you, the priest.

3. Developing community skills

Developing the 'Summerhill presence' – with the drop-in centre, craft centre and 'priesting' elements to it.

4. Co-operation.

Reaching out to other groups working in the area, and cooperating with them where possible, e.g. Tenants' Associations, Community Council, Eastern Health Board workers, etc.

Christopher Murphy CSSR

Fr Christy had a background of giving missions and retreats. This was his first full-time parish experience. His priorities were:

1. Doctrine

To preach the good news and the truths of the faith.

2. Family visitation and prayer

To visit the homes of the people, take an interest in the families and bless them. To promote family prayer in the parish.

3. Team support

To do back-up and support work for the rest of the team.

Fr Christy said of his role: 'I didn't see social works of any kind as my objective. I sought only to enable people to carry out their religious obligations of offering Mass, of receiving the sacraments, of prayer, of discharging the duties of their station in life and of neighbourliness.'

4. The team's belief and approach [7]

The overall approach of our priests team was based on the Vatican II model of Church, which predicated a cooperative, Christian community development type process.

Vatican II model of Church

We tried to promote the People of God model of Church, where all have different gifts and responsibilities, where no one has all of the truth and everyone has a little of the truth, where all the baptised have a say in their own destiny. From the beginning, we went for 'mission' rather than 'maintenance'. Since the traditional parish only dealt, in the main, with the 'practisers' (15%), we felt we had to change the structure of the parish and build an 'outreach' Church. Our main emphasis in practice was on housing, employment, skills training, relevant education and liturgy, and working with, rather than for, the people.

Christian community development

What we were really about was Christian community development from the ground up, and starting with basic human and community needs. We believed that the gospel could have great relevance and should have. We believed that the gospel could help change the situation in Sean McDermott Street a little. We believed that the gospel had been over privatised in Irish Catholicism, that it needed to be brought out to the streets, to the marketplace, to the heart of society and people's lives. That's where Christ brought it to in the first place – that's what the incarnation was about. He changed a priesthood which had been Church-based, cultic primarily, to one which was community-based. He also gave ministry and responsibility back to the people.

The priest: a different role?

We were aware that some people, both in the parish and outside, would say that our emphasis was all wrong, that we were 'social workers', not 'priests'; that the job of the priest and the Church is not about politics and economics and public morality and society, but about the Mass and confessions and devotions and 'spiritual' things. There is a great need for clarification and dialogue for us, priests and laity, about the relationship between 'public' and 'private' Christianity. We also need to clarify the role of the priest and the laity in the Church and in the world. I hope to clarify some of these issues in later chapters.

Conclusion

On reflection, I see that our being Christians, and being priests (ministers of the gospel of Christ), made us view the situation in Sean McDermott Street in a particular way. These factors also influenced how we acted. One's image of God, one's image of people and one's beliefs decide to a large extent how one responds to, or approaches, a situation. As leaders in the parish, the priest's team were attempting to make a Christ-ian response, in an imperfect way but nevertheless, a Christian response, in the Sean McDermott Street area. In chapters 3 and 4 we will see some of the effects of this Christian response and the response of the people, both as explicitly Christian and as people who might have had no explicit 'religious' motivation or allegiance.

Notes
1.   Peter McVerry SJ, 'Our Fourth World' in *Intercom*, Catholic
      Communications Institute of Ireland, Dublin, November
      1978.
2.   Ibid.
3.   Ibid.
4.   Ibid.

CHAPTER 3

Parish, People, Projects

When I set out to write up what we did in Sean McDermott Street, I felt I could do it with ten to fifteen concrete examples of what we did. For example, we set up a Parish Development Committee, a Craft Centre, Youth Training Programmes, opened a Daycare Centre, sent people on theology courses. It would be like describing how a building contractor built a block of flats: bought the site, got planning permission, cleared site, put in foundations, completed building, put it on the market, sold it, moved on – end of story!

But another parallel story could be written about the building of the same block of flats, or of a parish community – the human story, e.g. the contractor, who he was, his family, his company, its problems, the planning permission, how it was got, the red tape, the costs, the experience of building, the morale of the workers, the smog, the weather, the tensions on site. This approach to storytelling is what keeps *Dallas* going, and keeps lots of writers and film-makers in jobs. It's the human story behind the outward reality. The building of any parish or any community involved both realities, one more visible, tangible, more quantifiable, the other less tangible but equally real. When I started writing this chapter first, I was writing only the concrete, quantitative things. But then it dawned on me that there are deeper realities like human and community dynamics, the feelings and prejudices, the clashes of theologies and traditions, the conflicts of roles and personalities.

So, I have tried to take cognisance of both levels, the quantitative and the qualitative, the presenting realities and the deeper ones.

3 Ps

On reflection, I now realise that we, the priests' team, were engaged in three separate but related activities in Sean McDermott Street:

1. Parish Development.
2. People Development.
3. Project Development.

All three were part of our interpretation of what being priests in Sean McDermott Street was about. We engaged in all three in our role as priests. All three were a legitimate, and indeed necessary part of our vision of evangelisation in inner city Dublin in the 1970s and 80s. The role of the priest and the role of evangelisation, as we saw it, and practised it, was about full human development and therefore, full community development. It was about all aspects of the people's lives: personal, social, spiritual, economic, political, and about their culture, their history and the environment.

Questions

Lots of issues and questions arose during our work: The role of the priest? The role of the gospel? The meaning of evangelisation, care of people versus care of 'souls'? What is 'pastoral' care today? What is the role of the Church versus that of statutory bodies? Working with the Church-going people (15-20%) and/or working with the whole area? What is a parishioner? Everybody living in the parish area? People who do not believe in God or do not want to have anything to do with the Church or the Parish? Just the people who are committed to the Church and Parish? All of these are a very vital area of clarification and decision for pastoral work in the future.

1. Parish development

We, the priests' team, looked at the parish as it was and then tried to change it to be responsive to the needs of the people and the gospel. Pope Paul VI, in his famous apostolic letter, *Evangelisation*

Today, said 'The axis of evangelisation is faithfulness to the gospel and faithfulness to people.'[1]

Firstly, and most importantly, we tried to change the parish's vision of itself, or its self-understanding, from that of priests being really seen as the Church, with the people being the 'objects', recipients and helpers. We tried to change it to all the people being the parish with responsibility for it (for themselves), its governance, and its outreach (mission). What we tried to do for the parish was what Vatican II did for the Catholic Church – changed its self-understanding.[2] We tried to change the perception of what parish is and the reality by preaching and by dialogue, but most of all by the practice of partnership in ministry and action. This was a very slow process, primarily because of tradition and suspicion.

Most importantly, we changed the structure and focus of the parish from just dealing with the 15% to being open to all the people and the issues of the area. This was an attempt to make the parish a living, caring organism for all the people.

In trying to make the parish more responsive to the needs of the gospel and the needs of the people (my two basic criteria), we were always trying to be creative and innovative, to get the childrento understand the gospel and teaching of the Church better, to make the liturgy more meaningful, to bring the imperatives and vision of the gospel to bear on issues like unemployment, access to education, the injustices caused by the rich people of Dublin and Ireland. Here are some of the various initiatives we were involved in to bring the gospel alive and to meet local needs:

Liturgy
    The annual outdoor Stations of the Cross on Good Friday;
    dramatisations at the children's Mass;
    slide tape presentation of the homily on a monthly basis.

Work/Training
    youth employment schemes;

craft centre;
youth employment action group.

Education
alternative primary school;
women's personal development groups;
voluntary grinds for all second level students.

Justice
picketing and marching with street traders;
international conference on peace and poverty;
statements on housing, unemployment, drugs.

Maintenance and pastoral care
As well as trying to be innovative and making the gospel and religion more relevant in the people's lives, we did all the things
that traditionally are part of being a parish: baptisms, marriages,
funerals, Masses, sermons, home visitations, hospital and prison
visitation, parish fundraising, folk group, school visitation, First
Communion, Confirmation, school management.

2. People development

Over the eight years, the priests team, together with the Parish
Development Committee, engaged in a large amount of personal
and community development in the area. Personal development
aims at at full human development, or as Pope Paul VI called it,
'integral humanism,' the development of the whole person,
physical, psychological, emotional and spiritual.[3] This personal
development varied from skills-training in the Craft Centre to
leadership-training in youth employment schemes; from peer
ministry in the Folk Group or Youth Services to assuming parish
leadership in the Parish Development Committee. Personal
development and full human development ran through all our
youth services and parish programmes and was not too far
beneath the surface in anything we did. Neither was community
development. We saw community development as a natural

extension of personal development and full human development, and *vice versa*. In fact, after working for three years at multiple temporary Youth Employment Schemes (30+), Paul Lavelle, Frank Brady and myself saw that the most important and most needed effect of them was personal development – not manual skills or literacy skills, though vital, but the personal development that occurred through the acquisition of the other skills and the experience of working with others in a group.

A sense of dignity
I have no doubt that the most important thing we did in our time in Sean McDermott Street was to contribute, in some small way, towards giving the young people especially a sense of dignity, a sense of pride, a belief in themselves and in their ability to do things for themselves.

Local leadership
When we arrived in 1978, there was already a very dynamic and active group of community leaders, mostly local, who were asserting themselves and their leadership. Larry Whelan, Peg Byrne, Mick Rafferty, Tony Gregory, Fergus McCabe, Tessie McMahon, Noel Boland, Maureen Grant and others had formed themselves into the North Central Community Council (NCCC) in 1975, representing the twelve tenant groups in the north inner city. They were taking responsibility for who they were and they were asserting the rights of the local communities. They were also, rightly in my view, putting blame where it lay – on rich people in Ireland, on big business, on national and city decision-makers, and on the Church – though I didn't like it much when that involved me!

However, many of the people saw themselves, and their area, as failures, as almost a blot on the face of the capital city. The people, like most poor people, tended to blame themselves for being 'failures'; for failing the education system rather than it failing them by being irrelevant or unfair and loaded against them; for failing society and the country by producing delinquent and wayward children rather than the unjust and unequal and 'delinquent' national society producing them. An important learning for me in 1981 concerned the criteria for delinquency. If five criteria are present – low income, unemployment, poor housing, irrelevant education, poor environment – there will be delinquency.[4] This will happen in Sean McDermott Street or Foxrock or Dublin 6! One must separate structural and environmental causes from personal causes. Many of the people blamed themselves for being unemployed,unemployable, for being 'spongers' on society almost.

Certainly, 'successful' society never failed to tell the people of the inner city of their failure, especially via the media. Experts and leaders were, and are, forever pontificating on the problems of poor people, or offering them advice and solutions to their problem, without ever having experienced the savage and debilitating effects of real poverty, or without ever having walked the road of powerlessness, hopelessness and destitution. Or indeed without giving poor people the resources, know-how and say in policy and decision-making that would help them change their reality.

The experience of poverty

To experience real poverty, even only at second hand, is a real humbling and humiliating experience. To start your life minus basic needs, food, reasonable housing, education, health care, money, to live your life trying to get your hands on them for yourself and your children, and to end your life without your basic needs being met, is indeed a tragedy. It is the lot of many poor people and their children. It was, and is the lot of many people in Dublin's inner city today. My experience as a priest in Sean McDermott Street brought me in touch with that reality for the first time and it changed my mainly middle class and assimilated attitudes towards the poor. It also made me very angry and sad at the perpetrators of poverty in Ireland … the rich, the powerful, the upper-middle-class, the unresponsive national leaders, the 'don't rock the boat' Church people, or the decision-makers at all levels, like educators or civil servants, who did not respond. With so much national wealth and resources in Ireland, with such a small population, with our common experience of poverty and down-troddeness in the past, with such a large population of Church-going and believing people, should there be any poverty in Ireland? Is there any excuse?

Basic needs
Everything practical or concrete that we did in Sean McDermott Street was an attempt to respond to the people's basic needs, to help them to help themselves and to 'walk tall' as individuals and as a community in their quest for justice, equality, dignity, democracy and happiness in their lives. An excellent community development question is, 'Are you in the business of achieving tasks or developing people?' The best community development is about developing people through achieving tasks. Our team were primarily in the business of developing people, especially in trying to empower them to analyse their own situation, take steps to change it, and so achieve as much control as possible over their own destiny.

One of my 'insights' from ministering in the inner city is that the meeting of basic needs must be a constitutive element of evangelisation and parish work. The basic needs would vary from parish to parish. In a poor parish the need might be food, shelter, education, a living wage, and in a rich parish the basic need might be love, spirituality or community.

Another important insight is that the spirit and reality of the gospel incubate in the bones and marrow of working-class Dublin people. That fact may be obscured to many outsiders because of the growth of anti-social behaviour in many working-class areas of Dublin.

Ministers of the gospel
Though I consider the concrete things we did to be more like footnotes in the story of the development of Sean McDermott Street, enumeration of them will show what form we tried to give to our

vision and what emerged in practice from the meeting of two visions and realities, those of the team of priests and those of the people of the area. They will also give some idea about the practicalities and outcomes of a gospel response in a deprived community and maybe also about the relationship between evangelisation and community development. The gospel is alive; the gospel is a power, an energy, a change agent. Our gospel response to God (through our vocation) and to the people, caused some change and some things to happen. The gospel is also an inspiration ... it was to us a challenger, a vehicle of hope and indeed good news in practice. If we were not ministers of the gospel (priests) first of all we would not have been in Sean McDermott Street; secondly, we would not have been directed, inspired, encouraged to take risks, to be compassionate, to stand up and be counted. We often failed to follow the gospel fully, or even partially, but nevertheless it kept calling us, challenging us, cajoling us to be about 'our Father's business', and to walk as God's people together in faith, hope and love.

The real story
As we got involved with the area and with the people, we felt the great need to tell the 'real' story of the area ... to do what Tony Gregory and Mick Rafferty and the Street Traders and others had been so courageously doing before us. To try to do what Plunkett, Behan, and especially O'Casey had done more eloquently but with no less conviction from the foundation of the state.

Tough questions
As time went by, we began to ask tough questions like: Who caused the problems? Who was doing anything about them? Who cared? Why so many reports and commissions and pastorals?

And we tried to deal with these questions in our everyday work with the community – to place responsibility where it lay – locally or with some specific outside group or agency.

We also dialogued on these issues in the public forum. So we sought access to media or hardly ever refused a serious media person if we had the time or energy. This task alone took a lot of time and energy and took its toll. It also had a lot of risk attached to it and hurt at times.

We also got negative comments from priests and others like: 'Seeking attention.' 'Making an eejit of himself.' 'Hurting the Church.' 'Letting down the Church.' 'Letting down priests.' 'They're just social workers.' 'Why don't they get back to the spiritual – be *real* priests.' 'Meddling in politics.' 'Turbulent priests.' 'Trying to do professionals' jobs.'

And from some of the local leaders: 'Outsiders interpreting our lives ... telling us how to live ... controlling us for the Church ... middle-class manipulators.'

The media: an issue
My early experience of the media, mainly print, in Sean McDermott Street, was that it concentrated on cataloguing and condemning crime. There was little in-depth analysis of the situation or of root causes. In my experience, the media in the nineteen eighties, both print and electronic, progressed to a much more analytical and in-depth understanding of delinquency and anti-social behaviour, and their relationship to poverty, inequality and the stratification of society. *Today Tonight* programmes, radio current affairs programmes, major articles in the national daily papers, especially *The Irish Times*, stand out in my mind for their research and analysis. That is not to say that all the sensational and over-the-top presentations have disappeared.

There is great need for priests and the 'official Church' to work out their relationship with the media. The stance at the moment is a continuum from cooperation through suspicion to paranoia. Blanket feelings, for or against, are often the response of Church people to the media. Blanket responses are only O.K. for Rip Van Winkles!

Justice

Justice is also a major issue in any poor parish or poor area. The lack of justice is its reason for being poor. The lack of justice can be seen on people's faces, in their undernourishment, their anaemic look, their thinness, their ill health, their major and life-long anxieties. If I took photographs of whole sections of the population of Dublin or Ireland, I'm sure I could pick out the rich people and the poor people in eight cases out of ten. They look different. One group has access to high quality food and choices about it, to a high standard of healthcare and to choice, to choice as to where they will live; to be able to have holidays and to leave their environment regularly through means of their car. In general, poor people haven't got these choices. I heard an overworked, anaemic and trapped mother of seven children say her only holiday was her annual few days in the Rotunda maternity hospital!

The lack of justice can also be seen in the environment of poor people. If you travel through Dublin with a camera you can note the appalling contrast between rich and poor areas, the total grey or yellow drabness of the public housing areas of Dublin. Rich and better off people in general choose where they live. Poor people have to stay put or go where they are sent. Again, lack of choice or no choice. A reality in life!

Lack of justice also means lack of access to basic resources like health, education, housing, and ultimately a just share in the resources of God's creation.

Manna

So injustice is felt by almost everybody living in a poor area. People are angry at decisions being made for them and about them by politicians, public servants, people in statutory bodies, the Church, professionals and a host of 'outsiders'. They are angry at having so little say and at being controlled and used by so many groups and individuals. So justice is like manna to people living in poor areas. They can see, feel and touch its manifestation, e.g. if they get a real say in running the parish, in their own gov-

46

ernance or a say in parish policy and things that affect themselves about religion and life; if they get access to better education and training and therefore, a job, or a better job. Justice can take different forms, be it personal development for a mother who for the first time in her life could see herself as important, as separate from being a wife and mother, or community development, that helped a local group to analyse their own situation. In what ever form, people in poor areas know well the difference between justice and charity. Nobody, with choice, would make the acceptance of charity an option in life. Nobody. Nobody, except the oppressed.

We, the priests of the parish, made justice the major plank of our operation in my eight years in Sean McDermott Street. As with all the work of evangelisation, we were trying to marry the ideal of the gospel to the reality of life and society. And the real and imperfect often triumphed in our own lives and work, as it did in society.

3. Projects development

Over a period of five years, with the help of many local groups and individuals, and the support of statutory bodies, we developed projects in answer to parish and community needs. The projects were many and varied and some unusual. One of the projects, Lourdes Youth and Community Services (chapter 4), is seen as a very useful model of integrated community development in Ireland. It's known among community workers as 'the Lourdes Miracle' because of the amount of money we in the Parish of Our Lady of Lourdes squeezed out of the government Youth Employment Agency! It was a quarter of a million pounds per annum - a very good investment by the government.

The setting up and running of these projects was exciting. It was also hard work. It was survival for many young people, literally – money, work, a caring place, drug-free. It provided a choice, maybe for the first time for some. It also provided opportunities for skill training, education, literacy, leadership-training, full human development, enjoyment, involvement, democracy in action. All these projects at the micro or local level were run on a shoestring (except LYCS), and on a temporary basis. Temporary was the only enduring reality in Sean McDermott Street during those years!

The early years: concrete projects
For the first two years the priests' team did an apprenticeship of listening and learning. We were helped a lot by Paul Lavelle and Frank Brady SJ, who had already lived and worked in the area. We spent a lot of time in identifying community leaders and people with leadership potential.

I became a close apprentice of Paul Lavelle in meeting the youth of the area, assessing their needs and talents and, together with local youth leaders, we initiated approximately thirty temporary youth employment schemes in the area. As time went by, we developed a broad-based educational and community development programme for the youth of the parish, based on their needs and aptitudes. Out of many beginnings and failures, over the next five years would emerge a Community Craft Centre, an Alternative Primary School, a Youth Employment Action Group and a small Industrial Estate, a Skills Training Centre, a Furniture Co-Op, a Community Service Project (for training local youth and community workers), a residential Youth Care Hostel, Lourdes Youth Services (the parish youth services organisation), a Folk/Social Action Group and a Parish Newsletter Team. Out of some ugly caterpillars, the early disorganised projects, would come a lot of lovely butterflies! Adversity can be an anvil of alienation, or of affirmative action.

Cooperative efforts
A crucial factor about all of these projects is that they were cooperative efforts. They were suggested by a local organisation, a local Sean McDermott Street youth or adult, one of us priests, or a committed professional working in the area. For the first two years, there was a lot of suspicion between groups, and especially be-

tween the North Central Community Council and the parish. During this time, when the parish became very active and involved in community affairs, there were a lot of ripples and vibes, mostly negative! However, as the parish, through the priests' team and parish development committee, began to work at basic and practical local needs, barriers to cooperation lessened, I believe.

The role of the priest

Our role as priests in the area, especially in the earlier years, was that of initiators and, equally importantly, network convenors. We were trying, in the words of Helder Camara, 'to unite diverse minorities around primary goals.' In my view, the priest in the parish in Ireland is in an ideal position to be 'network convenor'. He has a lot of trust. He has a lot of power. He has control of a lot of property. Also, being a community builder and community convenor fits in very well with the nature and task of evangelisation and the role of minister of evangelisation. It fits in especially well with the role of collaborative or cooperative ministry inherent in the nature of the Church and parish, the ministry of all of the baptised to each other and to society, recommended by Vatican II. I will develop both of these points later.

At the time of writing, most of the projects mentioned above are still going strong. That is great. I am very proud to have been a part of their coming into existence, to have been a co-operator in their initiation or survival and development. Their survival is due to luck sometimes, but most of all, to the commitment and skills of those who are running them.

Community development

I would say that, as important as the service they are providing – jobs, skills, fulfilment – is the *way* they are providing it and the way they operate. All of these projects were set up with a community development philosophy. This was usually written into their constitution and the people hired to work in them and run them had to have it too. The people selected for their management boards would have this philosophy where possible. This means that, as well as producing good students, or good leaders or good furniture, all the projects tried to concentrate on personal development, involvement and leadership-training. It also meant that they did a lot of social and political analysis and usually were into networking with other groups and organisations. Some of these projects or programmes have been professionally evaluated or written up professionally[5] and this community development philosophy, with its emphasis on personal dignity, personal development, personal responsibility, as well as community and societal awareness and outreach, is very striking.

Conclusion

Our goal was to make the parish a more people-centred parish, to move beyond creeds, finances, buildings and activities, to placing a greater emphasis on parish as community than parish as institution and to meeting the basic needs of gospel and people.

In general we tried not to separate 'parish' from 'community'. Quite often people equate community with secular and parish with sacred. A holy but not wholesome thought! Not sound theology. Or is it? What's the difference between 'parish' and 'community'? Are they the same? Do they intermingle? Is community action parish action? What is the role of the priest? To run the parish? To develop community? Are both the same? Is parish development community development and *vice versa*? I will try to clarify some of these issues in a later chapter on parish and the role of the priest.

What we were about was Christian community development. I can see that clearly now. I described it at the time vaguely as 'integrated development', 'full human development', 'integral humanism', 'bringing the Church to the people', 'making the gospel live'. But Christian community development is the most apt description of our work. Christian community development happened in three ways – parish development/people development/project development.

50

Notes

1.   Pope Paul VI, *Evangelisation Today*, CTS, London 1975, No.4.
2.   Avery Dulles SJ, *Vatican Two: An Overview*, Liturgical Press, Collegeville 1986, p. 7.
3.   See Pope Paul VI, *On the Development of People*, Nos. 14, 42, USCC, Washington 1967.
4.   See Kay Carmichael, 'The Path of the Delinquent' in *Juvenile Justice at the Crossroads*, Dept of Social Administration, UCD, Dublin 1981.
5.   See:
      (1) Mary Whelan, 69, UCD Social Science Research Centre, Dublin, unpublished;
      (2) Pauline Faughnan, *Evaluation of Lourdes Youth and Community Services Project*, UCD Social Science Research Centre, Dublin 1986, unpublished.

CHAPTER 4

Some of the Projects

Walk not before me, I may not follow.
Walk not behind me, I may not lead.
Just walk beside me and be my friend.
(Motto of our parish youth work)

Approximately twenty-five major projects were initiated in the area during this period, under the auspices of the parish or by other groups in the area with the support of the parish. I will now give a brief account of six of those projects to reflect the variety of development, the type of needs, the type of response, the issues and some of the processes involved. Four of the projects were initiated by the parish, or developed under the auspices of the parish, and two, a residential child-care hostel and an alternative housing project, were initiated by other organisations. The six projects are:

1. Temporary Youth Employment Schemes.
2. Alternative Primary School.
3. Craft Centre/Community Service Project.
4. Industrial Estate.
5. Residential Childcare Hostel.
6. Alternative Housing Plan.

1. TEMPORARY YOUTH EMPLOYMENT SCHEMES

For the first two years in Sean McDermott Street, Paul Lavelle, Frank Brady and myself ate and drank TYES – Temporary Youth Employment Schemes, government sponsored work training schemes. Paul Lavelle had pioneered some of these schemes from

1974-1977, before official government ones began. And so he was trusted by the two people who ran them from the Department of Education, Tony O Dálaigh and Gerry Conroy. Both were very supportive in difficult circumstances. How difficult you shall see later!

No supervisors
There were 'miilions' of TYES projects, or so it seemed. We ran about thirty in all, over three years, with about ten young people in each. Most of the young people were the ordinary local kids who were not in trouble with the law, seven out of ten in each project approximately, and the others were the ones in trouble with the law, in trouble at home and with the community. We got a lot of flak from the locals and the parents of the 'good' kids for putting 'robbers' and members of the Bugsy Malone gangs on the projects. Many of the projects failed; people got hit with china dolls and pieces of furniture (whatever the 'craft' product was!) and, to make things worse, in those early years the government allowed for no supervisors on the projects. Since they were a new entity for them, the Department of Education didn't know enough about youth work projects to think of a supervisor! We in the parish had no extra money either, so, in an official project of ten young people, we hired nine workers, at £50 each (or less) and we skimmed £5 off each worker's salary to pay a supervisor at £95 per week. Of course, that didn't please the workers or ourselves but we had no choice.

Guarantors of trustworthiness?
The projects were as many and as varied as our imaginations and energy would allow. There was the Grafitti Project; the Wallpapering Project; the Scrap Metal Project; the Interior Painting Project; the Fibreglass Project; the Community Services Project; the Lorry Driving Project; the Education Through Sport Project. Each of those projects could form the basis of an excellent short story or of a book. The projects were interesting sociological phenomena – how they were set up, the balancing of the internal dynamics of

each, the interaction between statutory bodies, like Department of Education, ANCO (now FÁS), and the projects. Because there was often disagreement as to what 'work' was and what 'progress' was, Paul, Frank, and myself were stretched to the limits in patience, resourcefulness and spoofing, as go-betweens for the local projects and the statutory bodies. We were trusted by the statutory bodies because we were priests but, as time went by, we became less and less happy as guarantors of the trustworthiness of local communities and groups for statutory bodies as we felt that government agencies should be trusting local community groups more. They were hard times for all but the TYES were bridge-building efforts which would lead to better things like the North Inner City Co-op, the Craft Centre, the Youth Employment Action Group – whose reason for coming into existence was to go beyond TYES towards proper jobs and employment.

When I think of the TYES I laugh a lot now. For instance, the day the man from Amiens Street knocked on the door of the presbytery looking for Paul Lavelle. He was as pale as a ghost, Paul says, and looked as if he was going to get a heart attack. All he could say with a weak voice was, 'My car, my car.' Paul's heart sank to his ankles. He knew immediately what had happened. 'The car' would be as flat as a pancake down at the Hammond Lane scrap metal foundry by now. He was right, it later transpired. The Scrap Metal Project lads were running out of scrap in the immediate area and also running out of diesel in their lorry, so they pounced on the old man's 'banger'! The parish had to pay the full price of the car.

The Wallpapering Project

This was a TYES scheme which decorated the homes of elderly people. Paul had charge of this too. He was very busy for the three months prior to the Pope's visit in 1979. He and Peter Lemass set up an office in the Church to organise the parish for the possible papal visit. So he stepped back from the projects for a while. He had an arrangement with a large interior decoration firm in the area to pay for paint and wallpaper once a month. When he went back after the papal visit, he got an almighty shock. The bill was £3,000! Some of the lads had decided to do some 'voluntary' wallpapering for a little fee – as a gesture of goodwill from the parish on the Pope's visit!

The missing linoleum

I myself ran into what the Americans call some 'free flowing anger' from an old man whose flat the Painting Project had decorated while he was in hospital. He was very angry when he came into the sacristy to me after the Holy Saturday Night ceremonies. 'It's ridiculous, Father! It's ridiculous!' he kept repeating. It took me a while to get what was so ridiculous. Whilst he was getting better in hospital, Sr Gerard, one of the parish sisters, kept bringing him almost daily reports on how well the flat was coming along. He was thrilled and, of course, it was a very good service. He couldn't wait to get home to see the flat. Imagine his and sister's horror when they walked into the flat and saw the hole in the middle of the linoleum, five feet by five feet right at the centre. It transpired that the lads were rushing to finish painting the ceiling on the previous Friday evening and one of them knocked over a tin of paint on the linoleum right in the centre of the floor. The only quick solution was to cut the centre out!

The Graffiti Project

The Graffiti Project was Paul Lavelle's most risky and crazy project. It was just before the Pope's visit with the place receiving huge media coverage with NBC, CBC, BBC, RTÉ, *Time* magazine and many others flooding the area. Paul wanted to do three things: get rid of the graffiti, stop gangs repainting the walls in the area, and try to tackle the core of the Bugsy Malone gang. Well, it worked, for a few months. The head of the Bugsy Malone gang was made the supervisor and the leaders, his assistants, with four or five people who knew how to take paint off walls rather than spray it on. Everybody was happy with the project – the Department of Education, the police, us; the locals were thrilled but unbelieving; the gang were happy because they knocked every other gang's graffiti off and left one or two 'significant' ones of their own. Also they were being interviewed almost every day and could wink at the gardaí because they were now working with the priests and preparing the place for the Pope! I laughed later, on a visit to Mountjoy Prison, when the lads told me that they painted one huge Bugsy Malone slogan on the highest roof in the inner city because it could be seen from the roof of Mountjoy. Those who went on a protest on the roof of Mountjoy with the leader of the Bugsy Malones later on could verify this. One slogan was seen worldwide on the flats opposite the Church when the Pope passed through: 'John Paul Rules OK'. It came as the swan song of the Graffiti Project. A letter from one of the papal secretaries in the Vatican after the visit said John Paul really liked this slogan.

Failure: learning

Our project development started with small and tentative beginnings – and much failure. It was an experimental period, a time of learning for the statutory bodies and ourselves. This was 1979-80 and all these schemes were new. Failure is an important part of experimentation but it's hard to take. The pedagogy of failure is not dealt with very much in the Irish school system nor in the seminary system. 'Offering it up' is important, but not enough! Anyway, Paul Lavelle and Frank Brady and myself were often depressed with our failures during this period.

However, even though there was a lot of failure there were also worthwhile patterns beginning to emerge in the whole field of schooling, education, employment, community development. The jigsaw pieces began to fall together. For instance, being a 'failure' at school and dropping out was related to the fact that there was no future, no connection between educational achievement and employment, so the brightest often dropped out the earliest. If there are no jobs what's the point in preparing for one? Casual work by almost everybody (fathers, brothers in the docks and mothers and sisters as street traders) did not require formal education – so what was the point of it? Also, casual work is not good training for formal time keeping (school hours) or for the often over-formal structure and methodology of the school system. If you live an informal community lifestyle, strict and rigid formal structures can suffocate you. This is an important insight for educators, liturgists and community development workers, especially in a working-class area.

Experiential learning
In order to show some link between education and work we decided to locate whatever work project we could as near as possible to the school (Craft Centre/Skill Centre/Co-op).

We also saw that 'learning by doing' or 'experiential learning' is the preferred method of learning by working class adults and children. Perhaps it is by everybody? I feel that the Craft Centre and LY&CS could teach teachers and schools and education authorities about experiential learning and other methods of learning.

As the years went by, we began to formulate policies and practices and programmes which met some of the varied needs of the children, youth and the area and we tried to start where people were at, trying to enhance their innate abilities. This was inculturation in the broad sense. We were fulfilling the oldest principle in learning and education – 'You must start where the learner is at'. His/her needs, interests, aptitudes, environment, problems, all play a part in engaging the person's energy and motivation and hence involvement. This is a vital principle also for evangelisation and community development, just as it is for education.

2. ALTERNATIVE PRIMARY SCHOOL

The Youth Encounter Project is an Alternative Primary School. When I came to Sean McDermott Street in 1978, the Catholic Youth Council, through Fr John Fitzpatrick (Director), had been negotiating with the Department of Education about setting up a

Youth Encounter Project in Sean McDermott Street. I was asked to become the manager, find a building, find staff, a management committee and pupils, all in about three months! The Department of Education had money for four of these projects, one for Cork, one for Limerick and two for Dublin. If the money wasn't spent in that financial year it would go back into central government funds.

When we set up the YEP in 1979, there were sixty-one children from ten to fourteen years of age, running wild around the parish, who had dropped out of school permanently or had been thrown out. The YEP was set up for them and for other children from the north inner city who could not cope, or be coped with, in the ordinary primary school.

The YEP has been an enormous success.This success is due to stable funding, its flexibility, but above all the quality and variety of the staff. The principal, Brian Hackett was selected for his ability in the classroom as well as his outstanding track record in community, or out-of-school, aspects of education. With the other committed and skillful professional staff, three local parents were also chosen to be classroom assistants and bean-an-tí respectively. The three, Denis Kinlan, Christy Fagan and Annie Hopkins were excellent counsellors and role models for the children plus advisors to the staff in helping them gain a better understanding of the children and form links with home and community.

The start-up process
The YEP is described as follows in *Parish Alive, Alive O!*:[1] 'At first the YEP was like a drop-in centre, offering a warm welcoming atmosphere where children at risk could play pool, table tennis, go on trips, have an enjoyable meal together every morning and talk about 'their issues'.

When the habit of attendance was built up, and an atmosphere of trust built up, the young people expressed a desire to learn. This was after two to three months. Literacy classes were set up lasting initially not more than ten minutes (as concentration was low). Any sign of progress was praised to build up confidence in their ability to take part in longer classes.

The project became more like a conventional school when the days spent together became structured and included short periods of numeracy and literacy together with woodwork, crafts and cookery. In the first two years, the children who had dropped out of school from 1-5 years had a 93% attendance rate. That was a most encouraging start. By the end of the first year the YEP had developed to the stage where three formal groups or classes participated in an organised curriculum incorporating literacy, numeracy, home economics and physical education.

Other areas included music, sex education, environmental studies, personal evaluation, religious education and formation, community service.'

The YEP is in existence now for ten years and Brian Hackett is still Principal. The children do Group and Inter Cert. They go on work placements. There is a lot of liaison with the local community and the school stays open for the summer months with a slimmed-down staff. The YEP is an excellent model for primary education with disadvantaged children, though all the children in it are not disadvantaged. It has a lower pupil/teacher ratio than the ordinary school. (It is unfair to compare it with the ordinary school in the same situation, therefore.) It has a flexible curriculum and is in an inspector-friendly category. It costs just slightly more per pupil than the ordinary national school.

From a Church and parish point of view, I gave a lot of support to the YEP because:
(i) it gave a new life to fifty to sixty children;
(ii) all of them had been blamed for their failure – the victims had been blamed, not the system;
(iii) justice is being done;
(vi) a new, more integrated model of primary education is being developed for working class areas. [2]

3. CRAFT CENTRE/COMMUNITY SERVICE PROJECT

Lourdes Youth and Community Services, now with a staff of fourteen people, was the bringing together of the three separate projects which we had been developing from 1978 on. All three took blood, sweat and tears to set up and keep going. LY&CS is now doing excellent work not only in the parish, but also on a wider scale for women's groups, children and youth from all over the north inner city.

Origins of the three projects

1. Monto Skill Centre

Brother Liam Sheridan, from the north inner city himself, had practical manual skills to communicate to the young people in the area. Awareness of the need to build up their self-esteem and to inspire them to believe in themselves, led him to set up the Monto Skills Centre. He and the staff taught the basics of woodwork, metalwork and furniture-making in the Rutland Street school complex.

2. Community Services Project

The CSP has been described as follows: 'With four thousand young people in the area (1978-82), Fr Casey saw the need for setting up a locally managed youth service with local people as youth and community workers. Five young people, prominent in the folk-group, were selected to staff the project to be funded by Temporary Youth Employment Schemes under the Department of Education.

The aim was that, guided by the concepts of self-help, self-direction and self-reliance, young people from the community would run a relevant youth service using the community's own resources. The first CSP team of five, led by Martin Brennan, engaged in youth services, parish area youth development (getting a centre, adults and leaders in each area of the parish), peer ministry and peer counselling. They also produced the parish newsletter, and formed a general service to the parish and the community.'[3]

3. The Craft Centre

The Jesuits had run a small craft/drop-in centre for youth in Summerhill. When Summerhill was being knocked down, I, as parish administrator, realised it would be a great tragedy for the little craft/drop-in centre to die. Where to put it? At the time there was a cider gang problem in the basement under Rutland Street School – an open area under the first level classroom floor – so why not close that area in and kill two birds with the one brick wall? We did. In an area of 40 feet by 20 feet by 15 feet high, we built a two-storey four-room Craft Centre, a miracle achieved by Br Liam Sheridan, a member of the Holy Ghost community which had just moved into the area. The building of 'the wall' to close the area was a nightmare. It should have taken two days but took two months. The cider gang didn't want an 'effin' craft centre'! The 'workers' used to go out in sympathy with the gang – or due to intimidation. Half the wall would be built by day. Half the wall would be taken down that night. I said at the time it must have been easier to build the Great Wall of China!

I wanted a Craft Centre to serve the whole parish for children, youth, adults, the elderly, the schools and projects and youth leaders. That it did marvellously in time. The Craft Centre has been funded by the diocese, the Catholic Youth Council, Comhairle le Leas Óige, The Inner City Fund, the Corporation, the Youth Employment Agency, AnCo/FÁS, Belvedere students and the Ireland Fund.

Lourdes Youth and Community Services: evaluation

The Craft Centre, with the Skill Centre and CSP, which make up the LY&CS, have been evaluated professionally by Ms Pauline Faughnan, the Social Science Research Centre, UCD, in an excellent 560-page document covering all three projects in LY&CS.[4] What is most impressive in reading the document is the amount of learning and personal development done by the thirty-six trainees who go through LY&CS annually and also by the other groups who participate in its programmes and activities. Also the amount of confidence building, skill training, social and political awareness and community development that has occurred over the years. The skill, philosophy and commitment of the staff of fourteen comes through as well. David O'Brien, the first manager had done development work for many years in the Philippines; Anna Moore and Helena Caulfield have brought their love of art and crafts to the project; Aileen Foran, director of the Craft Centre, and now manager of LYCS, had learned her crafts and management skills in the Summerhill centre; Deirdre Clarke (Craft Centre) had come through her social science degree in UCD and brought a lot of group-work skills to the project. Denis Kinlan, Tessie McMahon, Seanie Lamb, Thomas Dunne and Raymond Collins, all involved with the CSP, were experts on local culture, local history and living in the city. They also had learned their community development and political skills through local involvement and transmitted much awareness and skill to the trainees.

I was very proud the day Shirley Williams MP came to look at the three projects on behalf of the OECD. She was impressed by the informal education and personal development aspect of the project and its innovative approach with working class youth. She was also appalled by the conditions in which the project was located and by the shoestring budget. Three 'global figures', Sean McBride, Bishop Desmond Tutu and Jesse Jackson (US presidential candidate), when they visited Sean McDermott Street for the International Conference on Peace and Poverty organised by Action From Ireland (AFRI) in 1982, were also high in their praise of the youth-to-youth work, youth involvement programmes and the politicisation of youth going on in the LYCS and the parish. It was very encouraging for us on the parish team and in the projects to get genuine praise and affirmation from such committed people. In our experience, affirmation was a scarce commodity except from some local people and the odd bishop!

4. INDUSTRIAL ESTATE

YEAG, the Youth Employment Action Group, was a group of fifty Sean McDermott Street youth, with a core group of ten, who came together in order to get a cluster factory and industrial estate for the area. YEAG was set up by Martin Brennan, co-ordinator of the Parish Youth Services, and five other local young people. Like the temporary youth employment schemes and the Craft Centre, YEAG was part of the overall parish response to needs in the area. One could not do justice to YEAG in two pages. It would take a book or more. Martin Brennan is writing the book at the moment.

The industrial estate/cluster factory was built in 1985 with eighteen units providing much needed employment. The factory was built by the IDA which had been completely against the project at the start, on land owned by Dublin Corporation who had opposed the project because there was no land zoned for industry in the area. In the end it had the unanimous approval of the forty-five city councillors most of whom had been against it at first. It must be said that the personal backing of the project by both Charles Haughey and Garret FitzGerald as taoisigh did no harm. The YEAG members got direct access to both on their own initiative.

YEAG first of all did an employment survey of the total parish, finding 70% unemployment very severe – by far the highest in Ireland then; they lobbied the forty-five city councillors individually, getting the approval of all except one, Alice Glenn; they did a skills profile of the area; I fasted with them for two days outside the GPO in O'Connell Street; they got 10,000 signatures of support for the factory; they wrote a song on unemployment which Liam Byrne, one of the YEAG members, sang on the 9 o'clock television news on RTÉ the night before the general election, a scoop which prompted a government minister to say, 'What our party wouldn't have given for that inside spot ye got on the night before the election!'

YEAG was important for six reasons:
(i) Local youth decided that they were fed up with temporary jobs and that they had a right to full-time jobs.

(ii) A group of local youth, about fifty, were politicised and learned many political and lobbying skills in the process.

(iii) They involved the local parish community all along the way in their fight for a factory and local employment.

(iv) The small industrial estate, though fairly insignificant in terms of jobs, was a sign of hope and success.

(v) The campaign showed who 'owned' jobs – the well off!

(vi) The YEAG campaign was another example of empowerment of the local community.

5. RESIDENTIAL CHILDCARE HOSTEL

Some adults from Sean McDermott Street and the north inner city of Dublin had spent their childhood in reformatories – Letterfrack, Clonmel, Daingean. It was a savage experience for any child of ten or twelve years, who had never been outside the inner city, not to mind the city.

Against the background of the reformatory experience of children from the inner city, we in the parish and the community felt we had to do something, if we could, about children in the community who needed residential care. Peter McVerry and others had set up Tabor House in Sheriff Street, a residential care hostel for teenagers. A place was also needed for younger children.

A pattern was beginning to emerge in our Youth Services and Youth Care: we had general youth services, we had crafts/skill centres, we had youth employment schemes, we had the alternative school and the teachers of the parish school, Rutland Street, were trying to adapt the curriculum and teaching methods of the formal education system. This was all good but we had nothing to help the pre-teenage children who were in serious trouble with the law. Now we were getting clearer about the need for what I termed, at the time, different levels of care for youth.

Mary Whelan, who was later to do a participative evaluation of the project in 69 Amiens Street, gives the genesis of the project and an insight into the attempt at co-operative pastoral and com-

munity development being engaged in by the parish and statutory and voluntary agencies at the time:

'On a morning in January 1980, two people met and stopped to
talk in Killarney Street, Dublin. Michael Casey, a local priest, and
Robbie Gilligan, an Eastern Health Board social worker whose
office was across the road from the presbytery, had plenty to talk
about. Four children, whom they both knew, had been caught
breaking into a shop the night before by the police. They had
spent the rest of the night in the garda station 'because there was
nowhere to bring them' and the senior social worker in Killarney
Street had just got a phone call from the gardaí to say that they
were still there. They were all under twelve years of age. Michael
and Robbie agreed that something had to be done as a matter of
urgency.

The present circumstances of these children crystallised the situation of a number of young children in the north inner city at the
time. As it turned out, the conversation they provoked was the
catalyst which brought together the elements of a new approach
to community-based residential care for children.' [5]

Through the co-operation of the parish, the Eastern Health Board,
local social and community workers and the St Vincent De Paul
Society, a residential childcare hostel for pre-teen children was
opened.

The St Vincent de Paul Society took on the main responsibility for
the project and established it in a house which they owned at 69
Amiens Street. They also provided funding and appointed an experienced and multi-disciplined management committee to get
the project off the ground. An initial staff of four, who between
them had wide and varied experience of both childcare and community-based work, opened the hostel which is still running for
the benefit of inner city children.

'69' is innovative and community-based, so that the children can
confront their problems and society's problems in the community
where they live. '69' also contributes a lot to community develop-

ment and parish support over the years. It has changed local parents' attitudes to residential care as well, a very welcome outcome considering the bad name reformatories had in the area – or any area for that matter. Instead of seeing time at the hostel as a punishment, as they did at the start, and feeling failures themselves, they now see it as support for themselves and the child. This has come about as a result of the painstaking and loving work of the staff and the openness of many of the parents. A most interesting project.

6. ALTERNATIVE HOUSING PLAN (NCCC)

'The year 1978 marked the beginning in the northside of Dublin of an urban renewal process which was market-orientated rather than people-orientated. This process would be made official with the publication of the Urban Renewal Bill in 1986. This market-driven urban renewal process, together with a severe overcrowding problem in Summerhill, just two minutes' walk from O'Connell Street, was the catalyst for Dublin Corporation's huge de-tenanting programme for the area in 1978.' So states Mick Rafferty, a charismatic local community leader.

Because of the outmoded and run down tenements of Foley Street, Sean McDermott Street and Summerhill, the Corporation decided to knock them down and move out five hundred families, have open spaces and build fifty houses as replacements. Everyone agreed some families had to be moved out because of the massive overcrowding and its consequent problems, but local people wanted a phased development (50% first) by which people could be moved temporarily and then allowed come back to the new houses when built. The 'Corpo' said no. 'All out, that's it.' So the shit hit the fan, as they say in the USA! We, the new team, got covered by it when we arrived! We had to make a decision in a hurry: Stay out of the issue? Inform ourselves and get involved and lose the goodwill of the Corporation if we joined the residents? It was a simple enough decision to make in the end.

The local people had responded angrily and in a very organised way to this major development by the Dublin Corporation. The local people wanted a say in what was happening. So, in response to this development and threat, Tony Gregory, Mick Rafferty, Larry Whelan, Fergus McCabe and other members of the NCCC (North Central Community Council), mobilised the people of the area. The NCCC blocked roads, went to court, its members went to prison, fought in the media and finally came up with a very imaginative alternative plan for the area. We in the parish and the Pro-Cathedral parish backed this very imaginative plan. We made written submissions, lobbied and sought every possible media outlet to promote this plan.

The Corporation, in its original plan, was only going to build fifty to seventy new houses in the north inner city. City managers and city architects did everything possible to block the alternative plan. They would only build fifty houses. They had the power. They would win, it seemed. But they didn't! The local community wanted two hundred and fifty houses. The local community was not supposed to know what's best for it – as most local communities are not, according to civil servants and professional policy-makers and planners. But of course most local communities and parishes know what is best for them (I believe that) and, anyway, they are the ones who have to live with the consequences of planning or the lack of it by policy-makers and planners. In any case, the local community, spearheaded by the NCCC, won the day.

270 magnificent houses
Today the two hundred and seventy beautiful red brick houses in the north inner city are a significant and inspiring testimony to the wisdom of the local community and to its people's commitment to what is good and beautiful and useful. It is also a tribute to the Dublin City's Councillors and to the Architectural Department of Dublin Corporation, although initially Dublin Corporation had done a lot to oppose it. It is, perhaps most of all, a tribute to the political acumen of Tony Gregory who, in master-minding the

famous 'Gregory Deal' in 1982, helped fund the building of the houses. Why did the civic authorities oppose the building of 270 houses? They had different ideas and priorities from the people of the inner city. The planners wanted open space and parks, the people wanted houses and an industrial estate for jobs. The planners wanted fifty houses and lots of parkland. The people got the two hundred houses, in fact two hundred and seventy, an industrial estate and less park space. A very good ending to a tough confrontation. A victory for local wisdom and the will of the people.

Notes
1. Ciarán Earley OMI, 'Sean McDermott Street' in *Parish Alive Alive O!*, The Columba Press, Dublin 1985, pp 40-41.
2. For a fuller account of YEP see Owen Egan, *Youth Encounter Project*, St Patrick's College, Drumcondra, unpublished.
3. See YEAG booklet, *YEAG*, Dublin 1982.
4. Pauline Faughnan, *Evaluation of Lourdes Youth and Community Services Project*, UCD Social Science Research Centre, Dublin, unpublished.
5. Mary Whelan, *69*, UCD Social Science Research Centre, Dublin 1986, unpublished.

CHAPTER 5

The Context of this Experience

Church and State on automatic pilot
Pursuing fixed goals
Saving souls in isolation
But losing the soul of the nation
(M. Casey, 1985)

In this chapter I will focus on the wider context in which my role and that of Christianity was being played out. That wider context is the Ireland, the Church and the world of the 1960s-90s.

A huge change came over Ireland in the 1960s. A huge change came over the Catholic Church in the 1960s. A huge change came over the world in the 1960s. All three coalesced to influence my ministry and its context, Ireland. These three tidal waves hit Ireland at the same time in the 1960s. Ireland was shaken to the roots. It would never be the same again.

PART I: IRELAND 1960s-1990s

It was a time of great social and cultural change in Ireland. Up to the 1960s Ireland was having a major effect on the outside world through its emigrants, its missionaries and, to a lesser extent, its literature. But the outside world was having little effect on it. It was a remote island on the edge of the Atlantic, largely untouched by the outside world, living a life of its own. Then in the 1960s a major change occurred. Television, rural electrification, industrialisation, free education, all combined to change the face of Ireland

and, of course, this change would have major implications for the role of the priest and for the role of the Church and gospel in Ireland.

For me, the two major signs and harbingers of change in that era were television and industrialisation.

(a) Television: the global vision

In the 1960s television brought global awareness and global communication to Ireland for the first time. The world, with its values, problems and potentialities, invaded our homes, our consciousness, and our consciences. From now on global affairs, good and bad, would effect our individual and national psyches. From now on our national agenda would be intertwined with the European and global agenda. We had become, almost overnight, part of the global village. Like the tide meeting the river, there would be a collision and mingling of ideas and ideals, of values and visions, of life-styles and cultures. It would be an era of transition, with its turbulence and its challenges and joys, for the people of Ireland. This would be a time of great challenge and threat particularly for the priests of Ireland as 'guardians of the faith' and 'pastors of the people'.

Within Ireland itself, television would play a major role from the 1960s on. Gay Byrne and *The Late Late Show, 7 Days, Today Tonight, On the Land, Tolka Row, The Riordans, Glenroe*, the soaps and pop would bring about change and be the topics of conversation and comment in pubs, villages, Churches, school – wherever people congregated. This would be a major challenge to the official Church and the priest – not all negative of course, in fact much of it positive, but nevertheless a challenge because it changed the context of their ministry and role. TV played a major, positive role in modernising farming in Ireland and in looking at social issues but it would also be seen by priests and many Catholics as competing with the Church for the heart and soul of the Irish people.

(b) Industrialisation

Rural Ireland

A huge change came over rural Ireland in the 1960s. Washing boards were replaced by washing machines, galvanised milking buckets and three-legged stools by milking machines, scythes by mowing machines, hay by silage. Open fires, candles, oil lamps and tilly-lamps were superseded by electricity and all its accompanying comforts and accessories. The radio and wet batteries, the gramophone and homemade music gave way to the television. The horse and the donkey and cart made way for the tractor and motor car. The 'comely maidens' left the crossroads and joined their more mobile Irish males at the larger dancehalls. The big bands – Mick Del, The Clipper Carlton, the Miami and Dickie Rock, Brendan Boyer, and others – replaced the smaller halls and local bands and these in turn would later give way to the discos, the groups, the electronic media. Change goes on. It doesn't wait for anyone. Perhaps the greatest sign of change in rural Ireland was the disappearance of the ban on foreign games. Soccer teams in Kerry, Mayo, Kilkenny, Newcastle West – who would have believed it? – all a symbol of tolerance, of modernity and of pluralism though the GAA has perhaps changed least of all in the past hundred years.

The City

City life, too, was not immune to this era of change and transition. With the increase in prosperity and mobility more people began to crowd to the city. The city began to expand. Industrial estates prospered. People followed the jobs. Prosperity and progress were in the air. More people bought cars and the number of buses increased. The greater mobility would change communities and parishes and thinking. This change from parochial thinking and living is well illustrated by the story of the fellow from the inner city who met a girl at the local dancehall in the 1950s and offered to give her a lift home on his bike. When she said she was from Ballyfermot (ten miles out) he said, 'Jaysus, it's a pen pal you need, not a fella with a bike!'

Uprooting

In Dublin the pawn shop almost disappeared, supermarkets prospered. With the advent of containerism dockers became an endangered species. Jobs disappeared in the inner city. A housing crisis brought people into the streets of Dublin in protest and, as Nelson disappeared into ashes and dust to be replaced by *An Lár*, Ballymun high-rise flats appeared like a phoenix, almost overnight. To deal with the population growth, Dublin Corporation and County Council embarked on a major and poorly-planned housing programme. The green fields of Tallaght and Coolock and Clondalkin were replaced by rows and rows of local authority houses with few amenities. As inner city accents were being heard out by the Dublin mountains, the Dublin diocese expanded and changed greatly to meet the needs of a mobile population in local authority housing, and also in the new satellite towns for the middle-class section of its community. The resources and creative imaginations of the diocese and city were stretched greatly. The rapid growth of urbanisation, the uprooting of communities and haphazard planning brought many social problems in their wake.

The Lemass Era: The EEC

In the 1960s a new prosperity came to Ireland. The Lemass era saw the growth of industrialisation, the mushrooming of advance factories and the growth of jobs. Emigrant ships did U-turns and became immigrant ships! With the new prosperity came a 'bungalow blight' all around Ireland and a population boom (half of the population of the Republic of Ireland under twenty-five years in the 1980s). Free education for all was a milestone decision in Irish history which would change many facets of Irish life, not least that of the Church and the role of the priest.

In January 1973, Ireland joined the European Economic Community, with Britain and Denmark, to form a partnership with France, West Germany, Italy, Belgium, Holland and Luxembourg, the original six who signed the Treaty of Rome in March 1957 to create the EEC. Even before the six countries of the original EEC expanded to nine, the six counties of Northern Ireland became embroiled in a sad saga of violence which brought pain to the people of Ireland and threw a major question mark over Irish Christianity in the eyes of the world.

Beyond the sixties

In the late seventies and early eighties, the first signs of questioning and displeasure began to occur about the economic miracles and the 'prosperity for all' prophecy. The poor still seemed to be with us, fulfilling Christ's prophecy, and they seemed to be growing more numerous and more poverty-stricken. Wealth was being created and was growing steadily on an annual basis, but so was unemployment – an apparent contradiction. (See Tables 1 and 2).

TABLE 1: Economic Growth And Employment Expansion Since 1987.[1]
Volume changes on previous year

Category	1987	1988	1989	1990	Cumulative Change 1987-1990
Real growth in GNP.	5.6%	0.8%	5.0%	4.0%	16.2%
Total Employment Growth.	0.6%	0.3%	1.1%	1.5%	3.5%
Increase in total numbers at work. (Annual average)	7,000	3,000	12,000	16,000	38,000
Total at work ('000) annual average.	1,087	1,090	1,102	1,118	

TABLE 2: Unemployment in Ireland since 1980 [2]
As measured by Live Register Unemployment
and by Labour Force Surveys

Year	Live Register Unemployment	Live Register Unemployment Rate	Unemployment measure by Labour Force Surveys	LFS Unemployment Rate
1980	101,500	8.1%	91,000	7.3%
1981	127,900	10.1%	126,000	9.9%
1982	156,600	12.1%	147,000	11.4%
1983	192,700	14.7%	183,000	14.0%
1984	214,200	16.4%	204,000	15.6%
1985	230,600	17.7%	226,000	17.3%
1986	236,400	18.1%	227,000	17.4%
1987	247,300	18.8%	232,000	17.7%
1988	241,400	18.4%	219,000	16.7%
1989	231,600	17.9%	203,000	15.7%
1990 June	224,800	e17.3%	N/A	N/A

e = estimate. The unemployment figure for June 1990 is seasonally adjusted.

Note: In both cases, the unemployment rate is calculated by reference to the size of the labour force at mid-April of the relevant year. Labour Force Surveys relate to mid-April.

The rich get richer but ...

The captains of industry, or the wealth creators, the politicians and the 'national handlers' all denied this reality, saying first of all, that it was impossible – a lot of them really believed the 'trickle down theory' or the 'rising tide theory' of economics. Many of them later reluctantly agreed, not because of the research figures of the Combat Poverty Agency or the Conference of Major Religious Superiors (CMRS) or the Catholic Social Service Conference (CSSC), all bodies that had distinguished themselves in fighting the cause of the poor with figures as well as policy statements. They had to change because a nationally recognised research agency, the ESRI, The Economic and Social Research Institute, showed the facts on poverty and unemployment to be incontrovertible. That, however, didn't stop politicians and national leaders controverting them!

These three major shadows of poverty, unemployment and emigration, which reappeared on the Irish horizon in the 1970s, are not merely phantoms, or figments of the imagination, as suggested by some national handlers and politicians, but are realities which have come to haunt and hurt our people, especially our poor and our youth. Out of a population of three and a half million people in the Republic, one million are poor, 240,000 are unemployed and 200,000 have emigrated between 1980 and 1990.[3]

A new awareness of poverty came with the bishops' conference in Kilkenny in 1971 and then the publication of *One Million Poor,*[4] a book by Sr Stanislaus Kennedy, the great prophetess of the poor and thorn in the side of successive governments. But awareness doesn't necessarily change people or solve the problems. People are more aware of poverty in Ireland today but there are no less poor as a result. My experience in Sean McDermott Street brought me into daily contact with these three harsh realities – poverty, unemployment and emigration. These realities cast a shadow over the lives of many families in Dublin's inner and outer city and in many other parts of Ireland, and are a huge challenge to the Churches and the people of Ireland today.

Challenge for the Church
Prosperity and poverty
Prosperity brought good and bad. We must be aware of both. It brought good housing, jobs, better education, better family life for many, fulfilment, more choice in life. Its bad effects are poverty, unemployment, emigration, marginalisation, alienation, secularisation, greed and competitiveness rather than compassion, co-operation and community. It has often made success at business an end in itself and made 'successful' people over-critical and judgemental of those who didn't make it.

In itself, capitalism hasn't got a conscience. Capitalism is not compassionate. By its very nature, capitalism's soul and goal is profit. Profit is its primary reason for being. Capitalism with a conscience, or a compassionate capitalism, is a reality that has yet to be experienced. The bad effects of multinationals and the international capitalist culture, as experienced by the Third World and the poor everywhere, are part of the downside of capitalism. Through industrialisation and 'modernisation', our Irish culture and society has become one like that of Europe and North America, which is more competitive, individualistic and materialistic. Christians and caring people are called to create a different focus. A modern society yes, but a non-caring society also? Surely no. The Irish social reality has changed rapidly and radically since 1960. It needs analysis in the light of the gospel in order to clarify and re-focus national goals and our priorities as a people.

The role of Christianity
The cultivation of a basic asceticism and provision of a prophetic critique which would counteract the luxury, consumerism, competitiveness and 'mé féin' so prevalent in Irish society today, could be Christianity's greatest contribution. A pendulum swing is necessary in Irish Catholicism to make our more individualised and privatised version of religion come alive in the community and in the affairs of the nation – not for control but for compassion and concern. It is imperative to make Christianity the conscience

76

of the people and the nation again. Christianity must be counter-cultural in our capitalist Ireland and Europe of today and tomorrow. It is only a Church that becomes a real sign of Christianity that will, or even can, attract a young Irish population to the message of Christ. They cannot separate the Church from the institutions of capitalist and secular society unless it *is* different in its values and way of being.

Coast-to-coast Catholicism
Another major change that has come over Ireland is that the Ireland of the regular family rosary, the Ireland of the sodalities and the penny catechism has disappeared. The devotional Ireland, which had produced thousands of vocations, male and female, for the local Church and for the missions, disappeared. The Ireland of the wall-to-wall, or coast-to-coast Catholicism, disappeared in the 1960s.

A new continent
A new era began for the country and for the Church in Ireland and for the role of the priest. A 'new continent' appeared. It would need to be traversed, looked at, analysed, and evangelised for and with Christ. Every new continent needs to be told 'come and see', every new continent needs the good news and every new continent will make the good news its own in a different way. 'The Church must constantly look for new ways that will enable her to understand more profoundly and to carry out with renewed vigour the mission re ceived from her founder.' [5]

The role of the priest and Christianity
Pre- and post-1960s Ireland would be in many ways as different as chalk and cheese. From the point of view of the role of the priest (and indeed others involved in spiritual or social change) it is important that these differences be examined. What has changed? What has not changed? What has changed radically? What has changed only superficially? Ireland is a new continent in many ways since the 1960s. Some issues which have effected religion and the role of the priest are:

1. The changed social reality

Progress, prosperity, technology, and higher levels of education have brought about a changed social reality in Ireland. Andrew Greeley in the USA, Bishop Donal Murray, Frs Liam Ryan, Harry Bohan, Michael Paul Gallagher SJ, Sean Healy, Sr Brigid Reynolds, CMRS, Combat Poverty, and the ESRI have dealt with many of the issues arising from this changed reality.

2. Change from a Catholic to a pluralistic society

What are the implications? Andrew Greeley's research and writings are very informative in this field. The experience of the Catholic Church in the USA also throws light on this subject. (See chapter 9)

3. The electronic age

How does a TV generation think, look at things, evaluate, hear and receive religion? In other words, the effects of the electronic age must be evaluated. McLuhan and Mike Warren have looked at some of these issues.

4. Religion in a secular society

What are the effects on the Church, the faith and religion of a secular, materialistic, capitalist/consumer society? The study of the Catholic Church in Europe and the USA can enlighten us about that experience. In the USA, especially, we see the survival and growth of religion in a culture that does not cushion and support it as it did so strongly in the pre-1960s Ireland.

PART II : THE CATHOLIC CHURCH 1960-1990

A huge change came over the Catholic Church in the 1960s. On 25th January 1959, Pope John XXIII called an ecumenical council to bring together the world's 2,500 Catholic bishops and many of the world's best theologians. Their task was to reflect on the Church and the world in order to see how best the Church could serve the gospel, the world, and its peoples. It would be a time of review, evaluation and renewal, the first major one for four hundred years in the Church. On December 1st 1962, after three years preparation, and much public speculation both within and outside the Church, the world's 2,500 Catholic bishops and Pope John XXIII came together for Vatican II. The Church would never be the same again.

Vatican II was a time of great excitement for the Church. It was a review of the Church's two-thousand-year history, a reflection on its origins, especially its early life in the first Christian community and a reflection on its journey through history. This reflective journey through the total history of the Church was a great form of enlightenment for the assembled bishops and theologians, as John XXIII, the historian, well knew it would be, and indeed for members of the Church worldwide.

Hierarchical, clerical Church
At the start of Vatican II many of the Church's theologians and bishops saw the Church as it had been operating in reality, and therefore described in theology, for the previous five hundred years: an institution made up of the Pope, bishops and priests. They were the Church. The Church was clerical. This hierarchical, juridical, institution is best described as a pyramid with the Pope on top, then the clergy and then the laity, who 'prayed and paid and obeyed.' This was the Church of the 2%, as it was later described.

This 'above-down', almost upstairs-downstairs Church reflected the self-understanding, and understanding by the people, of the Church. There was a strong division between clerical and lay – the altar rails expressed it in Church architecture; the priest saying Mass with his back to the people and the people looking on passively – the opposite of *communio* expressed it in the liturgy. This thinking was also represented by putting priests and bishops on pedestals. A Cork comedian half jokingly reflected the reality when he said, 'Bishop Connie Lucey gave a new word to the English language, boy! Connie coming down a stairs – condescending!' Another Irish bishop, not too far from Cork, unwittingly did the same when he called his whole household staff together to explain to them his new insight about Church as *communio*. 'I want to tell ye we are all equal in this house from now on, everyone from myself right down to the cook!'

At Vatican II, the speech of Cardinal Suenens of Belgium, one of the great theologian-bishops at the Council, was the decisive one in rejecting the old hierarchical, clerical, first class/second class citizen description of the Church. In outlining the new and revolutionary definition of the Church, he said:
(i) the Church is all the baptised (the 100%);
(ii) the Church is not just the clergy (the 2%);
(iii) there are two ways of being Church: clerical and lay;
(iv) all (100%) are full members of the Church;
(v) all (100%) are responsible for the Church ... not just the clergy.

'Cardinal Suenens, in rejecting the clerical vision of Church, proposed that the Council should first consider what it is to be a Christian, a member of God's people, before going on to the two chief ways of being Christian, clergy and lay. The lay person, in other words, was not a second rate Christian but a full Christian with all the rights and responsibilities of bringing Christ to the world.'[6]

The four hundred years sleep
Under the heading 'The Four Hundred Years Sleep', Edmund Flood says that many bishops and cardinals still resisted the new definition of Church, but that the majority were very much in favour, as had been shown by the vigorous and prolonged applause from the bishops at Cardinal Suenens' intervention. The Bishop of Pittsburg USA summed up the welcome for the new definition of Church when he said, 'The faithful have been waiting for four hundred years for a positive conciliar statement on the place, dignity and vocation of the layman.'[7]

A twentieth-century revolution
This seemingly simple core-change in the definition of the Church, from the Church being the Pope, bishops and priests, to the Church being all the people of God, has brought about a revolu-

tion in the Church in practice in the twentieth century. Under the guidance of the Holy Spirit, and contrary to all expectations, the Church has been re-defined. This was really a paradigm shift for the Church, almost like the shift from the flat-earth view of the world to that of it being round. This re-definition would have many major implications and raise many questions:

1. All the baptised were described as full members of the Church. What did this mean in practice?

2. The 'priesthood of all the laity' was re-asserted after centuries of inertia. What did this mean?

3. How does the ministerial priesthood relate to the priesthood of the laity? How are they different?

4. Pope, bishops, priests, and deacons are servants of the people of God. How can a change come about in practice, from being the Church, being in charge, to being servants of the people and developing a partnership Church?

5. What would the new definition of Church demand in terms of restructuring and re-definition of roles at all levels of Church?

The Church as communio

Cardinal Basil Hume, in his marvellous book, *Towards a Civilisation of Love: Being Church in Today's World*, takes us deeply into the nature of Church, and gives us some insight into the epoch-making importance of Vatican II's re-discovery of the core meaning of Church: 'The Church since the Second Vatican Council has been engaged in an intense experience of self-discovery. We have moved beyond the former emphasis on the visible, the structural, the hierarchical to a sustained meditation on the unfolding mystery, the inner reality of the Church (as a *communio* of the baptised).'[8]

The change could be summed up in Bonhoeffer's very deeply meaningful phrase, 'The Church is Christ existing as community.' What does this mean in reality? If the Church is Christ existing in the world or Christ existing as community, then the Church must look like Christ, must think like Christ, must act like Christ. The Church must not look like, think like, or act like a multinational or a bank or other business concern whose *modus operandi* and reason for being is profit. If the shape, the thought pattern and culture or way of being of the Church is that of institutions and organisations of the secular, consumer society, then it is not a sign of Christ. It is not the 'sacrament of Christ' in the world, as Schillebeeckx would say.

This very issue brings us to the heart of evangelisation, especially of youth, and to the heart of the vocations issue today. Are parishes *communios*, i.e. caring families of people who try to see all as members and equal before God? Are parishes and the Church a sign, a clear sign of Christ's teaching and way of life? Is the Irish Church a sign of contradiction in the consumer society of Western Europe and Ireland today? Are the Irish Catholic and Protestant Churches an outward sign of Christianity? The fact of the split or division of the Churches is the first and most obvious contradiction of the meaning of Church as *communio*, as a family representing Christ.

Putting Vatican II into practice
The Church in practice throughout the world has been wrestling with the implications of the re-definition of Church at Vatican II. The same would apply to myself, to parishes and to many priests. While I know that Vatican II is still a closed book for many Catholics and parishes, nevertheless I believe that the practice of Vatican II, and the deeper self-understanding of the Church over the last twenty years, is transforming the Church in many areas of the world. Many parishes in Ireland (chapters 2, 3, 4), in Latin America (chapter 8), in the USA (chapter 9) and worldwide (chapter 14) are trying to incarnate, or put in place a People of God model of Church, with its emphasis on the parish as *communio* responsible for its own governance, care, mission, and united around the word and sacrament, especially the eucharist. No one parish is a model of this type of Church, but many parishes are practising different aspects of it.

Conclusion
A major change came over the Catholic Church in the 1960s. This

revolutionary change, initiated at Vatican II, has continued to influence the Church worldwide and in Ireland since the 1960s. My priesthood has been practised during that period of major change in the Church. That change has influenced my person, my role and the Church in which I minister – both people and structures. The Church as defined by Vatican II is meant to be more about people, community, equality and partnership rather than about structure, institution and hierarchy. The pastoral reality of everyday is the magnetic field (or minefield!) in which the constant tension and struggle exists between the two poles of Church as people/community and the Church as hierarchy/institution. It is the constantly changing arena in which the 2% and the 98% struggle, sometimes for control, sometimes for partnership, as part of the evolving history of Church and ministry in the world.

PART III: THE WORLD 1960-1990

Some major changes came over the world in the 1960s and the 1970s. The world became for the first time a global village through the dawn of the electronic age or the era of television. The microchip and the computer were creating an information revolution. No person and no country would be an isolated island any longer. The civil rights movement in the USA, the stirrings among students worldwide, flower power and the peace movement worldwide were all movements towards democracy and assertions of the importance of the individual. Maybe the most important and significant of all was, and is, the women's movement. What has been most striking for me over the last thirty years is how these movements, which were small or localised at first, gathered momentum and spread rapidly. Equally striking is the fact that all of these movements coalesce like mountain streams to form a great and powerful river. The liberation of Eastern Europe in the 1980s and 1990s would seem to have been influenced by the domino effect of many trends, inccluding the civil rights movement, media power and global awareness.

Major trends

In 1982, John Naisbitt published his book, *Megatrends*.[9] It sold eight million copies. As the title suggests, it was about major trends. The identification of these megatrends, 'large social, economic, political, and technological changes which are slow to form, and once in place influence us for some time,'[10] was described by the *Washington Post* as a 'field-guide to the future'. In *Megatrends*, Naisbitt identified ten major trends or patterns in the forces transforming the world in the late nineteen-seventies and made his predictions for the 1980s. There would be shifts from:

1. industrial society to information society;
2. national economy to world economy;
3. centralisation to decentralisation;
4. institutional help to self-help;
5. representative democracy to participatory democracy;
6. hierarchies to networking;
7. short term to long term;
8. north to south;
9. either/or to multiple option;
10. forced technology to high tech/high touch.

These megatrends, or macro forces, change the way people live, the way they perceive things and the way their lives are affected at a deep level. The industrial revolution, the civil rights movement, the women's movement, the media revolution, the growth of capitalism and the consumer society and its negative effects like poverty, unemployment, emigration, all change people's circumstances, their relationships and, indeed, their culture and patterns of living. These megatrends effect at a deep level religion, spirituality, evangelisation, the role of the priest and the Church (chapters 7, 8, 9, 10). This is especially clear from *The Parish Project* in the USA and the *Notre Dame Study of Parish* (chapter 9). It was very obvious in our ministry in Sean McDermott Street. Naisbitt's findings are interesting in terms of the major trends that are influencing people and parishes in America and the world, including Ireland. In this context, I'm reminded of Bishop Carroll's famous words about Irish people's tendency to adapt everything good and bad from the USA and progressive countries: 'Every heresy comes to die in Ireland.' A great saying! But, of course, mega-trends, good and bad, come anyway.

Naisbitt's predictions in 1982 have been proved very accurate. Now in 1990 John Naisbitt and his wife, Patricia Aburdene, have produced *Megatrends 2000* which is an equally fascinating book about the major trends influencing our lives in the 1990s and be-yond. In this 'road map to the twenty-first century' Naisbitt and Aburdene outline:

The millennial megatrends [11]
1. Boom in world economies – increasing interdependence.
2. A new golden age for the arts.
3. Emergence of free-market socialism.
4. The world will become increasingly alike in lifestyle and culture.
5. The welfare state will decline.
6. The decade of women in leadership.
7. The age of biology as opposed to physics.
8. A great religious revival.
9. The triumph of the individual.
10. The rise of the Pacific rim (countries touching the Pacific).

What is being predicted here is a more democratic, humane, holis-tic, spiritual, peaceful, prosperous world with more respect for the individual and greater global interdependence and solidarity. It is a very optimistic and positive picture, based on facts and the 'signs of the times' as they appear at the moment. *Megatrends* and *Megatrends 2000* would be an important *vade mecum* for priests and policy makers, in terms of understanding some of the major forces effecting people and parishes today.

Some implications
All of the above megatrends are important since they influence our lives and life-styles, and our ways of thinking and acting. If megatrends didn't happen, if the world at the deeper or macro

level didn't change, then the role of the priest and the role of the parish, Church and gospel would be the same.

It seems to me that we in the Church have concentrated on the micro issues and forces while the macro has been changing under our feet. We are analysing the footnotes without reading the text or the large print. We're re-arranging the bedroom furniture upstairs whilst the house is on fire downstairs! We have continued to do more of the same with less effect. These different images of mine are saying the same thing: we need to spend a lot more time reading the larger text and analysing it – the megatrends, the values and beliefs of people today, their thought patterns, the major issues influencing people and their social reality. We need to focus on the changed reality and adapt our structures to meet the needs of that reality.

Ministry to macroforces
It is not just sufficient to be aware of, and identify the megatrends or macroforces affecting society and people's lives, though that is vital too. It is necessary to go beyond identification and analysis to critique them and to contradict them if they are contrary to the gospel and the needs of people, or piggyback on them if they are positive. All four steps – identification, analysis, critique and contradiction (or affirmation) – are necessary parts of evangelisation today.

Vatican II made this exercise of identifying, analysing and critiquing the modern world, a major part of its work, and CELAM, the Latin American Conference of Bishops, followed its methodology (Chapter 8). Pope John Paul II, in Knock 1979, spoke of it very clearly regarding the mission of the Church, when he spoke of each new generation as 'a new continent' to be understood and won for Christ.

Roles, patterns, structures, priorities must change in the Church to meet the changing 'continents' and realities. Otherwise the Church becomes a museum. The Church has been changing and adapting in Ireland and elsewhere since Vatican II especially: new roles in the liturgy, lay ministries in parishes, parish and pastoral councils, new social ministries, running renewal programmes. But I think that a deeper response is needed, a radical gospel response.

PART IV: MEGATRENDS AND EVANGELISATION

Let us now look at a number of megatrends which have had influence on the Church and the world over the past hundred years and are likely to affect and shape people's lives in Ireland and in the rest of the world in the 1990s and the third millennium. These may be positive or negative forces, or contain elements of both.

Within the Church the biblical, catechetical, liturgical and ecumenical movements at the start of the twentieth century were megatrends which culminated in the Vatican Council, the major megatrend in the Church at the end of the second millennium. Its central aim and focus, the reactivation of the laity, 98% of the Church, will have a huge influence on the Church and it's work in the 1990s and third millennium. All five megatrends, biblical, catechetical, ecumenical, liturgical and Vatican II, continue globally and locally. The biblical movement will, in my opinion, play an even greater role in the future in terms of ministry, evangelisation and the direction of politics, economics and society in the third millennium, as all the Churches concentrate on evangelisation.

Liberation theology, another megatrend, which emerged in Latin America in the 1960s, will continue to grow with the Latin American and third world Church which will be the major part of the Catholic Church in the third millennium. Its methodology, starting with the social reality rather than theory, and its content, with its emphasis on justice and equity for all God's people, will have a greater influence on the Church and world in the third millennium. Irish theologian Enda McDonagh says:

'In the last few decades, particularly since the Vatican Council, the local community of the Catholic Church has become more significant. This was expressed in a number of ways by emphasising bishops' conferences, by development of priests' councils, by synods and other assemblies of the laity. The best known of these developments occurred in Latin America with their Basic Christian Communities at the immediate local level and the Latin American Bishops' Conference (CELAM) at continental level. Their meetings at Medellin in 1968 and at Puebla in 1979 have become bench marks in the development of local Churches and of local theologies. Latin American liberation theology, which developed out of the basic communities and was endorsed and promoted by the meetings of the Bishops' Conference, has become the most influential form of Catholic and, indeed, of Christian theology today. It is not without its critics, including some at the Vatican. However, as a theology emerging out of a particular context and out of a particular geographical region, admittedly on a grand scale, it has restored to theology its original sense of place and time.'[12]

The new spirituality

Another very significant megatrend in the Church is the New Spirituality. The new spirituality, like many new discoveries, is 90% old! The new spirituality has many strands or tributaries, all of which coalesce to form a new megatrend. One strand, the spirituality of Vatican II, the best of the old and the best of the new, brings us back to the Bible, especially the New Testament and Jesus, and it emphasises the relationship of the word, sacrament and life in the world. The world is the place where holiness is to be achieved. The world is one world. The secular and the sacred are not two separate worlds. They meet in and, intermingle in, God's creation. The Church is not an end in itself. It is God's people, all of whom are called to be witnesses to the kingdom in the world.

A second strand is the spirituality of liberation theology which has justice and equity at its core. The justice of God, the elimination of structural and social sin which destroys people and the growth of spiritual and fraternal communion are part of its spirituality. Spiritual growth is possible only where people are liberated from sin and its effects, individual and structural, through Christ. This new spirituality of liberation theology is very challenging and effective since it starts with the social reality and applies the gospel to life.

A third strand of the new spirituality is often called creation spirituality since it re-emphasises creation as the first gift from God and that redemption is not the first or original blessing but the second. This spirituality is ecological, God-centred, Biblical and holistic. The fact that it is holistic counters a lot of the fractured and schizophrenic spirituality of the past few hundred years, one that separated soul from body, one that separated right brain from left brain in people and so emphasised logic, reason, propositional religion, creeds, catechism – all important but imbalanced and only a part of Christianity and life. It neglected the right brain areas of story, myth, community, feelings, art, the creative, the imagination as parts of spirituality and religion. Matthew Fox and Thomas Berry are two well-known proponents of creation spirituality. Fr Andrew Greeley, in discussing 'a theology of the religious imagination' because 'religion is an imaginative activity before it becomes a cognitive activity,'[13] emphasises the reality and the search for God in story, myth, culture and community. Fox speaks of spirituality and theology getting away from 'the departmentalising of theology that took place in the eighteenth century à la Newton. The creation-centred spiritual tradition cannot be taught within the confines of cartesian, left brained, academic structures alone. There is a need for 're-connecting science, mysticism, art, and social transformation'. Creation spirituality is 'about liberating Christianity from its patriarchal self, from its overly introspective and fearful self, from its dualistic self, from its fear of passion, prophecy.'[14] Fox sees the development of the more holistic, integrated spirituality, with its emphasis on mysticism as well as creed, on community and prophetic commitment in action, as a great counter to the success of fundamentalist religions today. They are fulfilling a need which the more logical, propositional, institutional, patriarchal, hierarchical Church is not meeting. The holistic departs from the *either/or* to a *both/and* balance which sees the values of creed *and* community, logic *and* feelings, dogma *and* mysticism, unity *and* equality, imagination *and* reason.

Machine as metaphor

Joe Holland in his recent book, *Creative Communion*, draws out the implications of a movement from an atomistic, mechanistic, 'fractured' world in science, education, philosophy, theology, to a more holistic one. It is really a megatrend or major shift from the industrial era (1815-1950s) with its root metaphor and major influence, the machine, to the post-industrial era:

'Our age is witnessing the end of the modern era and final breakup of the dualism of spirit and matter that has marked western culture since the time of classical Greece. This period of crisis is felt particularly keenly in the first world where technological progress has been built on a foundation of rationalism and materialism. Yet our age is also witnessing the dawn of a new era, holistic in character, ecologically-centred, moving towards a new integration of science and spirituality. As citizens of this new era, we can assist in the birth of the dawning culture in our families and in our work.' [15]

Fourteen megatrends

In this section I have mentioned fourteen megatrends in the Church and world which are, in general, very positive in terms of the development of religion and of people. The megatrends are the biblical movement, the ecumenical movement, the catechetical movement, the liturgical movement, liberation theology, the new spirituality, Vatican II, all in the Church; the civil rights movement, the students' movement of the sixties and seventies, the peace movement, the green movement, the media revolution, the women's movement, the movement from a fractured world to a more holistic one. Note especially the relationship between these megatrends and how they build momentum for each other, if they are not contrary ones.

We must locate the Ireland of the 1990s, and therefore the Church in Ireland and the role of the priest, within these macroforces of the Church and of the world and bring the light of the gospel to bear on them and on the Church which has been influenced by them. That is the challenge at the end of the second millenium and the beginning of the third.

Summary
Ireland, the Catholic Church and the world changed enormously from the 1960s to the 1990s.

In my view, Ireland prior to 1960 could be described primarily as insular, rural, Catholic and nationalist in its culture and way of life. The Ireland of today would best be described as capitalist, industrial, Christian and pluralistic in that order, certainly in the urban setting. Our society has experienced major change. The macro forces are different. Its a different 'ballgame' for gospel, Church, priest and the people of Ireland. It is time we started facing that reality in a more organised, committed and creative manner.

Notes
1.	ESRI, *Economic Commentary*, April 1989: 'Medium-Term Prospects for Ireland: An Update.'
	John Bradley and John FitzGerald: Table 1, ESRI *Commentary*, April 1990.
2.	Central Statistics Office, Department of Finance, *Economic Review and Outlooks*, Dublin.
3.	See article in *The Sunday Tribune*, July 29 1990 by Paul Tansey.
4.	*One Million Poor*, Ed. Stanislaus Kennedy, Turoe Press, Dublin 1981.
5.	John Paul II, *The Pope in Ireland: Addresses and Homilies*, Veritas, Dublin 1979, p. 52.
6.	Edmund Flood OSB, *Vatican Council in Practice*, Living Parish Pamphlets, London 1966, pp. 29-30.

7.   Ibid. p. 31.
8.   Cardinal Basil Hume, *Towards a Civilization of Love*, Hodder & Stoughton, London 1988, p. 15.
9.   John Naisbitt, *Megatrends*, Warner Books, New York 1984.
10.   Quoted from John Naisbitt and Patricia Aburdene, *Megatrends 2000*, Sidgwick & Jackson, London 1990.
11.   Ibid. p. 3.
12.   Enda McDonagh, 'Between Westport and Asia Minor', *The Furrow*, Maynooth, April 1990, p. 232.
13.   Andrew M. Greeley, *God in Popular Culture*, Thomas More Press, Chicago 1988, p. 3.
14.   Matthew Fox, *Original Blessing*, Bear & Co, New Mexico 1983, p. 25.
15.   Joseph Holland, *Creative Communion*, Paulist Press, New York 1989.

SECTION II

Parish and Evangelisation

CHAPTER 6:
Parish: History, Issues, Realities

CHAPTER 7:
Re-defining Goals and Roles

CHAPTER 8:
The New Definition in Practice

CHAPTER 9:
The Parish in the USA

Parish:
History, Issues, Realities

In Section I, I have described my experience of 'priesting' (chapters 1-4) and its context (chapter 5). In Section II, I will now take a deeper look at the normal *locus operandi* of 'priesting' and of living the Christian life, i.e. the parish or local Church.

Some Important Questions
Was there Church life before parish?
How did the Church organise itself in the early centuries?
Was there Church life outside parish in Ireland?
What will be the form and shape of the local Church of the future?
Is the territorial parish the best model for evangelisation and being Church today?

The best model of local Church is the one that :
a) answers peoples' religious and spiritual needs and best helps them to find meaning in their everyday lives;
b) gives them a sense of dignity and belonging as a caring Christian Community;
c) best facilitates evangelisation and the living out of the gospel imperatives.

In this chapter we will look at how the Church has organised herself 'as Church' through the ages at local level and, especially, as parish. Specifically, we will be looking at four things:
1. Before parish: four examples.
2. Origins and development of parish.
3. The parish today, 1960s-1990s.
4. The parish at the crossroads.

PART I: BEFORE PARISH: FOUR EXAMPLES

For the first four centuries after Christ, the Christian Church thrived and the concept of parish hadn't yet been thought of. The first Christian communities, as described in the New Testament, were dynamic and well organised. Like any new movement, Christianity had certain basic elements which it got from its founder, Christ. We read in the Acts of the Apostles (Acts 2:42-47) an account of the first Christian community:

'These remained faithful to the teaching of the apostles, to brotherhood, to the breaking of bread and to the prayers. The faithful all lived together and owned everything in common; they sold their goods and shared out the proceeds among themselves according to what each one needed. They went as a body to the temple everyday but met in their houses for the breaking of bread.'

People, proclamation, brotherhood, eucharist and ministry were the core elements. These core elements would have been part of each local community but the local Church would vary in form and structure. The Christian Church in these early centuries was very much a house Church or a Church of small communities which gathered in the homes and small Churches or catacombs, under various leaders – travelling apostles or prophets or teachers or elder-presbyters or, from the third or fourth century, bishops and priests.

1. The first Christian community
Once I became administrator (parish priest juridically) in Sean McDermott Street in 1981, my vision or model for development of the parish was the first Christian community. The first Christian community was attempting to incarnate the vision and teaching of Christ. It is the expression of 'being Church' in the first century after Christ.

Here is a caring Christian community. One senses, first of all, a great dynamism in it. There is a strong community emphasis. It is all about the community, the people together sharing, living, worshipping and caring for each other. There is an integration of gospel and life, secular and sacred, theology and fellowship, teaching and practice, equality and sharing. This Church is, primarily, based around the homes of the people – house Churches, *ecclesiola* (Vatican II) – and around small communities.

2. The local Church in Corinth

What was the Greek and Gentile experience of local Church, or being Church, in an urban and alien or pagan setting? Here we get our information from the letter of St Paul which was written in order to give advice on particular problems or issues which had arisen. But as Enda Lyons says in his book, *Partnership in Parish*, 'The letters were not written with us in the twentieth century in mind, and so do not give us a plan for organising parish life today ... (they) do, however, capture something of the atmosphere and the spirit which pervaded these Churches.'[1]

The first letter of St Paul to the Corinthians makes very interesting reading in terms of today's parish and today's diocese. It is really like a pastoral letter dealing with the issues of the day, both within the Church itself, and in the society in which the Church is called to exist and to witness. Paul's letter deals with dissensions within the Church, true and false wisdom, incest, marriage and virginity, worship of idols, decorum at public worship (women wearing headscarves in Church – God be with the days!) and, finally, about special gifts, about which there is dissension in the community. We will focus on the latter, special gifts, since they give some insight into the nature of the local Church in Corinth. Paul writes:

'There is a variety of gifts but always the same spirit; there are all sorts of services to be done, but always the same Lord; working in all sorts of different ways in different people ... for a good purpose. One has the gift of preaching with wisdom, another the gift of instructing, one healing ... another prophecy, one discernment, another the gift of tongues ... Just as the human body, though is made up of many parts, is a single unit, so it is with Christ ... God put all the parts into the body on purpose. If all the parts were the same, how could it be a body? (*Or a community?*) (1 Cor 1:24-21)

Many gifts, many, many gifts; all different for different needs and services to the community, all to build up the community, the Body of Christ. Where have all the ministries in the Church gone?

Many gifts, many ministries

The first thing that strikes me about this passage is that so many gifts have been stifled in the Church over the centuries. The second thing is that God has given gifts to many, many people for the development and the good of the Church and of people, and following from this is the fact that the Church cannot develop fully without the gifts of all the members of the Church (the laity) being tapped. I find it fascinating to read this passage now because I haven't read it in one piece for about ten years. And during those ten years I have become firmly convinced that we priests haven't enough talents to develop the Church in each parish … we just haven't enough gifts and talents – full stop. When I hear a lot of criticism of priests about preaching, and lack of understanding of youth, or lack of leadership abilities for developing collaborative ministry or involvement, or that priests are not perfect leaders, I am saddened because,

(i) I know we haven't all the gifts, we're not perfect;

(ii) yet we created a Church where all depended on us;

(iii) and the critics are often the least likely to get involved and take responsibility.

But in every parish there are all the gifts, between priests (2%) and people (98%). The Church has all those skills available to it. The gospel needs them and the Church and the people need them. I believe that was one of the great insights of the Vatican Council: the giftedness of the People of God and the need of the gospel and the Church for those gifts to be tapped and revitalised. The ministry of Church leader is to call forth and bring forth those ministries and gifts of the People of God. St Paul and the early Church, before parish and the clerical model of Church were heard of, were very much aware of the fact that people *were* the Church, that each person had been given certain gifts for the good of all;

97

that there was a diversity of gifts; that no one had a monopoly on all the gifts; that all come from the one source, God, for the good of the total community, the Church.

Lyons concludes his study of the local Christian community in Corinth: 'The unity of a body, consisting in the variety of its organs, the diversity of their functions, and the mutual co-operation between the organs – that is Paul's model for life in the parish* of Corinth, and, indeed, in any parish. Another point which the reader might notice about the passage from Paul's letter is the emphasis on service rather than rank, on action rather than office, on what people were doing rather than who they were.'[2]

3. When in Rome

In his letter to the Romans, St Paul gives a very interesting list of activities which were obviously part of the local Church. First of all, as in his letter to the Corinthians, Paul uses the same imagery of the one body and many parts (using the same sermon for every group!)

'Just as each of our bodies has several parts and each part has a separate function, so all of us, in union with Christ, form one body, and as parts of it we belong to each other.' (Rom 12:4-6)

All the gifts and all the ministries do not reside in one or two, or three, people. There is a multiplicity and a diversity of gifts and ministries. And all are united with Christ, not just bishop or priest. All are part of Christ's body through baptism. All the baptised have a share in Christ's priesthood.

Then he goes on: 'If your gift is prophecy, then use it as your faith suggests; if administration, then use it for administration; if teaching, then use it for teaching. Let the preachers deliver sermons, the almsgivers give freely, the officials be diligent and those who do works of mercy do them cheerfully.' (Rom 12:6-9)

---

* Lyons says that the experience of Church life described in Corinth is closer to our experience of parish life than our experience of diocese and for this reason he uses the word 'parish'.

He mentions there seven ministries practised in the community. Which is the priest? Who gives the sermons?

It is obvious that in this local Church in Rome:
1. the Church is a community;
2. there is a great variety of ministries;
3. there is friction between the ministers ... role conflict, and perhaps role confusion.

What is, perhaps, most striking is the similarity in structure between the two local Christian communities in Rome and Corinth, a thousand miles apart.

4. The Monastic Model

The Irish Church has always been acknowledged worldwide as one of the great Churches of Christianity. Since the time of Patrick it has been a great 'sending' Church. This great and dynamic Church was primarily a monastic Church. A Church of charismatic founders and leaders like Columba of Derry and Kells (and Iona), Finian of Clonard, Enda of the Aran Islands, Brendan of Clonfert, Bridget of Kildare, Comgall of Bangor, Finbarr of Cork, Kieran of Clonmacnoise – all saints and scholars of the Bible, spirituality and evangelisation.

In this Church of the monasteries, where the abbots were more powerful than the bishops, the Bible was at the core. This great love of the Bible is exemplified for posterity in the *Book of Kells* and the *Book of Durrow*. But the monks and the monastic Church did not only revere the Bible and biblical spirituality. They lived it. Prayer, sacrifice, fellowship, evangelisation, mission and devotion to the eucharist were biblical virtues that were the hallmarks of the Irish monastic Church.

From the eighth to the twelfth century, before dioceses and parishes were formalised, the Irish Church was primarily, and almost totally, a monastic Church. The 'monastic model' was the local Church model.

The monastic model of 'parish' or local Church was an integrated model of life and religion, of community and worship, and of secular and spiritual service. The model of Church seemed to follow the model of social organisation at the time. Of course it wasn't a perfect model – too much control by families and local landlords at times. But nevertheless, it was most successful as a model of inculturation and pastoral care. It survived and thrived in hard times in Ireland during periods of crisis and transition. This model also proved its worth during the Dark Ages (500-800) in Europe when religion almost disappeared. The strengths of the monastic model were primarily the strengths of its leaders and their followers. Single minded, independent in spirit, missionary in outlook, the monks had the flexibility to follow 'need' and not be slaves of 'territory'.

Charismatic leaders
It is interesting to note that, when structures and institutions floundered in the Dark Ages, it was charismatic individuals, like the Irish monks, who brought about renewal and new hope. It is also interesting to note that with the collapse of parish in Europe other charismatic leaders filled the breach – the rise of the great religious orders in Europe. The same tended to happen in Ireland with the decline of the monasteries. Some charismatic and single-minded individuals, the *Céli Dé*, began a reform movement in the 700s from two great monasteries in Dublin, Tallaght and Finglas. Maybe Paddy Wallace and his Parish Development and Renewal team are the *Céli Dé* of today?

The point about the need for charismatic leaders or new pathfinders is also made very strongly today with regard to the decline in vocations to the religious orders.[3] The religious orders were originally founded by charismatic personalities who went outside the structures and thought-patterns of the time and made an original response to a new need. Must the same be done about parish today?

Characteristics of change
More generally, two things tend to happen in periods of major

change or transition. The first is a period of break-up of society, institutions, community, and of patterns and meanings. It is a period of turbulence, confusion and chaos. Also old definitions, creeds and conventional wisdom get questioned. Such is the period in modern society and in the Church today. The second happening in periods of major change and breakdown is that charismatic and creative leaders begin to search for new meanings, new patterns and help to create new structures.[4] People begin to group around these new prophets and pathfinders, to share their vision and meaning. People also gravitate towards small groups for security and community in answer to the insecurity and alienation created by the upheaval of society. New meaning, new definitions, regrouping and charismatic personalities are part of the pattern of response to a time of crisis and transition. John XXIII and the Vatican II, the new Code of Canon Law and the restructuring of the Church, are good examples of this in ecclesiastical terms at the macro level.

Lessons for today

We, in today's period of major change, can learn from the monastic model of evangelisation and being Church at local level:

(a) By copying the example of flexibility, sense of mission, and the need for identifying and encouraging pathfinders or creative and charismatic leaders, clerical or lay.

(b) By studying its model of being 'parish' or local Church and applying some of its learnings to the redevelopment and restructuring of the Church. Of particular interest would be the 'inculturation', building around existing patterns of place, community, culture, and ways of worship. The same successful pattern was adopted by the founders of the new religious orders in Europe – developing shrines, customs, local leadership. The most striking things about the 'monastic model' of parish was that it was Bible-centred, life-centred, Mass-centred, and missionary.

Conclusion

We have seen that there *was* Church life before parish. All of these four models of being Church at local level can throw light on how best the Church can serve the gospel, the People of God and the world, at local level today. All four examples were in different situations, cultures and environments, and adapted or developed in dialogue with the local circumstances. All have the same core elements of the Christian community: People of God, the teaching of the apostles, eucharist, brotherhood and ministry. But they also have different leadership structures (governance), different ministries and a different shape or form. One community is in Palestine, the homeland of Jesus and the Jewish religion, becoming independent of it and being in relationship with it. One is in pagan Corinth, meeting the advanced Greek culture and society. One is in the heart of the other great culture and civilisation of that era, the Roman empire. And one is in pagan, fairly violent, tribal Ireland. What strikes me, above all, about them is:

(i) Their flexibility and differences, taking into account each local culture and environment;

(ii) Ministry and governance was the responsibility of the whole community, not the clergy alone;

(iii) Christianity was in the community, in life, in the marketplace.

PART II: ORIGIN OF PARISH

Fr Thomas Sweetser SJ, and Carol Wisniewski Holden, who have spent the past sixteen years evaluating parishes in the USA, make this introductory comment on their study of parish:

'The origins and development of parish life provide a perspective for judging the present situation and future direction. Parishes did not begin until the fourth century.

By the fourth century, most Christians were clustered around a central worship centre (basilica). Some, however, lived at a distance from the place of worship, and the leaders were concerned about those who could not get to the bishop's Mass. We have evidence from the correspondence of Pope Celasius 1 (492-496) that the solution to the problem was to divide up the rural areas into

102

parishes, each of which was placed under the jurisdiction of a resident priest (presbyter). The Pope's correspondence dealt with the correct disposition of parish revenues. He stipulated that one-fourth of the revenue should go to the upkeep and maintenance of the parish, one-fourth to the poor and dependants, one-fourth to the pastor, and one-fourth to the bishop.'[5]

Here we see that the chief reason for the setting up of parish is the importance for the Christian community to be able to gather round the table of the Lord, to celebrate the eucharist. Eucharist and Christian community can never be separated in the eyes of Christ and of the Church. Some of the elements one can glean from the very first account of parish are Christian community, eucharist, a priest, an area (not yet defined exactly) and sharing (support of the poor and the parish priest).

The origin of parish is also the origin of the 'pastor', or the parish priest as we know him today. He was to be an *alter ego* for the bishop in rural areas in order to make the eucharist available for the People of God.

Who elects the pastor?

One hundred years after Pope Celasius adapted the idea of parish, Pope St Gregory the Great took a hand in developing parish. He elected some priests to parishes in Tuscany and so changed the Church's policy up to then, where the people chose their own pastor. From 591 the bishops selected the parish priest and the appointment was for life.

Role of the pastor

Under Pope Gregory's reform, the pastor was also given the following duties to perform: solemn baptisms, to enact the Easter penance duty, to perform burials, and to require parishioners to attend the parish Mass on Sundays and feast days.

In 787, the Council of Nicea ratified these duties of a pastor and gave him further rights: he could not be removed from office by the bishop and he was given title to parish property for his support.

Sunday obligation

It is very interesting to note that Sunday obligation – the obligation to attend Mass on Sundays and feast days – began in the eighth century, not because people weren't attending Mass, but because many were going to shrines set up by religious in honour of local saints. So to counteract the loss of members and of revenue, the people were obliged to attend Mass in their own parish on Sundays and holy days of obligation. Only the pastor could release people from that obligation. That pattern of attendance of the Sunday parish Masses continued almost unbroken through the centuries till the advent of evening Masses after Vatican II.

The secular priest

A most radical development occurred in the concept of parish, and in the role of the priest, during the reign of the Emperor Charlemagne at the beginning of the ninth century. Charlemagne exempted pastors from paying taxes and attached twenty acres of land, called the altar plot, to each parish for the support of the pastor. This made the pastor quite independent of the Church and of the people. Charlemagne also influenced the method of selection of the parish priest. He took it out of the hands of the bishop and gave it back to the people, in theory. In practice, the parish priest or pastor was elected by the local monarch. This secularising of the position of pastor gave him more status and stability but it also tended to change the parish into a more political and business entity. As Sweetser and Wisniewski Holden say:

'The outcome of Charlemagne's decrees on parish life was that the pastor became not only the spiritual, but also the secular leader of the area. Parishes became the place for conducting local business and exercising political power. The term secular clergy applied to priests, derives from this practice.'[6]

Serving Christ or Caesar?

I think this change of emphasis during the reign of Charlemagne is one of the issues at the core of the problems concerning the role of the priest or pastor today. He has two jobs, one evangelical or spiritual, and one secular, that are quite contradictory and at log-gerheads with each other in his role and within himself. Was the priest of Charlemagne's time able to fulfil his role of spiritual leader and secular leader satisfactorily? Can the priest of today fulfil his call by Christ to be an evangelical/spiritual leader of the People of God, and have so many 'secular' responsibilities? Can the priest be servant of Christ and of Caesar? Can the parish? Can the Church? I will look at this question of the role of the priest in chapters 11 and 12, when I will try to clarify that role.

In terms of the role of parish, it is interesting to note, as Sweetser and Wisniewski Holden do, that parishes declined during the Dark Ages. And what happened? 'Charismatic individuals and groups sought to fill the vacuum. A number of religious orders were founded during this period.'[7]

Is this a pointer for today, with all our new needs? Will there be creative responses, new ministries, new Church structures, pro-phetic people?

Conflict leads to development
With the rise of these orders came inevitable clashes between sec-ular clergy and religious orders. (Could never happen today!)

Sweetser and Wisniewski Holden tell us of the important inter-vention of Pope Sixtus IV, which continued the development of parish, and finally the contribution of the Council of Trent (1563) and the Code of 1917 to the development of parish.

Pope Sixtus IV (1471-1481) tried to manage the conflicts between secular and religious clergy by setting down some compromise guidelines:
1. Masses offered by the religious orders satisfied the people's obligation to attend Mass on Sundays and feast days.
2. Bishops had control over the list of approved confessors. Priests had to have 'faculties' in order to hear confession. This provided some control over the activities of religious orders in a diocese.
3. Charitable institutions were separated from parishes so that

religious orders could care for the physical needs of people independent of the pastors.

4. A pastor still had the final authority over the people under his jurisdiction and could impose censures on those who got out of line.

The Council of Trent

Pope Sixtus' guidelines, however, did not clear up the conflicts. The pontiff was unable to clarify the boundary problem: Who belonged to what parish? Where did one pastor's jurisdiction end and another's begin? This dispute continued until the Council of Trent.

The twenty-fourth session of the Council of Trent, held in 1563, addressed parish life and organisation in the following ways:

1. It clarified parish boundaries so that every parish within a diocese had a territorial definition. This stipulation had many exceptions, however, as the ethnic, non-territorial parishes of American cities manifest.

2. It gave pastors control over the sacraments administered to their people to such an extent that marriages performed without the pastor's consent were invalid.

3. It guaranteed pastors an income: no longer did one-fourth of the parish income go to the bishop.

4. It specified that pastors were to be selected by the bishop and had to pass an examination to show they were equipped for the job. Once appointed, they were guaranteed that pastorate for life.

5. It noo longer confined the Sunday obligation for attending Mass to the local parish. Any valid Mass would do. Pastors could no longer impose censures on their people.

The Code of Canon Law

In 1917, the Code of Canon Law systematised the centuries of adaptation and development of parish by spelling out the duties and rights of pastors. Pastors are expected to do the following:

1. Reside in the parish and have only one parish at a time.

2. Have jurisdiction over the sacraments administered to the people.

3. Offer Masses for the people and provide for the education of the youth.

5. Administer the money of the parish under the bishop's supervision.

6. Grant dispensations to the people whenever necessary.

7. Be examined and approved by the bishop if they have been appointed for life.

Notice that the needs and rights of the parishioners are not mentioned, only alluded to, in official correspondence and papal decrees. The pastor was the focus of the parish life and development.

In the next chapter, we will see the latest development in the Church's understanding of parish, as encapsulated in the new Code of Canon Law.

PART III: THE PARISH TODAY, 1960s-1990s

The old style parish
The old style parish worked very well. Why didn't John XXIII leave the Church and the parish alone? Weren't we doing fine?

I believe the old style parish worked very well. That was my experience as a young person growing up in rural Ireland. And, I believe, it was also the experience of most of our older priests and people.

Why did the old style parish work well before 1960? And what has changed? I believe five words explain the reasons for change, and therefore, the problems of parish today. The five words are: mobility, education, cultural 'progress', media, Vatican II.

Mobility
The first reason why the parish worked well in the old days was

that the people were born into a certain area, lived and died there and moved very little in the intervening sixty or seventy years. Parish and the neighbourhood community coalesced perfectly. They were a natural community and the idea of geographical parish built on that. All the people knew each other, too well at times, and were a family. Mobility, transport, lack of jobs, etc., have changed all that today.

Education
The second reason why parish worked well in the old days, or more correctly the clerical model of parish worked well, is that the people were less educated and therefore, in general, more accepting of what they were told. Of course there were exceptions but they kept quiet, dropped out quietly or were kicked out if they became troublesome. As people became more educated in Ireland and elsewhere, the relationship of people with the priest and with the Church has inevitably shifted. Andrew Greeley has documented this change better than anybody else in his research and writing with The National Opinion & Research Centre, Chicago, and, indeed, the massive *Notre Dame Study of Parish* adverts to the same. (chapter 9)

'Progress'
The third reason why parish worked well is that change in society was at a much slower pace. In general, institutions were respected, the world of work was local, the pattern of extended family and roles in a community were fairly clear and unchanging.

In the 1960s, the pace of life and the nature of society changed rapidly, with urbanisation, industrialisation, breakdown of community all contributing. A major strain was put on institutions, authority, and the role of the parish and the priest.

Media
The fourth reason for change was the advent of television and the growth of the media industry and its influence. In the old parish the home, the school and the parish (priest) worked in unison and

gave the same clear message. That was the reality. For children and youth there was a clear message, whereas today young people are getting a host of different messages from all three, with the media as a fourth source. Young people, and adults, are getting mixed and often contradictory messages, like a radio station suffering from interference. Young people are confused – and adults! And priests! The reality for parish, for priests and for evangelisation is different because of the information explosion.

Vatican II

The fifth issue is the Vatican Council. The old parish was built around the priest, with patterns and structures devised by him. The people, for the most part, were willing helpers. The home, the school and the Church were the chief vehicles of evangelisation with a large variety of devotions, sodalities, missions, sacramental and other holy things or exercises, as vehicles of holiness. That type of parish seemed to work well. Doctrine was clear, roles were clear, responsibilities were clear, ways to holiness were clear. So why change? Or what went wrong? Who with any sense would give us instead the parish today? Doctrine is confused, roles are confused, the people are confused, the priests are confused!

Why Change?

Well, of course, the answer is that the underlying realities have changed. The old-style parish worked well because (a) people tended to live in the one place, (b) they listened to authority more, (c) community was strong, and (d) structures were more static. Because these underlying realities had all changed, Pope John and Vatican II set out to deal with the new reality. A new reality brings new challenges and demands new responses. In an era of transition like the 1960s-90s, roles, patterns, structures and ways of looking at things all change. Old wineskins cannot adequately contain new wine. Neither can old and static parish structures deal with new and changing social realities.

The question of parish

A major issue that came up between younger and older priests in the Dublin diocese in the 1970s and early 1980s was the choice between emphasis on working with small groups or running the parish as an institution. That, for me, is the presenting problem of the deeper question of parish. Is parish relevant? Is parish succeeding? Is parish about large numbers or small groups? Is there an alternative to parish? Worldwide in the Church this question is being asked about parish – about its ability and appropriateness as a structure or vehicle to meet the needs of evangelisation and of the Christian people today. This question is being asked in the Philippines by the Columban Fathers and the local bishops.[8] It is being asked in Latin America by the Latin American Conference of Bishops (CELAM) and in thousands of parishes where Basic Christian Communities are becoming more and more the way of being 'local Church'. It is being asked in the USA where the bishops set up *The Parish Project* in 1978 to look at the relevance of parish. It is being asked in Europe where there is a great shortage of priests, as in North and South America. And it is being asked here.

The role of the parish

I want to try and clarify the question of parish for myself and the reader. What is parish asked to do? It is meant to be the place where people today meet their spiritual and religious and 'meaning in life' needs as individuals and as community. It is where they are to be Church with, and for, each other. It is where they are expected to worship with meaning and fulfilment, to get a deeper understanding of the word of God, to examine the questions of life and society in the light of the gospel, to live as a community, to 'act justly, to love tenderly and walk humbly with their God.' (Micah)

A lot has been expected of parish. In the past four hundred years, along with the diocese, it has been the major way of being Church at local level. So the question of parish is a vital one for the Church today. Whether it is addressed, and how it is addressed, will have vital implications for the Church and for the gospel.

PART IV: PARISH AT A CROSSROADS

The parish is at a crossroads, especially in urban settings, where there is a lot of mobility, and where groups may be more important than geographical location. There is a lot of alienation in such situations, and outdated parish structures can come in the way of community-building and evangelisation.

Before we can come up with a worthwhile answer to the question of parish, and therefore continue to invest a lot of personal resources and energy into parish in its present structure, I believe that we need a lot of information, real information, about parish. Some things that we need to know are in the areas of:
1. Community;
2. Spirituality/meaning;
3. Evangelisation.

1. Community
a. If we are to build caring Christian communities through parish, we need to know how community happens today.
b. We need to know how parish is succeeding or coming in the way of forming community today.

2. Spirituality/meaning
We need to know how people today, educated or non-educated, youth or adult, rural or urban, working-class or middle- and upper-class, meet their spiritual, religious and meaning needs. The *Notre Dame Study* and *The Parish Project* in the USA have looked at this aspect of Church life. Every diocese needs to do the same.

3. Evangelisation: research
We need to know from empirical research, both qualitative and quantitative, as well as from informal gathering of information

and experience, how parish is succeeding or not as a vehicle of evangelisation and pastoral care. Have we done any research in Dublin, in our 194 parishes, as to how parish is working? Not that I know of. We need to, urgently. There is a wonderful fund of pastoral experience among our priests, some of whom have been practising it for fifty years. We have fifteen *thousand* years of evangelising and pastoral experience among our seven hundred priests alone! One good study of their experience, and that of their parishioners, would be worth a mountain of 'hunch' information and guesswork. We owe it to the priests who are working so hard to tap this reservoir of pastoral experience. We owe it to the many community and parish groups who are trying to be Church in a meaningful and responsive way today. We owe it to the gospel to read the 'signs of the times' exactly, and to know the attitudes, values, aspirations, and changing life patterns. There are obviously ways of measuring parish as a tool of community-building and evangelisation, or if there aren't, we have got to devise them. We need to come up with some tools for evaluation of parish and evaluation of evangelisation.

Professor Conor Ward and members of the Social Science Research Centre in UCD have been doing some very interesting qualitative research and evaluation, especially in community situations, over the past five years. That type of expertise, and that of people like them, would be invaluable in evaluating parish as the major vehicle of evangelisation, and of being Church, today. Fr Conor Ward's own internationally recognised study, *Priests and People,*[9] a study of parish, the role of the priest and the people of the parish, done in the 1960s in Liverpool, is a model in this field. Fr Thomas Sweetser and his parish evaluation team in Chicago have been evaluating parish for seventeen years now and Fr Phil Murnion has been evaluating dioceses – or, more correctly, helping dioceses to evaluate themselves.

Vital information
The people in the parishes have a wealth of vital information that

must be tapped. As well as through formal professional studies, we can collect exact information and facts in other ways through parish assemblies, parish self-surveys, meeting with specific groups. The important issue is that the diocese needs exact inform-ation and facts and therefore it needs to establish, on an ongoing basis, an information-gathering mechanism as a vital and neces-sary part of evangelisation. It is part of any successful business or-ganisation today. It should be part of Church. Access to factual in-formation in the area of values, ideas, beliefs, behaviour and practices, becomes even more important in an era of transition. In a word, pastoral research and planning are a vital pre-requisite for an effective pastoral plan today.

Parish from personal experience
Team ministry
When I finished working in Sean McDermott Street I was appoint-ed to lead a team ministry experiment in the parish of Bonny-brook, a large, mostly working class parish on the north side of Dublin. In 1986 the diocese had decided to launch team ministry in three parishes: St James' in the south inner city, Ballymun and Bonnybrook on the north side of the city, as part of an experiment in ministry and pastoral care.

The idea of team ministry was that a mixed group of priests and sisters would co-opt lay people from the parish on to the team, and then that team would have responsibility for involving the whole parish in developing itself into a caring Christian commu-nity.

This would be a parish geared to mission, not maintenance, in the eyes of the diocesan authorities and the team. We, the team in Bonnybrook, were trying to gear the parish towards the Vatican II model. It was slowly moving towards that in some areas of its life, but despite the clear efforts of the diocese and the parish develop-ment team to gear the parish towards evangelisation and the building of Christian community, I still believe that the very struc-ture of the parish came between us and achieving a lot more in

113

terms of evangelisation and development of the people of the area. I know that the structure of parish inhibited and stopped evangelisation. This had been my experience, especially in Sean McDermott Street.

I believe the new Code of Canon Law, which has redefined the role and nature of parish, is voicing some of the same concern and need for change of direction and structure. I believe the Holy Spirit is at work here in a very deep way because the Code of Canon Law is the Church itself re-defining and re-structuring itself, based on its new self-understanding at Vatican II. In other words, the Code's definition comes as much from the new self-understanding of the Church, as from the needs of evangelisation and society today. The Code reflects, as Vatican II does, the outcome of the Church's exercise of analysis *ad intra* and *ad extra* on the nature of the Church itself, and of its analysis of the changed world of the twentieth century.

In the next three chapters we will hopefully deepen our understanding of parish by looking at the parish (a) in the new Code of Canon Law and (b) at the development of parish in Latin America and in the USA.

Notes
1. Enda Lyons, *Partnership in Parish*, The Columba Press, Dublin 1987, p. 65.
2. Ibid. p. 70.
3. Gerald A Arbuckle SM, *Out of Chaos: Refounding Religious Congregations*, Paulist Press, New York 1988.
4. Ibid.
5. Thomas Sweetser SJ & Carol Wisniewski Holden, *Leadership in a Successful Parish*, Harper & Row, San Francisco 1987, p. 5.
6. Ibid. p. 7.
7. Ibid.
8. Niall O'Brien, *Revolution of the Heart*, OUP, New York 1987.
9. Conor K Ward, *Priest and People: A study in the sociology of religion*, Liverpool UP, 1965.

CHAPTER 7

Re-defining Goals and Roles

At Vatican II, the Church reviewed and re-defined its goal and role in the world in the light of the gospel and the needs of people at the end of the twentieth century. The re-defined goals and roles of the Church are contained in the New Code of Canon Law. In this chapter, I will look at the re-defined role of the parish and diocese in the New Code.

THE PARISH IN THE NEW CODE OF CANON LAW

I was right in the middle of my writing about the role of the priest and his place in the parish, his *locus operandi*, when I got an article on the role of the priest and the role of the parish as defined in the New Code of Canon Law and I was absolutely delighted.

I had asked Alex Stenson, our Diocesan Chancellor, for articles about the New Code's definitions of priest, parish, parishioner, diocese. I hadn't yet read the New Code itself. I had been too busy trying to survive, trying to deal with everyday issues of parish life and not definitions. The busy practitioner takes little time for theory!

My experience in Sean McDermott Street and Bonnybrook had clearly brought home to me that the structure of parish, as we now have it, often comes in the way of evangelisation and the work of the gospel. The present parish is cumbersome, and ill-focused as a vehicle of evangelisation and community development today. The parish, with all its paraphernalia of tasks and jobs and demands, urgently needs to be changed, re-focused and re-structured. In fact it needs to be re-defined theologically and sociologically. That's exactly what the New Code of Canon Law has done! It has radically and drastically re-defined parish, based on Vatican II and the needs of the Church today. I think this re-definition is prophetic and far-reaching. The parish, as we know it, will change drastically, I believe, over the next fifty or hundred years. It will change for two reasons:

a. The changed life patterns and lifestyles of people and society today;

b. The re-definition of parish by the Church itself.

a. Old realities: new needs

Industrialisation and urbanisation have changed the patterns and lifestyle of people in modern society. In earlier times, the area or geographical location were paramount. In general, people were born, lived, worked and died in the one neighbourhood or area. And parish fitted that area. The 1917 Code definition of parish matched this thinking and reality. In the 1917 Code, a parish was two essential elements: a territory and an endowment. As Bertram Griffin says, 'A parish was essentially defined as a territory with people attached. Saul Alinsky once said how he envied the Catholic Church because of its territorial divisions. The entire planet earth was divided into squares called diocese, and each square was divided into other squares called parish, and there was somebody responsible for every square inch of turf and, for a community organiser, that was a marvellous way to organise the planet Earth: namely, in terms of territory.'[1] The parish, as a group of territorial cells, unifying the Church globally, was a masterful invention. It formed a tightly organised network, useful for communication, for organisation, for canonical control and for accountability. The priest was responsible for the parish; he was in turn responsible to the bishop, who in his turn was answerable to the Pope. Organisationally and canonically, it was a very strong and effective model of Church.

As the *Notre Dame Study of Parish* says, there is huge amount of such cells worldwide today in the Christian Churches:

'The first Christian congregation gathered in Jerusalem fifty days

116

after the resurrection of Christ, on Pentecost Sunday around the year 30 AD. Today, over nineteen and half centuries later, there are some 1.8 million local congregations throughout the world with an estimated 1.5 billion adherents. Over 380,000 of these local Churches are in the United States, 19,500 of them Catholic and over 360,000 non-Catholic.' [2]

In times past, parish boundaries were very important. Each parish was an island with its own life, its own ground rules, its own identity, a strong sense of community and a strong hierarchical structure. Also, as we have seen, each parishioner used to be bound to attend their own parish Church for their Sunday Mass obligation. Territory was the key element of parish. Control was tight. There was little mobility. Evangelisation, sacramentalisation and pastoral care followed a well-tried and well-tested formula. Each parish had its own full life. I believe we could learn some invaluable lessons for evangelisation and pastoral care for today from many of our more senior priests who did pioneering work in their parishes. Their model of pastoring and pastoral care was, in my estimation, a very well thought-out and integrated one, and, above all, very suitable for the culture and way of life at that time. Many of its strong points can be applied to the new reality of today.

Parish as priest-centred

As territory was the first essential element of parish, the second, in the 1917 Code, was that of endowment, or as it was called in Canon Law a 'benefice'. 'The parish was an endowed office and the pastor was the holder of benefice or endowment. Pastoral care was attached to the benefice. Theoretically, all that the parish owned belonged to the pastor.' [3]

In their book on the parish, Sweetser and Wiesnewski emphasise the fact that in the 1917 Code definition, parish was, in effect, synonymous with pastor. It was built around him. He was the central figure and authority, canonically and in practice. This reflected the Church's pre-Vatican II self-understanding as primarily an hierarchical, juridical institution made up of the Pope, bishops and priests, with the laity as their assistants.

b. New definition

But Vatican II changed all of that, as we have already seen, at the first session of the Council. It was a drastic change, a reversal of fifteen hundred years' history. It shifted emphasis and power in the Church. By changing definitions it changed perceptions, roles, relationships, and emphasis.

The 1983 Code of Canon Law, as a codification or putting into law of the teaching of the Church at Vatican II, has completely re-defined parish. This new definition of parish, the local Church, reflects the new self-understanding of the Church of itself – the Church is a *communio*, a people of God committed to love each other and care for each other as a reflection of the Trinity. There is no mention of 'territory' or 'benefice' in the new definition of par-ish. This is a major change. As Griffin says:

'In the revised Code, the two essential elements of a parish are not territory and benefice, but rather 'community' and 'pastoral care'. Community is now primary in the revised code, not only in the parish, but on every level of the Church. The Church is no longer a series of squares drawn on the planet earth.'[4]

Definition reflects Church

From a pastoral point of view, the definition of parish as commun-ity plus pastoral care, rather than territory plus benefice, is much closer to what we priests are trying to create with the people of our parishes today. The definition is closer to, and in tune with, the desired goal of parishes to create caring Christian commun-ities. The new definition is also closer to the Church as *communio*, as the people of God, and as partnership in mission rather than the clerical, hierarchical, jurisdictional Church.

The 1983 Code defines parish as a 'definite community of the Christian faithful which is established on a stable basis within a particular Church.'[5] Canon 518 of the 1983 Code reads, 'Personal parishes should be established based on rite, the language, or even nationality of the Christian faithful within some territory, or even upon some other determining factor.'[6]

Parishes may be set up around groups of interest, neighbourhood groups, or any natural groups of people today. And even if one does not set up a parish around such groups, the direction has been given. Flexibility of focus, freedom to 'follow the fleet,' has been given to ministry. The ministry is not to a territory but to a people and to natural groups and communities. It will take priests and other pastoral workers a long time to re-focus away from territory and tasks and plant, because that is what our primary focus has tended to be. The responsibilities and roles given to priests will have to be re-examined in the light of the new definition of parish in the Code. This new definition would point to much greater flexibility in the appointment of priests and greater flexibility in ministry. As well as running the territorial parish, with less priests and more full-time lay ministers, one could also have the parish of the youth or the unemployed in a particular area, for example, in a deanery, and special teams, evangelisation teams, youth teams, family ministry teams, ministry to the unemployed, to women's groups, to the alienated, like the parish of the travelling people which already exists in Dublin. The 'new parishes' could be any of the above groups, with a priest and team appointed to serve them.

Co-responsibility

Griffin makes a very good point about diocese and parish. The bishop and priests are pastor together. The new model of ministry of and with the people of God is one of unity and partnership. Since all the baptised are responsible for the Church, and not just the 2%, the clergy, partnership has to be the way forward.

'To understand the parish, first it is necessary to look at the diocese in the revised Code. Canon 369 defines the diocese: 'A diocese is a portion of the people of God' (not a territory). It is a portion of the people of God entrusted for pastoral care not to a bishop only, but to a bishop with his presbyters. It is a 'bishop with his presbyters' who are in charge of the pastoral care of the portion of the people of God called diocese. This portion of the people of God is gathered in three ways: in the Holy Spirit, in the gospel, and in the eucharist. By being gathered in the Spirit, by the gospel and the eucharist, that portion of the people of God becomes a particular Church in which the one, holy, catholic and apostolic Church of Christ is truly present and operative.'[7]

The new parish: new roles

Where does the priest fit into the new definitions of Church, diocese and parish? The 'new diocese' and the 'new parish' in the 1983 Code of Canon Law is more about community than institution, pastoral care and mission than territory, collaborative ministry rather than clerical ministry on its own. In this definition, the 'priesthood of the presbyterate' is at the service of the people of God, as it was in the apostolic Church. The priest is to be the minister of ministries of the laity, who in turn will be the servants of the gospel in the world. This model of Church and relationship of roles would seem to be that put forward in *Christifideles Laici*.

Is the new definition of diocese and parish, a recipe for continuous conflict between clergy and laity, between the 2% and the 98%? Will it mean a down-grading of the priest's role? When I told a priest colleague in Dublin whom I had not met for some time that I was writing on the role of the priest today he said, 'Is there any role left?' – half seriously!

Chapter 10 will be on the origins, nature and history of priesthood and Chapters 11 and 12 on the role of the priest. Maybe we'll get a few answers to those important questions then!

New theory, new practice

When the Church reviewed and renewed its theology at Vatican II, it set out a new vision, new priorities, and new goals for the Church in the world. That meant the same for the Church worldwide – episcopal regions, dioceses, parishes. All would have to try to re-adjust their corporate goals under the promptings of the Holy Spirit and in keeping with local needs. Pope John XXIII saw the revision of the Church's Code of Canon Law as a vital pre-requisite for facilitating local renewal. A framework was needed and so was legislation and clarification. The New Code gives flesh to the new vision and theology of Vatican II by re-defining the nature of the Church, the diocese, the parish, the role of pastors, bishop, and the role of the laity. So, it points towards the shape of the 'new' Church at global and local level.

At the same time as the Code was reframing the theology of Vatican II, in canonical and juridical terms, for the whole Church, local Churches, regional, diocesan and parochial, were reviewing and renewing themselves in practice. This happened in Ireland, in Dublin, in Sean McDermott Street and elsewhere at local level. In the next chapter, we will look at the Church in Latin America because, I believe, we can learn a lot from its experience and models of renewal, especially at the macro level – region and diocese.

Notes

1. Bertram Griffin, 'The Parish and Lay Ministry' in *Chicago Studies*, Vol 23 No. 1, April 1984, p. 45.
2. *Notre Dame Study of Catholic Parish Life*, University of Notre Dame, Report No. 15, June 1989.
3. Griffin, p. 48.
4. Ibid., p. 49.
5. *The Code of Canon Law* (1983), Canon 515.
6. Ibid., Canon 518 (American Edition).
7. Griffin, p. 49.

CHAPTER 8

The New Definition in Practice

THE CHURCH IN LATIN AMERICA

The changes in the Latin American Church between 1960 and 1990 are both mind-boggling and mind-blowing. For five hundred years the Latin American Church had been seen as both the chaplain to, and the canoniser of the *status quo* in Latin America. At the Vatican Council it was called the 'Church of Silence' because it had little or nothing to say, even though it was the largest regional Church at the Council. It was out of its depth in terms of theology, or of having creative ideas about the relationship of the Church and the world. Its history had not prepared it for this. It had been a Church of devotions, nominal Catholics, 'an unchanging, other-worldly monolith' and 'for centuries part of the ruling hegemony.'[1] It was a Church that had lost touch with the people in general and therefore with the social and everyday reality of their lives. It had been a clerical Church, predominantly cocooned in privilege, paternalism, and privatisation of religion. Delegates from twenty Latin American countries at the historic Catholic Action Conference in Chimbote, Peru in 1953 (a fore-runner of Medellin and Puebla) described the Latin American Church as follows: 'They agreed that most Latin American Catholics were only nominally Catholic. They could be expected to reflect but nominal acceptance of the spirit and dictates of the gospel. Their Catholicism consisted of a traditional set of pious customs, a superficial substitute for those demands of a vital nature that the Gospel made on their lives.'[2]

Edward Cleary, a Dominican priest, who has studied the Church in Latin America for the past 20 years, says: 'Neither ambassadors, nor military leaders, Latin America watchers nor media people, theologians or Church leaders would have predicted or even imagined, the profound changes that came over Latin American Catholicism and the Latin American parish between 1960 and 1985.'[3]

The events of eastern Europe in 1989 are the closest one can come to the type of unpredictability and unlikeliness of outcome. The key events and dates in this wholly unforseeable and unlikely transformation are CELAM (Latin American Episcopal Council, 1955), Vatican II (1962-65), Medellin (1968), Puebla (1979). The key issue is about being Church in Latin America. The key outcomes are liberation theology and Basic Christian Communities and a whole new approach to parish and ministry in many parts of the Latin American Church.

CELAM
The organisation of the Latin American Bishops into a strong transnational body (CELAM) in 1955 gave a new sense of unity, a sense of purpose, and a new strength to the Latin American bishops. CELAM held an ordinary meeting annually and an extraordinary meeting about every ten years – Rio de Janeiro (1955); Medellin, Columbia (1968) and Puebla, Mexico (1979).

Medellin
Medellin, famous today as the headquarters of the Cocaine Cartel, was the location of a revolutionary Church conference in 1968. The Latin American bishops and their experts had learned a lot from Vatican II. They had got to know each other well over the four years and, though many of the questions discussed at the Council were not 'their' questions, but those of the First World, like questions of faith or the lack of it in a scientific age, they had been influenced largely by John XXIII and his call for *aggiornamento*. In their own time, they would ask their own questions, see how *aggiornamento* Latin American style might happen and do it their own way.

Three things were new and different about Medellin:
1. The representation;
2. The methodology;
3. The outcome.

1. *Representation*

For the first time CELAM would have: '... pastoral representation (delegates from functional or apostolic sectors) rather than canonical representation (delegates from each ecclesiastical region). This decision was crucial: it meant that the Church would be analysed and defined from the bottom up. It was a conference of 'The People of God' rather than the 'Hierarchy of God'.'[4]

2. *Methodology*

The new methodology used at Medellin has changed the way of being Church in Latin America in many ways. Many theologians believe that this new methodology, introduced at the Second Vatican Council in the document *Gaudium et Spes* (*The Church in the Modern World*), is as important as the content of that great document.

'The methodology used in that document turns traditional theology on its head. Instead of proceeding in the time-honoured fashion, discussing theological and biblical principles and then applying them to a present day situation, *Gaudium et Spes* reverses the process: it begins with a careful analysis of the *de facto* situation, then turns to sacred scripture and theology for reflection on that situation, and finally, as a third step, makes pastoral application. Theological reflection thus becomes the second, not the first step. Tradition, established theology, and the magisterium of the Church had been used as the starting point in previous papal teaching, other Vatican II documents, and in traditional theology. In the description of the Church in the world, *Gaudium et Spes* makes use of the social and behavioural sciences. Previously philosophy, the preferred 'handmaid,' guided the theological enterprise. The Church now searches the given socio-cultural situation for the 'signs of the times', to hear the voice of God in them.'[5]

'In *Gaudium et Spes* the Church also returns to sacred scripture more directly than it was accustomed to doing. It thereby employs a more thorough hermeneutic, that is, a contemporary search for the meaning of the world and world events in the light of the scriptures.'[6]

CELAM used this radical new methodology (for the Church) at Medellin:
Social reality;
Theological and biblical reflection;
Pastoral recommendations.

'The change in methodology was monumental: it represented a shift from a perspective that was dogmatic, deductive and top-to-bottom to one that was exploratory, inductive and bottom-to-top.'

Preparation
A two-year period of preparation for Medellin took place, during which Vatican II was assimilated and the new methodology was applied. Social scientists took on the task of describing and analysing the Latin American situation, theologians reflected on the reality and the theology of Vatican II, dioceses, pastoral groups, experts met to do their bit. The Medellin Conference would not be a clerical conference and it would not be a theological conference. It would be a pastoral conference, as Vatican II was a pastoral council, starting with the social reality of Latin America and making recommendations based on that social reality and the gospel. Shades of Pope Paul VI's core of evangelisation, faithful to people and gospel!

A Latin American theology
As Cleary says: 'The first task in constructing a Latin American interpretation of Vatican II – analysis of the human and religious situation – was taking definite shape. The second task – a theological re-interpretation of Latin American theology in the light of Vatican II – was also beginning. Based on social analysis, Latin American theology began to shape itself. Faced with domination

125

and dependence, the Latin American theologians turned to the theme of liberation. A new theology was taking shape.'[7]

Philosophy and the social sciences

Cleary then goes on to mention their use of the social sciences. This helped them better understand structures, systems and the reality of society itself. The marriage of theology and the social sciences can be most productive, in my opinion, when both are used critically. I do not see the social sciences replacing philosophy as the handmaid of theology, but as being used in conjunction with it. Good analysis is as important as straight thinking, and *vice versa*.

Cleary makes another valuable point when he refers to the convergence at Medellin between theologians and social scientists. '... it occurred at precisely the time when sociologists and economists were focusing on the fact of dependence. The kind of development that many Latin American analysts saw taking place was uneven and inequitable. The poor were getting poorer. By May 1968, the CELAM group meeting at Itapoanbahia, Brazil, incorporated the description and analysis of the socio-economic realities of Latin America as formulated by many economists and social scientists. The Medellin Conference would accept and enlarge on that line of thinking.'[8]

The methodology of Medellin, in starting with the social reality, would change the theology and pastoral approach of the Latin American Church.

3. The outcome

The methodology undertaken, starting with the social reality of Latin America, would change the direction of the whole conference. The conference couldn't just talk theory, no matter how elevated or elating. The question from the start had to be: 'What are we doing about this terrible reality?' What has the Church done for the past five hundred years? What must the Church do to be credible or to reflect the gospel?

'The sociography of the continent showed the participants a stark and realistic picture of the social and religious situation in Latin America. The situation was much worse than we thought, bishops recalled later.'[9]

The interaction of the social reality with the gospel and theology gave a new dynamic to the conference. This has been my experience in Sean McDermott Street too. As I have already stated, the power of the gospel, when it is brought to bear on reality and life issues, creates a new and powerful dynamic. Starting from the 'bottom up' at Medellin meant that the Church had to make choices – major choices. It had to decide whose side it was on. It couldn't sit on the fence like the politician with both ears to the ground! The Church chose the side of the poor. They made a 'preferential option for the poor'. The Church must reach out to the poor and give them preference in order to make them equal. To be Church demanded that. To be a disciple of Christ demanded it. This would be achieved through evangelisation and lay participation (*pastoral de conjuncto*) from which grassroots communities (*comunidades de base*) would sprout. The option for the poor, or the choice to be on the side of the poor, was a monumental decision with inevitable results. It would change the nature and role of the local Church.

Medellin: The relevance of gospel and Church
The gospel imperative had to be followed. The basic issues of poverty, equality, irrelevance of the Church and gospel, the loss of intellectuals and the ordinary people, especially the poor, – these all had to be dealt with. They could dot the 'i's and cross the 't's later. Moreover, a commitment to a horizontal, rather than a vertical Church, had to be made and it was. That decision would have major implications for any Church. As Cleary says: 'During Vatican II, it had become clear that communal ordering of the Church (Church as communion, people of God, partnership in mission and ministry) was called for to bring it in line with the original mandate of Christ to his apostles.'[10]

That decision to operationalise the 'people of God' or 'Church as *communio*' model of Church, with the people of God, laity and clergy, reflecting on their parish or diocese or national Church, would have major implications for the outcome of any reflection or pastoral plan. The post-1960s Ireland as 'new continent' would, it strikes me, benefit greatly from a Medellin-type reflection and review just now.

Summary
The Latin American Church at Medellin:
1. Enunciated a new theology which would blossom into liberation theology;
2. Used a new and revolutionary methodology for the Latin American Church: social reality, theological reflection, pastoral action;
3. Was the first major meeting of CELAM as Church – the people of God – not as hierarchy or as clergy;
4. Took a stand on the side of the poor – a prophetic and conflictual versus consensus position for the Church in society;
5. Strove to re-model itself, and developed priorities, in keeping with Vatican II;
6. Created a Vatican II Church milieu at the macro level in Latin America, and so supported dioceses, parishes, priests, religious and 'people of God' ideologically, theologically and emotionally in their quest for renewal and revitalisation at local level.
7. Embarked on a partnership-in-ministry model of Church for Latin America.

Parish in Latin America
It should be easier to understand Basic Christian Communities, their origins and development, and the possibility of applying them to other local Church situations, after looking at CELAM and Medellin. Basic Christian Communities have to do with 'social realities', 'being Church as the people of God', giving the laity responsibility, applying the gospel teaching to life and the world in which people live or try to survive. Basic Christian Communi-

ties are living mini-parishes. They are not magical and fanciful pastoral DIY-kits pulled out of a hat that are likely to disappear just as quickly as they appeared.

Parish not working

Basic Christian Communities are community and pastoral initiatives that, first of all, come out of the failure and frustration of existing Church and parish structure. In parts of Latin America, immense parishes, sometimes 40,000-70,000 with 90% nominal Catholics, were totally unmanageable, unsuccessful and unfocused. What was the point of maintaining a dead structure, playing the numbers game, over sacramentalising without evangelising, multiplying rituals without meaning or relevance?

'To respond to the situation, several major changes were called for: reduction in scale, instruction in depth, a sense of community, new ministries, and emergence of lay leaders.'[11] The shortage of priests is not seen as the chief reason for the emegence of Basic Christian Communities. There has always been a shortage of priests in Latin America.

'Jose Marins, a key figure in the spread of the base communities, recalls the beginning in the 1950s, and, more evidently in the 1960s: priests working in various parts of Latin America began feeling the malaise that comes from working with a parish structure that was out of alignment with pastoral ideology. The parish structure was not achieving the results that enlightened pastors sought. Marins, Aldo Gerna, both in Brazil, and Leo Mahon (from Chicago) in Panama, began experimenting with alternative parish structures.'[12]

Cleary says that the same type of experimental structures began to appear in many parts of Latin America. Reduction in scale, neighbourhood groups, developing the natural community, working mostly with adults, as children and youth were not mature enough to give the commitment needed, making worship meaningful; concentration on evangelisation as against sacramentalisation, starting with the social reality and putting the Bible back in people's hands, were all aims and elements of Basic Christian Communities.

The mushrooming of Basic Christian Communities in Latin America is one of the miracles of the Church. 'If someone had told me twenty years ago that I would be witnessing Catholics, ordinary ones, reading the Bible and caring for one another on the basis of scriptural reflection, and doing it in large numbers, I would have told them they were seriously misled,' said Reverend William Wipfler, an Episcopalian priest who studied the Latin American Church for many years.[13] Cleary says that two or three million Latin American Catholics (one million in Brazil) are part of Basic Christian Communities.

b. The local Church

The growth of Basic Christian Communities, as well as being an answer to pastoral need, also exemplifies the shift in thinking in Vatican II, Medellin and Puebla, about the nature and structure of the local Church. Trying to get the 'people of God' to live in the world, and in their local areas, as *communio*, and as gospel people, meant a new shift of emphasis and a shift in ministry and methodology – from vertical to horizontal Church, from individualism to partnership in ministry, from committees to community, from sacramentalisation to evangelisation, from maintenance to mission, from a 'two world' view to a 'one world view' of the unity of history, from an other-worldly to a this-worldly theology and practice.

New corporate goals

'The impact of these new ideas (says Cleary) would result in new corporate goals. In sum, major objectives would include: instruction in depth; direct use of the Bible, a sense of community, new ministries, the emergence and empowerment of the laity, and emphasis on working on the side of the poor. Grassroots Christian communities fulfil all of these objectives, to one degree or another.'[14]

No wonder CELAM said at Puebla: 'We are happy to single out the multiplication of small communities as an important ecclesial event that is peculiarly ours, and as the hope of the Church.'[15]

Some reflections

1. Wouldn't it be useful in every diocese to work out new corporate goals for the parish and the diocese, using the Medellin methodology and structure? How valuable it would be to have diocesan and parish assemblies planning from the ground up, setting corporate goals and priorities for the Church in the third millenium.

2. The growth of Basic Christian Communities shows the value and the need for small communities, as was also shown in the USA studies of parish and the experience of Renew, as well as our experience in Sean McDermott Street. Will the parish of the future be a community of communities? Will the role of the priest be a minister of ministries? A minister of ministries in a community of communities – not a bad basic definition of the role of the priest in the future.

3. Good liberation theology – rooted in reality and rooted in the gospel, with its special methodology – would make the link, so necessary in Ireland, between the spiritual and social gospel and between people's everyday lives and their religion.

4. One is struck by the major contribution of scripture scholars and theologians of liberation as partners with priests and people in the development of the local Church in Latin America. Future pastoral development would benefit greatly from having trained scripture scholars and theologians working on the ground, involved in reflection, training and pastoral ministry.

5. The congruence between the goals of the Latin American Church at macro and micro level has been a great influence in renewal of the Church and parish in Latin America.

MAJOR IMPLICATIONS FOR IRELAND

I see implications from my study of the local Church in the new Code and of the Latin American Church at two levels in the Irish Church: the first is at the macro level - the vision, the goals, the planning, at national level by the Church in Ireland; the second implication concerns the diocesan and local level.

1. The national level

Reflecting on the Irish Church, in the light of the gospel and the needs of the people of Ireland, especially for the future, I feel that the Irish Hierarchy as individuals have made many important and significant contributions, but that, as a body, they have not given visionary or prophetic leadership to the Irish Church or Irish people. I believe that is what both the Irish Church and Irish society need.

The Latin American Bishops (CELAM) did come up with a very worthwhile corporate gospel response which forms an excellent framework at the macro level for the development of people and communities at the micro level. The Irish Hierarchy as a body have produced some of the elements but not a gospel mission statement or blueprint with goals and priorities which are so much needed by the Irish Church and Irish society today.

The priests

I believe the same can be said of the priests in Ireland as a corporate body. The National Conference of Priests of Ireland is a possible exception in the sense that it is trying, with limited resources, to be a corporate voice for Irish priests. But like the cuckoo, it is heard only once a year!

At diocesan level, how often do you hear a group or association of priests speak out about major issues like unemployment, emigration, poverty, centralisation of government and lack of local democracy, or the place of women in the Church and society? What about priests of a given diocese speaking out?

132

Rainbow coalitions: corporate voices

If the corporate voices of diocesan priests' groups or associations, the NCPI, individual religious orders, the hierarchy and other concerned groups, were joined to those of the Combat Poverty Agency and CMRS and CSSC, the most consistent voices on behalf of the less well off, then a continuous corporate concerned voice would rise in our land. This would be ministry at the macro and media level also. The Sr Stans, the Peter McVerrys, the Cahal Dalys, the Des Wilsons, the Denis Fauls, the Brendan Ryans, are great, but if only these individual prophets were complemented by corporate prophetic voices and stances!

2. The diocesean level

In my estimation the diocese is a very important and vital entity in the development of Church today. In the total Church, there are four levels:

(1) The global;

(2) The regional;

(3) The diocesan;

(4) And the parish.

All four levels are vitally interrelated. That was an important insight of the Latin American bishops: they saw the interrelationship and devised a method for dealing with it creatively in practice. As well as planning for the total continent of Latin America, cardinals and bishops began to be inspired by CELAM and to do a number of things at diocesan level also:

(a) Restructure the dioceses to be better able to be 'Church' or a communion of people;

(b) Have ten- and twenty-year diocesan plans with priorities;

(c) Re-examine parish, in terms of being Church and as a medium of evangelisation;

(d) Review the diocesan model of evangelisation and pastoral care. A very good example is the 'Sao Paulo Experiment', which you could read about in Bulletin 99 of the *Pro Mundi Vita* magazine (1984/4).[16]

(e) Hold diocesan synods. The 'synod', a Greek word etymologically meaning 'the way – what we do together', is part of a very ancient tradition in the Church. The synod or 'assembly' was held every two years in the eighth and ninth centuries. The Council of Trent prescribed a diocesan synod each year, and Vatican I suggested every ten years.[17] The New Code of Canon Law, 1983, reflecting the mind of Vatican II, says: 'The diocesan synod is the meeting of the delegates of priests and other faithful of the particular Church who assist the diocesan bishop in ensuring the well-being of the whole diocesan community.'[18] The diocesan synod is a very ancient and yet very new method of consultation, corporate planning and co-responsibility in the local Church.

Notes

1. Edward L Cleary OP, *Crisis and Change*, Orbis Books, New York 1985. p. 1.
2. Ibid., p. 5.
3. Ibid., p. 1.
4. Ibid., p. 22.
5. Ibid., pp. 60-61.
6. Ibid., p. 61.
7. Ibid., p. 33.
8. Ibid., pp. 32-33.
9. Ibid., p. 41.
10. Ibid., p. 42.
11. Ibid., p. 106.
12. Ibid.
13. Ibid., p. 105.
14. Ibid., p. 109.
15. Ibid., p. 104.
16. Pierre Delooz, 'Pastoral Care for Supercities' in *Pro Mundi Vita*, Bulletin 99 (1984/4), Leuven, Belgium.
17. 'Ministries and Communities', *Pro Mundi Vita*, No. 61, 1989.
18. *The Code of Canon Law* (1983), Canon 460, American Edition.

CHAPTER 9

The Parish in the USA

In this chapter, I will focus on the experience of parish in the USA, because:

(i) The US Catholic Church has been operating in a pluralistic and openly secular society for many years, and very successfully;

(ii) A lot of reflection and research has been done on parish and its underlying issues in the USA;

(iii) The first Catholic parishes in the USA were lay-centred and governed.

During the summer of 1989 I spent two fascinating months in theUSA studying the role of the priest and the parish, and the Church in general. I travelled coast to coast visiting nine dioceses and doing eighty-nine interviews as well as collecting lots of literature, the two most interesting pieces being *The Parish Project* and the *Notre Dame Study of Parish* .

The findings of *The Parish Project*, the Parish Research and Development Project of the United States Catholic Conference of Bishops, and the *Notre Dame Study of Parish* would, I think, be very useful reading for any diocese or people trying to renew its approach to evangelisation and pastoral care today.

1. The Parish Project

In September 1977, the National Conference of Catholic Bishops in the United States, in order to focus attention specifically on parish life, established an *ad hoc* committee on the parish. The committee would 'approach the parish not as an organisational problem but as a people attempting to express the life of Christ which they share.' Does parish help people to live the life of Christ today? Can it? If not, why not? If so, how best? What are the issues? What are good models of parish? These are some of the questions the committee would be dealing with over a period of five years. Fr Philip J Murnion was appointed director of what was to become known as *The Parish Project* from 1978 to 1982. The first contribution that Phil Murnion made to this enterprise was to produce a paper called *Forming the Parish Community*, an essay on the sociology of current parish developments. In this very valuable little booklet he tells us how and why *The Parish Project* was initiated and what were the major issues underlying the call to critique parish as the way of being local Church. He saw two major problems underlying the question of parish:

a. Erosion of community.

b. Secularisation.

a. Parish and community

Murnion first of all quotes sociologist Robert Nisbet: 'The loss of a sense of visible community in Christ will be followed by the loss of the sense of the invisible. The decline of community in the modern world has as its inevitable religious consequence the creation of masses of helpless, bewildered individuals who are unable to find solace in Christianity regarded merely as a creed.'[1]

Murnion then goes on to give the precise reason for the initiation of *The Parish Project*, the intervention of Bishop Albert Ottenweller at the annual meeting of the US bishops in November 1975. He quotes Ottenweller: 'A parish is an institution ... But a parish is also a community. Members of a parish have a need and a right to be like an extended family, to know each other, to care for each other and so to grow in the love of God and of one another. My contention is that right now, organisationally, parishes are very heavy on institution and very light on community.'[2]

b. Secularisation versus spirituality

In an article entitled *The Community Called Parish*, Fr Phil Murnion wrote the following:

'Catholic Americans, like the majority of their fellow citizens, are a believing people in spite of our secularity. We continue to profess faith in a personal God, in Jesus Christ, and in the work of the Holy Spirit. The American Catholic continues to believe in a life after death, in heaven and hell, and in prayer as a way of being in communication with God. In this respect, American Catholics are much like the Irish of both the south and the north of Ireland; they too have retained their faith. On the other hand, fellow Catholics in the rest of Europe have considerably less faith in those realities that are explicitly supernatural. Study after study, comparing the United States with Western Europe, finds that people in the United States, and Catholics in particular, remain people for whom God is important and religion is significant.

We would, nonetheless, be foolish to deny the significant problems we face in living regarding to that faith. Profession of faith is not the same as living the faith, it takes spirituality to turn the profession of faith into a life of faith. And spirituality is our challenge.'[3]

The problem of parish

Against that background that he located the 'problem of parish'. Spirituality versus secularity is the basic issue for the Church and the parish today. Is our living and society God-referenced and gospel-referenced or ruled by pragmatism, 'progress' and materialism or hedonism? Archbishop Desmond Connell, in his talk to priests in Clonliffe (February 13th 1990) on pastoral development, said that the major issue is between secular humanism and a God-centred society. The question of parish is about two major issues:
1. The question of community: Church as *communio*, and the people's need of community as against alienation and disintegration;
2. The question of spirituality, relating faith and life, as against secularisation.

As Murnion says: 'There is a seriously growing gap between faith and life. Belief, then, is not the characteristic American problem, but the scope of spirituality, the extent to which our understanding and behaviour are guided by our belief, surely is. I'm talking, of course, about the process of secularisation. For secularisation does not mean specifically loss of faith, but the isolation of faith and religion from the rest of life. It signals the compartmentalisation of life into various segments and the removal of religious norms from our everyday activities.'[4]

Christianity as creed or as communio?

Christianity just as creed, or Christianity as institution, does not fulfil the needs of the people today, especially in urban settings, nor does it fulfil the meaning of Church as *communio*, as a People of God sharing a heritage, a vision, or a way of life as well as a creed. The true Church and the vital parish is the Church living as *communio* (communion), primarily, that believes in God and love (creed) and has an organisation and authority structure which facilitates both (institution).

Personalising the parish community

Murnion, in his booklet *Forming the Parish Community* says: 'Bishop Albert Ottenweller's call for a restructuring of the parish has elicited an extraordinary reaction throughout the country ... because it has struck a deeply responsive chord in today's Church. I suggest that Bishop Ottenweller's proposal 'that we search for new models of parish life' expressed the need for personalising the parish community and its ministry – that more than mere revision of roles and rites have occurred in the Church and also that the changes in the role of the parish minister and in the rites and structures of parish life have not so much solved the problem of relating the Church to contemporary life as they have exposed the problem in its many dimensions.'[5]

So Murnion has identified the problem of parish as not just about the revision of rites and roles, but also about the revision of relationships of people to each other, of people to God, of religion to life, of structures to vision and goals, with community and secularisation as the underlying issues.

New models of parish

Murnion addes two other voices to that of Bishop Ottenweller on the question of parish. In a talk to the New York clergy, Baltimore theologian Ralph Kiefer recommended: '... a new model of local

Church community that would enable the Church to fulfil the purposes for which it takes root in an area. There are four major areas where conventional parochial ministry is not really adequate to the task of evangelisation.'

The four areas are:
1. development of a life of prayer and relationship with God;
2. establishment of a supportive community of discipleship in faith;
3. energising of social action;
4. enablement of people in their lives and work-place to give testimony to the hope that guides them.

In response to the inability of conventional structures to develop these areas of life, Kiefer proposes the organisation of small diverse groups within the parish.' [6]

Membership versus territorial approach
The third voice was that of Rev. Franklin Fitzpatrick. 'Responding, as did both Ottenweller and Kiefer, to the problem that the local Church community seems stifled in its life and purpose by the organisational and institutional constraints and burdens, Fitzpatrick suggests that we explicitly adopt a 'membership' approach to parish structure as opposed to the present territorial approach ... His approach takes the much discussed trend towards voluntarism in Church participation and turns the trend into a principle, arguing that the retention of the territorial principle is anachronistic, given general social patterns of affiliation and association.'[7]

Murnion completes the first section of his booklet by referring to the fact that: 'the World Council of Churches some years back (1967) point in the same direction when they speak of 'zonal groups', or organising ministry in terms of certain 'zones' of human life and of identifying certain points of assembly to which ministry should be directed; issues, statuses, life conditions, movements, around which we will find people assembled.' [8]

Rahner's 'Extra Parochial' principle

He concludes by quoting the great theologian, Karl Rahner. 'Rahner, in an essay entitled 'Peaceful Reflections on the Parochial Principle', acknowledging the importance of the 'parochial principle,' i.e. the territorial basis of parish development, argued that current urban life requires a complementary 'extra parochial' principle. He urged that we relate pastoral ministry to the bases on which people find their most significant identity and on which they convene.'[9]

The Parish Project: Issues and Outcomes

Over its four year history Phil Murnion and his committee produced many reflections and writings on parish. The dynamism of *The Parish Project*'s literature comes from the clear awareness of the theology and the reality of parish. The material reflects the coming together of practitioners and theorists – a good combination.

There are five booklets produced for, or by, *The Parish Project, which* I would recommend as very worthwhile reading for anybody engaged in parish work or the renewal of parish.

1. *Forming the Parish Community*, Philip J Murnion, USCC, 1978.
An excellent introduction to the issue of parish today.

2. *The Parish: A People, A Mission, A Structure.*
Vision statement by the committee on Parish 1980,
National Conference of Catholic Bishops (NCCB).
The purpose of the committee in publishing the vision-statement was to produce a focus towards which the renewal of parishes might be directed. The booklet was reprinted six times between 1981 and 1986 such was the demand for it.

3. *Parish Self-Study Guide*, USCC, 1980.
A workbook to help a parish evaluate itself in relation to the booklet *The Parish: A People, A Mission, A Structure.*

4. *Parish Life in the United States*, NCCB, 1982.
The final report of *The Parish Project* committee to the bishops is a

compendium of the history, the context and the different styles of parish in the USA. It also deals with the issues for parish today, various responses by parishes to the needs of its people, the role of the diocese, the present state of parishes in the USA and creating a future for parishes. This is quite a focused reflection by *The Parish Project* committee though it covers a wide canvas. Valuable background material for illumination of the 'parish issue' or parish question.

5. *Big or Small: Parish is still Possible*, National Parish Life Centre, 299 Elizabeth St, NY 10012, 1987.

This booklet is an account of a meeting of representatives of ten of the largest and most effective Catholic parishes in the USA. It surprisingly shows that small is not always best but that 'big is beautiful' and can be most effective in terms of parish achieving it's goal as a people, a mission and a structure. This surprised me a lot, as it did Phil Murnion who convened the three-day meeting of the Parish Teams in his capacity as director of the National Pastoral Life Centre. The reason why some larger parishes are very effective in developing a sense of community, a sense of involvement and a sense of mission is that they have a larger staff, a greater variety and skill in leadership and therefore greater choice and greater variety in programmes and processes of development. Big parishes can foster a constellation of small communities, uniting diverse ministries around primary goals.

Reflection

The Parish Project and its successor, the *National Pastoral Life Centre*, both under the directorship of Phil Murnion are tangible signs of the reflection of the US Catholic Church on the parish during the past fifteen years. There has been a lot of debate, a lot of reflection, a lot of renewal on the part of bishops, priests and laity. In general the findings would be: Parish is in; Parish is important; Parish is under question; Parish has problems; Parish can work.

RENEW: *Parish Renewal*

Parish needs 'partners'in mission, other ways of being Church today, other methods of evangelisation. Small groups or small communities is the primary answer. My meeting with Mgr Tom Kleisler, founder of Renew, the international parish renewal programme operating in 165 dioceses on the five continents, absolutely confirmed that small groups and small communities is the best way forward. Renew has fostered thousands of such small groups and its second phase is supporting small groups and moving them on to be small communities. The diocese of Baltimore, with its new diocesan office for nurturing and fostering small communities, is a good example of how many American dioceses are taking small group/community seriously.

USA Parishes: *Personal impressions*

Some aspects of good American parishes that struck me very strongly were:

1. They are very focused. They know clearly who their parishioners are and enrollment is very common. People choose to be parishioners. This has a positive domino effect.

2. There is a great emphasis on preaching. Research says it's crucial. I asked Andrew Greeley last year, 'What is the most important thing the American Church needs today?' And he answered without hesitation and without qualification: 'Good preaching.' I would take that advice very seriously though it surprised me in terms of the overall needs of the American Church.

3. American parishes seem to me to be very weak on mission and outreach. Perhaps they see the consolidation and development of their own members as a community as a necessary first stage. I'm not so sure.

4. The American parishes also seemed to be weak on social justice. They tended to be self-sufficient communities with a strong 'in house' sense of participation and partnership, democracy and equality, but are the better off being challenged in the light of the gospel with justice as a priority? I don't think so. That was my ex-

perience from talking to a lot of priests and parishioners and also my impressions from the *Notre Dame Study* of parish.

National concerns about parish: A vision

Bill Bausch, in his writings on ministry, says: 'Based on the studies of Andrew Greeley and others, the report entitled *What do People Want?*, produced by Philip Murnion and his staff, enumerates these national concerns about the parish. People want:

1. Liturgies that nourish their faith, and above all, good sermons that do the same.

2. That the parish have as its agenda everyday practical concerns: family life, children, teens, etc.

3. A democratic form of leadership.

4. That the parish should be an alive and dynamic place.

5. Priests should be able to work well with others.

6. There should be a sense of community.

7. There should be opportunity to develop spiritually.

8. There must be care for people who are hurting.'[10]

That list seems to me to be a good summary of the priest's role as priest, teacher and shepherd. A parish is a place where the People of God listen to the Word of God, celebrate their love of God together, care for each other, especially the weak and hurting, live as a community in the middle of secular society and all take responsibility for being a part of the local Church.

Most effective parishes

Bausch continues: 'If these are the concerns, research from the same group found that the country's most effective parishes to meet these needs were those which:

1. Provided organisational activities such as adult education, liturgical planning, youth ministry, help to the elderly;

2. Had a definite pattern of shared responsibility and ministry;

3. Had many opportunities for the people to participate in parish;

4. The quality of the parish staff – larger parishes had a more varied staff and therefore more skills, ministries;

5. Had a vision of parish – what it was to be the People of God.'[11]

Necessary ingredients for parish renewal
The Parish Project team also drew up a list of ingredients for parish renewal based on their experience of parish needs and of concerns about parish. The ingredients are:
1. Participatory leadership;
2. Awareness of people's needs;
3. A clear sense of priorities;
4. More people being trained (formation);
5. Personal commitment to Christ and the Church;
6. The opportunity to meet in small groups;
7. Attentiveness to relationships, especially to the male-female ones in ministry;
8. The enablement of all to minister to each other;
9. The availability of resources.[12]

2. *The Notre Dame Study of Parish*

The *Notre Dame Study* is probably the biggest, most indepth and most unique study ever done of the parish. It is a study of the 19,500 parishes in the one hundred and ninety Catholic Dioceses of the USA which have fifty-three million Catholics on their census registers. The *Notre Dame Study* was an eight-year project carried out in three phases between 1981 and 1989.

Everywhere I went in the States during my summer visit I was referred to the *Notre Dame Study of Parish*, starting with Mgr Tom Kleisler at Renew, Joe Vancio of Newark Diocesan Research and Planning Office, Ruth Doyle, Director of New York Archdiocese Research and Planning Office and finally by her predecessor, Fr Philip Murnion. I decided that I had to get this report.

I was delighted when Fr Bob Pelton presented me with a copy of the report at Notre Dame and told me to use it as I wished, but especially for the benefit of the Irish Church.

The *Notre Dame Study* is valuable because:
a. it is an indepth study of parish;
b. it produces facts about the changing reality of parish;

c. it clarifies issues and roles and puts them in context;

d. its findings are sometimes unexpected.

Setting the scene

The report begins by setting the scene or the context of the radical change in US parishes since the Council:

'The Second Vatican Council focussed on the broad questions of the nature, life and ministry of the Church, on ecclesial relations among the Christian communities and on the role of the Church in the modern world. Its two principal documents, the *Dogmatic Constitution in the Church (Lumen Gentium)* and the *Pastoral Constitution of the Church in the Modern World (Gaudium et Spes)*, provide theological fundamentals and pastoral principles which have brought significant and continuing changes in the Catholic Church at all levels, global, regional and national, especially among dioceses and within parish communities.

Where have the twenty years of reform taken the American Catholic parish? Is it a place where the people find their God, where they join together in meaningful worship and prayer, where they satisfy their yearning to know God and serve their neighbours? What ministries do parishes perform well and where do they come up short of people's needs and God's expectations?'[13]

Phase 1 of the study, a questionnaire sent to 1,850 parishes (10% of the parishes at the time), elicited valuable information about structure, staffing and parish life for 1,100 parishes. The results of Phase 1 suggested:

1. A rich mosaic of parish life. Lay leadership and involvement well begun but new mechanisms of governance not yet clearly formed.

2. American Catholic parishes differed greatly by region, urban and rural location, by size, by structural complexity and by dynamism of programmes.

Methodology

In trying to penetrate deeply into the dynamics of each type of parish, the *Notre Dame Study* in Phase 2 became an indepth study through multiple approaches. Most previous research surveyed beliefs, attitudes and practices of parishioners and, in a few cases, parish structure had been examined. But no study had as yet systematically investigated both basic areas.

'The first unique quality of the *Notre Dame Study* is that it combines analysis of parish structure, leadership and performance with study of parishioners' views and behaviour.

A second unique factor is the interdisciplinary character of the research: it involves sociology and history, liturgy, doctrine and theology, together with organisational analysis and community power studies, parishioners' beliefs, practises and communal faith experiences past and present.

Finally, a third significant element is that Phase 2's indepth study focuses on a sample of thirty six parishes chosen as representative of the original 1,100 who responded to the questionnaire.

This complex sample design yields sufficient cases to generalise about each of the thirty-six parishes with a high degree of accuracy. But it also allows valued comparison of different types of parishes.'[14]

Core Catholics

It is important to note that the study is based on the survey of parish membership lists (probably the most common way of running parishes in the US – one registers in order to become a parishioner). The study decided, after much reflection, to define 'parishioner' as a registered member of the parish who voluntarily chose to be a member. It called those surveyed 'core Catholics,' i.e. the core population served by parish. The study results do not tell you anything about inactive or alienated Catholics – a pity! However, it is a very valuable study of Catholics who see themselves as part of parish in one way or another. The *Notre Dame Study* decided to study and compare Catholics within the context of their local parishes: 'For it is within parishes that we are baptised and come to learn about God, we marry and raise families, we enjoy friends and argue about programmes, we offer our help or shirk our responsibilities, and we die.'[15]

Survey results: A summary

1. Vatican II is succeeding

'If a major purpose of Vatican II was to re-institute the sense that all Christians – lay, priests and religious – are responsible for the corporate life of the Church in the local parish, Vatican II is succeeding in the United States. The American Church is participatory not only in religious ritual but especially in shared responsibility for ministry. Parish policy-making and governance patterns are not yet clearly demarcated but the effort to find parish governance mechanisms as effective or more effective than parish councils continues. The picture of a parish where Fr O'Brien took care of God, Sr Cerita ran the school, and people met their mass obligations and said 'Hail Mary's' would be a woefully inadequate stereotype of US Catholic parishes in the 1980's, if ever.' [16]

2. Lay responsibility for ministries.

'The most striking feature is that unpaid lay persons conduct many of the important ministries of the parish. The results showed that beyond the pastor, 83% of the leadership within Catholic parishes are lay persons, paid or unpaid. Responsibility for ministries (for running the parish) is clearly shared. In none of the parishes sampled in Phase 2 (36 parishes) was leadership exerted by the pastor alone or the pastor in concert with religious. In 36% of the parishes leadership was shared by pastor and laity with no involvement of religious. In 64% of the parishes leadership involved a combination of pastor, religious and lay.'[17]

3. Parish Councils – governance.

'Lay responsibility does not necessarily bring with it policy control. The American Bishops had encouraged the development of parish councils where the People of God – pastor and laity alike –

would share governance in parish life. Based on our sample of 1,100 parishes, we can say that 75% of the parishes currently have a parish council, 5% are forming them, and 7% once had them but they are now defunct. Usually council members are elected by the laity but most councils also include *ex officio* staff members. Several parishes are evolving mechanisms for popular consultation such as parishioner assemblies, annual surveys, larger advisory councils to a smaller parish executive committee, etc. The issue is not the existence of parish councils but their effectiveness, i.e. whether they have much impact on policy and the shaping of ministries.'[18]

The report concludes this section by saying: 'Conflict does not appear to be any more likely between pastor and council than between pastor and staff or staff and council. And generally people active in parish leadership feel so strongly about their parish – particularly if they 'share its ownership'– that they find ways of resolving disputes amicably.'[19]

4. Loyalty to parish

The report says: 'Despite all the talk about parish-shopping and parish-hopping, parish boundaries continue to orient the parish life of most US Catholics. About 86% of American parishes are territorial and 10% are nationality parishes. About the same percentage (86%) of Catholics in one sample claim to attend the parish within whose territorial boundaries they live, while slightly under 15% cross boundaries in selection of a parish. About 60% cite the territorial definition as the factor that 'attracts' them to their parish. 20% claim that what attracts them is the quality of pastoral care and slightly over 10% refer to the friendliness of the people. About 6% refer to the style of worship and 4% the quality of preaching. Thus, even though there is considerable fluidity in attendance patterns, nevertheless the notion of parish as neighbourhood Church remains dominant for American Catholics.'[20]

5. Lay participation.

'Besides Mass, in what ways do Catholics participate in their parishes? Almost 50% of the respondents in Phase 2 are participating

148

in one or more parish activities beyond Mass. 24% are involved in spiritual renewal programmes or prayer groups, studying the Bible, or instructing the Catecumenate. 4% are Eucharistic Ministers, 3% are lectors. 5% are serving on parish councils or equivalent parish governance mechanisms.'[21]

The report ends this section with the comment: 'For many Catholics, religious practices in the parish cannot be likened to pulling up at the service station on a Sunday and gassing up in holiness. Religion involves a sustained effort to serve and learn. Gone are the days when learning was left to the abbeys and serving left to the priests and sisters. They are sufficiently satisfied with the parish programmes and their involvement in it that over 85% of our respondents feel their parish meets their spiritual needs well.'[22]

6. The parish as social community.

'Whether contemporary American parishes are meaningful social communities is another matter. Within our 36 parish sample (Phase 2), over half feel their parish has a strong sense of community, but nearly half do not feel very attached to parish. Despite the larger proportion who feel the parish meets their spiritual needs well, 45% claim that it fails to meet their social needs very well. While half have frequent conversations with fellow parishioners, about one in three do not list any of their five closest-friends as being from their own parish. Catholics in suburban parishes feel far less attached to their parishes than do Catholics in rural areas, inner cities and small towns respectively.'[23]

7. Different types of parishes

From a historical survey of the 36 parishes it was found that parishes have a variety of parish pasts. 'In the US there has never been one typical parish that has dominated the landscape during the course of the last two hundred years. St Peter's Parish in New York, founded in 1785, has served a variety of communities throughout its two hundred year history – though the building has stood on the same spot, the nature and style of parish life has changed with changing times.' [24]

8. Lay parish.
'In the early nineteenth century a distinctive type of parish did exist in north eastern United States where the bulk of Americans and Catholics lived. Since in many instances the people had preceded the priest, leadership in the parish initially fell on the shoulders of laymen. Once the priest arrived, people and priest had to learn to work together for the benefit of all. A system of governance, common in American Protestant Churches, was worked out whereby laymen, elected by the people, worked with the priest in managing the affairs of the parish. Called trustees, these laymen were the recognised leaders in the parish. Though the system had some problems because of irascible laymen or authoritarian priests, it worked well where, in the words of Bishop John England, 'the laity are empowered to cooperate but not to dominate'. In a sense, the post-Vatican II American Church is now returning to its roots.' [25]

9. Clerical parish
The *Notre Dame Study* continues: 'But as the number of clergy increased and the institutional Church became better organised with the establishment of numerous dioceses, bishops and pastors assumed control of the local Church and the laity were left to 'pay, pray and obey' as one pundit put it. With the demise of lay leadership in the parish, the focal point of the peoples' involvement shifted especially to the devotional arena but also to benevolent societies.

10. Devotional parish
Throughout the Catholic world a devotional revolution had taken place in the second half of the nineteenth century, promoted by the papacy and the hierarchy. It was received with enthusiasm by most of the American Catholic community. An elaborate network of devotions, both public and private; churches were decorated with numerous statues and paintings depicting local saints; mission preachers promoted devotional Catholicism; and parish confraternities, organised around a particular devotion, sustained the

peoples'interest. Devotional Catholicism and devotional parish were central in defining American Catholic identity at the neighbourhood level. Another key element in defining this identity was the parochial school.'[26]

11. The contemporary parish

The contemporary American Catholic parish reflects much of its many 'parish pasts' – lay and clerical governance, a strong relationship to its existing context or milieu, changing with the times, an evolution in devotional needs and trends. The report concludes with the observation: 'The Catholic Parish of the nineteenth century could not resist the social impact of immigration and urbanisation; if it did it would have been an anachronism. Today much the same is true. To be a living force in society the Church will have to adapt itself to this changing social environment. As human beings stumble and falter towards a loving God, so the American parishes try to adapt their many traditions to further our individual and collective journeys.'[27]

Some observations on the study

The *Notre Dame Study* is a very interesting and informative study of the different aspects of parish life. It shows that the American Catholic Church is working hard at trying to be Church. The Study itself in the changing circumstances of today has been criticised for its sampling – a study of only 'core Catholics' – but nevertheless, it provides much useful information for those who wish to study parish and the Church today.

Though its results regarding parish would be optimistic because it only samples involved Catholics, it shows, nonetheless, that parish can work in today's environment of change, urbanisation and secularisation.

It also shows the American Catholic parish to be very focused, close knit, vibrant, though not always strong on mission, outreach and social justice.

151

3. Overall impressions

The major finding of my two months research trip across the USA is that small communities or small groups is the way of the future for the Church. Sometimes the small group was a neighbourhood group, sometimes an interest group, sometimes an ethnic group, a gospel or religious group, or a small community itself. Despite exceptions, there was a clear pattern right across the 3,000 miles of the USA and this pattern was propounded by Diocesan Planners, Renewal Coordinators, Parish Evaluation Teams, researchers, groups of priests, individual priests, sisters and lay members of parishes. It was most interesting to find this consensus.

As a result of this American experience I realised that there is an even wider consensus on this issue. My own experience in Sean McDermott Street would say the same thing – small communities or groups is the major way forward. The Basic Christian Community movement in Latin America is saying the same thing as indeed is the New Code of Canon Law in its re-definition of parish. The New Code, the US Church, the Latin American Church and my experience in Sean McDermott Street all point along the road of small communities or groups. These might be geographical, or groups of interest, or vocational groups, or groups based on need. This insight must point to a more flexible approach to local Church and a different definition or re-definition of local Church as diocese, parish or other grouping.

Three R's of Local Church

This in turn must lead to a re-structuring of local Church, the diocese, and a re-distribution of resources and personnel based on the new vision and needs assessment. The three R's of diocese and parish must be *re-definition, re-structuring* and *re-distribution* of resources and personnel. Vatican II, the New Code of Canon Law and local need have moved the local Church in this direction. Identification of small groups and communities, creation of the same, and ministry to these small groups and communities, whether within the parish structure or outside of it, would seem to be the way of the future.

Priesthood and parish

Another major and related issue in the US Church is the shortage of priests and sisters, though the priests issue was much more discussed probably because of the connection between priesthood and parish, with the continued existence or otherwise of parish seeming to depend on ministerial priesthood. Many parishes were being closed, some of them one hundred years old, because of the shortage of priests. Roughly, there were three different views taken of the vocation crisis and the shortage of priests:

a. Laity model

That the phenomenon of declining vocations is a sign that God wants a new type of Church to emerge, with all of the ministries of the People of God being redeveloped as in the apostolic Church. This would mean the whole People of God taking full responsibility for the Church again. The male, celibate, seminary-trained model of priesthood may be disappearing for ever.

b. Clerical model

That God will provide priestly vocations soon but we don't know when as we don't know his plans. This was described as the more spiritual view and was supposed to be that of half the bishops of the USA.

c. Partnership model

The third view, supposed to be held by the other half of the American Bishops and many Church people, was that we must plan for the present based on the information we have got. The Holy Spirit through Vatican II has told us that we are all the People of God, the *communio* of God in the world, all with different gifts, all with responsibility for the Church and that the way forward is a partnership of ministry between the ministerial priesthood and the priesthood of the faithful.

Parish closures

Another issue, which was related to the priest shortage issue, was the closure of many parishes, a very sad experience. The American Church seemed to have stumbled on this issue too quickly and too late. Why? I don't know exactly. The Americans are very pragmatic and good planners and one would have expected them to be better prepared. Maybe the clerical Church is slow to admit its own greying and diminution or to see that it must decrease, so that the other Church, the partnership Church, can increase.

A vibrant Church

I found a very vibrant Church in the USA. It is a growing church: 18,500 Catholic parishes in 1981, 19,500 in 1989. Roughly 53 million Catholics in 1970, 65-75 million in the year 2000. The vitality of the US Catholic Church is of interest to us since it is dealing with all the issues and realities of a first world Church and has been doing so for many decades.

The recurring question for me was: will the Irish Church go the way of the US Church with growth and involvement, and problems of course, or go the way of the Church in Europe, the 'four seasons Church' as it has been called – contact with Church at the four seasons of life, birth, youth, middle age and death – baptism, communion, marriage and burial?

Notes

1. Philip J Murnion, *Forming the Parish Community*, USCC, Washington 1977, p. 2.
2. Ibid., p.2.
3. Philip J Murnion, 'The Community Called Parish' in *Church Winter '85*, National Pastoral Life Center, New York.
4. Ibid.
5. *Forming the Parish Community*, p. 4.
6. Ibid.
7. Ibid.
8. Ibid., p. 7.
9. Ibid.
10. William J Bausch, *Ministry*, XXIIIrd Publications, Mystic CT 1984, p. 121.

11. Ibid.
12. See Ibid., p. 122.
13. *Notre Dame Study of Catholic Parish Life*, University of Notre Dame, Report No. 1, December 1984.
14. Ibid.
15. Ibid.
16. Ibid.
17. Ibid.
18. Ibid.
19. Ibid.
20. Ibid.
21. Ibid.
22. Ibid.
23. Ibid.
24. Ibid., Report No. 2, February 1985.
25. Ibid.
26. Ibid.
27. Ibid.

SECTION III

Ministry, Priesthood and Evangelisation

CHAPTER 10

Nature, Origins and History of Priesthood

Having dealt with my own experience of 'priesting' in Section I, and having looked at its *locus operandi* in Section II, I will now explore the nature of the Christian priesthood itself and look at its origins, history and changing role in the Church and in society.

PART I: THE CHRISTIAN PRIESTHOOD

When I sat down last year to write about the nature of priesthood and especially Christian priesthood, I decided to put down a list of words on a page which reflected that reality for me, my images of priesthood in words. I wrote about thirty words altogether and when I had written them as they came into my head, I discovered that they clustered around certain elements of priesthood and the life of Christ.

The words were *mystery, transcendence, God, higher power, love, service, sacrifice, bible, eucharist, sin, forgiveness, reconciliation, alpha and omega, unity of history, pontifex, prophet, disturber, morality, truth, justice, community, people, leadership, kingdom of God* .

I notice now that there is nothing about boards of management, plumbing, bingo, parish halls, or signing passports! These things are certainly not an integral part of the essence of priesthood for me, nor a constituitive element of the preaching of the gospel according to my subconscious or deeper reflections on priesthood. They may have something to do with its practice.

Just as the bunch of words quoted above were a reflective mirror of priesthood for me, so also were the titles of the books I had accumulated on my shelf around this topic. They give a colourful kaleidoscopic image of different aspects of priesthood: *The Wounded Healer, The Vowed Life, God's Witness in the Heart of the World, The Christian Priest Today, The Church with a Human Face, Ministry, They Left Their Nets, Sign of Contradiction, Labourers in the Vineyard, A Shepherd's Care, Being Priest in Ireland Today, Partnership in Parish, Priests on Trial, Ministry: Traditions, Tensions, Transitions, Revolution of the Heart, The Emerging Pastor, Servants of the Lord, Take Heart Father, Priesthood and Ministry, Towards a Civilization of Love, Drawn to the Lord, Out of Chaos, Carers for the Kingdom.*

PART II: PRIESTHOOD AND MINISTRY IN THE EARLY CHURCH

The first four centuries

Ministry in the early Church consists of a rich mosaic of gifts and ministries all in the service of the People of God. Ministry took many forms in this early period guided by peoples' response to the Holy Spirit and to the missionary needs of the gospel at that time. In the infant Church, devoid of any existing structures at its beginning, there was naturally great flexibility of structures and of response. From a single beginning in one area and one culture, the Church developed readily into different areas and different cultures. For this reason, the Church developed differently, taking on different forms, as it has through the ages since. Often these different forms of structure and ministry are related to each particular area's context, culture and social forms. (See chapter 6, Pt 1) The new Christian Church in Palestine did not originate from a vacuum, but was a product of a long Jewish religious and social history, of which Jesus was a part. The new Church and its ministries has a relatedness to earlier Jewish forms and also, at times, deliberately chose to be different from the Jewish religion for reason of identity and purpose.

What I am saying overall is that ministry then, as ministry now, is influenced by the gospel imperatives, and the imperatives of evangelisation and the social reality of the time. By looking in this chapter at the biblical, theological and historical data we might be able to see what is essential, what is not essential, and therefore clarify the accretions of history around ministry in general and priesthood in particular.

I would recommend two books to the general reader as sources on ministry and priesthood in the early Church, one for its popular but comprehensive presentation of the subject and the other for its scholarly presentation of the history of the issues and the sociological and theological realities. The first book is *Ministry: Traditions, Tensions, Transitions* by William Bausch;[1] the second is *The Church with a Human Face* by Edward Schillebeeckx.[2]

Beginnings: A Church

When we look to the founder of Christianity, Jesus, and the founding documents, the New Testament, we get a very rich and varied picture of ministry and ministries. Christ left us as his basic gifts: (1) the Church, (2) the eucharist, (3) the gospel, (4) the ministry and priesthood and (5) a way of life. His mission on earth, his incarnation, was to reveal the Father to people and to establish the kingdom of God on earth. God's family had been given the basic gifts through the power of the Holy Spirit, to establish this kingdom of justice, peace and love on earth and to live as God's family in peace and love.

Ministries

So Jesus established ministries to serve this mission of the kingdom. Did he start with the triad of bishop, priest, deacon, the ministerial priesthood, the official ministries of the Church as we know them? No. 'When we turn to the New Testament pages we discover that Jesus did not directly institute bishops or priests or deacons in either the ancient or modern senses of these terms.'[3]

Jesus selected twelve laymen, twelve apostles, who would become his itinerant followers to be moulded into the spirit, thought patterns and ways of the kingdom. They would represent the twelve tribes of Israel of the New Age.

The first ministers of the Church of Jesus would have a very different origin, form, lifestyle and *locus ministerii* from the priesthood of the Old Testament which was elitist and separate, primarily cultic, and confined to a specific holy place, the sanctuary. The first apostles' sanctuary was the world, their ministry the gospel, and their mission would be accomplished on the highways and byeways of life. God, the gospel, the kingdom and the needs of people were the stuff of ministry for those first ministers of the fledgling Christian Church.

Jesus would seem to have made a complete break with an elitist type of ministry for his Church. He was the Pope John XXIII of his time and his change of emphasis concerning ministry and priesthood was more radical than Vatican II! Ministry is for service and is open to all members of the Church on whom gifts have been bestowed by the Holy Spirit. In a sense, Jesus 'democratised' priesthood and freed it from its elitism by choosing the twelve apostles and the seventy-two whom he sent out in pairs to evangelise. (Lk 10:1-12)

Bausch makes the point that there is no attempt made by the early Church to replace the twelve as a college or the seventy two. There is 'a clear indication that Jesus obviously did not provide a blueprint for his Church. He left his intentions, genius and desires but gave the Church total freedom to develop what form would best fulfil these hopes.' [4]

Jesus also gave very exact teachings and instructions to the twelve and the seventy-two. But he did not impose a structure or a form for all time on his Church. Thank God! Building the kingdom was paramount. Flexibility, adaptability and the giving of responsibility would be important in the building of any kingdom or organisation. Even a cursory reading of the New Testament shows Jesus as primarily a people-person and a God-centred person rather than an institution person. He did establish an institution, the Church, but it was built around people, for people and the living of the message in community.

162

Development

'From the beginning of the new Church the controlling ideal of ministry seems to be communities' needs arising from their grounding in Christ and the apostolic tradition. The Church did not consider itself bound even to forms that Jesus used. Rather it took from him that perfect freedom to build up his body, the Church, and to proclaim the Good News in those forms and structures that best seem to do the job.'[5]

Different Ministries

Christ the High Priest, the mediator between God and people is the founder and foundation stone of ministry in the Christian Church. He shared his ministry directly with the apostles. Ministry in the early Church would be developed in conjunction with or in reference to them. 'They are a kind of founding fathers, an apostolic college, the living witnesses to Jesus. They are direct touchstones with his will and his ministry. (see 1 Cor 15:5; Acts 6; Rev 21:14)'[6]

Bausch goes on to mention others, also called apostles, who were not members of the original twelve. These travelling apostles, like St Paul, would bring the gospel to people, minister to them and encourage them. Then there were teachers and prophets who proclaimed the Word of God, celebrated it in liturgical assembly, and gave inspired utterances. Next there were deacons. This ministry was instituted by the twelve apostles and arose out of the circumstances of the time. The Church was growing, authority was over-centralised in the apostles and problems arose around a very important 'secular' matter:

'The Greek-speaking Jews claimed that their widows were being neglected in the daily distribution of funds. So the twelve apostles called the whole group of believers together and said: 'It is not right for us to neglect the preaching of God's Word in order to handle finances. So then brothers, choose seven men among you who are known to be full of the Holy Spirit and wisdom and we will put them in charge of the matter. We ourselves, then, will give our full time to prayer and the work of preaching.' (Acts 6:1-5)

The institution of this ministry brings up some important points about ministry and priesthood in general:

(1) This ministry arose out of friction, not some holy thought;

(2) The ministry was in answer to a community need;

(3) The apostles realised that they had become over involved in secular things. They were becoming 'secular priests' with the emphasis on secular!

(4) Ministerial priesthood (that of the apostles) is primarily about proclaiming the gospel and mediation between God and people, which gets concretised in service (ministry) and fellowship in the Christian Community.

Thomas O'Meara's definition of ministry emphasises the fact that it is service of a special kind – that done by people of God's family in response to the Holy Spirit and the real needs of fellow-family members: 'Christian ministry is the public activity of a baptised follower of Jesus Christ flowing from the Spirit's charism and an individual personality on behalf of a Christian community to witness to, serve and realise the kingdom of God.'[7]

Schillebeeckx makes the same point about ministry when he says: 'Early Christianity was a brotherhood and sisterhood of equal partners: theologically on the basis of the baptism of the Spirit.'[8]

Role development

Deacons did works of charity and looked after corporal and social needs, but their role also developed and widened. They worked miracles and wonders among the people (Acts 6:8) and in fact their role blurred with that of travelling apostles, prophets and teachers in preaching, leading prayer and founding new communities.[9]

Within the chapter 'The Fellow Workers of the Apostles,' Max Thurian says: 'It is not accurate to see in these seven what the Church was later to call deacons. Admittedly they were ordained in the first place for this ministry of the agape, but two of them were revealed as having fuller gifts: Stephen appeared as a prophet (preacher), 'a man full of faith and of the Holy Spirit ... full of grace and power, doing great wonders and signs among the people' (Acts 6:5-8); and Philip as an evangelist (a missionary and apostle's helper, Acts 21:8), who preached, taught, baptised and performed miracles of healing (Acts 8: 5-8, 12-13, 26-40).'[10]

Already, we see five ministries in operation in the early Church: the apostles, travelling apostles, teachers, prophets, deacons. Their roles differed but were interchangeable.

Variety of Gifts: Variety of Ministries
Paul in his letter to the Corinthians gives us a very powerful image of ministry in the early Church. It is the variety of gifts – one spirit, one body, many parts – image. 'There are different kinds of spiritual gifts, but the same spirit gives them. There are different ways of serving, but the same Lord is served. There are different abilities to perform service, but the same God gives ability to all for their particular service. The spirit is shown in some way in each person for the good of all.' (1 Cor 12:4-8)

Ministry or service is from God for God and the community. It is his gift for the good of the community of his people. And Paul lists a number of other ministries here: healers, miracle workers, interpreters, preachers, discerners. That makes ten ministries to date.

Bausch concludes: 'There were, then, a variety of agents and officers who engaged in ministering to the small communities and house-churches of the first century.' [11]

Many gifts, many ministries; developing roles and relationships; unity without uniformity; organisation without stagnation; authority with autonomy. That is the picture of ministry in the first century of Christianity.

Bishop and priest
The two other important ministries which appear in the New Testament are presbyter and the 'guardian' of the community or

bishop. 'And sometimes the words presbyter and guardian are used so interchangeably that it's hard to tell if and when there is a distinction.'[12]

Presbyter: origins

The word presbyter literally means elder. The elders were advisors to the king or prince, usually older men steeped in ancient lore, full of wisdom, and noted for integrity of life. They formed an advisory council to the king in ancient Egypt and Israel and among other ancient peoples. In the history of the People of God in the Old Testament, these elders were called presbyters, 'established by Moses whose father-in-law told him to choose able men from all the peoples and let them judge the people.' (Ex 18:18-22) In another tradition Moses is directly approached by God who tells him to gather seventy elders 'and I will take some of the spirit which is upon you and I will put it upon them'.'[13]

Bausch tells us that around the second century before Christ the elders had developed into a type of senate, the Supreme Council of Jerusalem, the *synedrion* or sanhedrin, and each territory in Palestine had its sanhedrin.

'These elders or presbyters were 'ordained', i.e. they were installed by the laying on of hands: they were not priests nor were they connected with the temple in any way. They were simply invested in their roles by the laying on of hands, which was an old symbol of the transference of power ... The tasks of these elders-presbyters lay mainly in the role of judging, guiding, and in general presiding over the local community. Some of the elder-presbyters, collectively called the presbyterate, were sent out to carry messages to various Jewish communities and promote piety and learning ... Such 'sent members' were called apostles.'[14]

Bausch then makes the point that all the first Christians were Jews. As Jews they would instinctively follow their ancestral social forms. That is why they largely adopted the presbyterate model of ruling their first communities, especially in the first

Christian community at Jerusalem. Note the letter sent out from the Council of Jerusalem. 'The brethren, both the apostles and the presbyters to the brethren who are Gentiles ...' (Acts 15:23)

Local variety in ministry

'In due time, as we begin our variety of tradition, not all communities beyond Jerusalem followed this pattern ... In Antioch, Syria, Barnabas, sent by the Jerusalem sanhedrin, ... winds up organising the local community around local prophets or charismatic figures. (Acts 13:1) These local leaders have no special title and are referred to by Paul as 'those who labour for the community' ... Some communities had presbyter-councils but with a single person in charge, others with no specific lead.'[15]

Bishop

'The Presidency' is a distinct development after Paul's death around the years 58 to 62 at Philippi and Ephesus. Among the ruling elder-presbyter body, one of their number begins to stand out as a leader. This is somebody 'more equal' than others even though he works with them. He is called the 'guardian' or the 'bishop' and he is assisted by his deacons. In the pastoral epistles (1 Peter, John) on the other hand, he appears to be someone quite distinct from the elder-presbyter.'[16]

Was he appointed by one of the twelve apostles or the elders-presbyters? We don't know. But we do know that he gradually began to dominate the scene and to be separated from the elder-presbyters.

Plethora of ministries

During the first four centuries there was a plethora of ministries, *munera et ministeria*, different forms of ministry which were a reflection of the Church's or the Christian community's way of living and carrying out the mission of Jesus. Such was the case for four exciting and intensely developmental centuries of the Church's history. The variety of ministries and forms of mission which originated and developed in different contexts and cultures, in the practice of the Church, included the twelve apostles, the seventy-two disciples, teachers, prophets, travelling apostles, guardians/bishops, presbyters, deacons and a variety of leaders, administrators, discerners, and community leaders.

This apostolic Church had some very important characteristics which clearly reflected the mind of Christ passed on through the apostles.

(1) It was faithful to Christ and the apostolic tradition. 'They remained faithful to the teaching of the apostles, to the brotherhood, to the breaking of bread and to prayers'. (Acts 2:42-43)

(2) There was a very clear and definite authority structure. There was constant reference back to the apostles or to Jerusalem. The writings of Paul confirm this constant dialogue between the more centralised authorities and the local communities. The local leaders would ask for advice or discernment or a ruling from Paul and Paul would reply or check out with Jerusalem. The Council of Jerusalem (Acts 15:22-30) was a formalised form of this constant dialogue, decision making and exercise of authority. Autonomy and authority, centralisation and decentralisation seemed to be very well balanced.

(3) The early Church was a 'community-based' Church. It was run by the local people with the support and guidance of the central authority, the apostles at Jerusalem. They, the locals, took full responsibility for its governance, its ministries, its support and its doctrine. The Church was the people and the people were the Church. It would have been unthinkable to try to separate the two. At this stage the 'Church' had not been divided into two, the lay Church and the clerical Church.

(4) The many ministries in the early Church were all 'official' ministries. Inspired by the Holy Spirit, all of these gifts and ministries were the inspired and practical response of the followers of Christ, as individuals and communities, to the imperatives of the gospel and the needs of the community.

The monarchical bishop

1. Survival and centralisation

How did 'the one' take over from 'the many'? How did the single person of the bishop come to dominate? How did his office become separated from that of the elders-presbyters? How did the elders-presbyters end up as dependent extensions of him? And, most importantly of all, how did the ministry of the single monarchical ruler come to absorb so many of the charisms and ministries of others in the early Church? The emergence of the guardian of the community or bishop was a good thing. The church needed good shepherds and pastors. But how did the monarchical office come to supplant most of the others?

Bausch raises many of these questions, and answers as follows: 'It is not too simplistic to respond by saying that the office of bishop was propelled by the pressures of history. First of all, the twelve apostles had died and fierce pressures descended on the Church. There were heresies for one thing. Persecution would take its toll. The second coming of Christ was apparently being delayed. With all of these factors there was a need to retrench, to dig in for the long haul. Survival was at stake. There was a desperate need for direction, for a living rule of faith, a living guide to what was right and wrong. There was a need to preserve the genuine apostolic tradition. In a word, there was need to centralise.

To all of these needs the early Church responded with two basic reactions. One was the writing down of the normative Jesus story, with all of its variety of interpretations and traditions, and that is what we call our New Testament. The second reaction was to turn to a centralised source of leadership. The emerging guardian-bishop was just the one for this. Crises had assured his ascending and firm position.'[17]

2. Governance: various models

Bausch further reminds us that there were at least five models of governance or local Church leadership in the first century. 'The epistle of James tells us that the elder-presbyter Church order was in vogue. The Johannine communities started out as spontaneous charismatic communities but wound up with authoritative leaders. Matthew's gospel reflects a Church community, perhaps in Syria, that still seems to be under the individual prophet's and teacher's leadership, and they do not seem to be aware of the elder-presbyter model. In general, the Roman sources speak of the elder-presbyters who seem to be appointed for life, have cultic functions and preside over the community. The Asian Churches seem to have bishops surrounded by an elder-presbyter council of advisors.'[18]

3. Multiple ministries to monarchical bishop

Then Bausch goes on to speak of the transition from multiple ministries to the full emergence of the dominant monarchic bishop: 'Whatever the variety, there is a distinct trend, in the face of heresy and the need to pass on the apostolic tradition intact, to depend less and less on the charismatic prophets, teachers and wandering apostles, and more and more on stable resident bishops. ... By the time we meet a writer like Ignatius of Antioch (d. 117) and his disciple Polycarp, and some decades later Irenaeus of Lyons (d. c.202) we have the end product of what was begun in the pastoral epistles, the centrality and triumph of a strong monarchical bishop. Older patterns remain and ruling by elders-presbyters is still common, so much so that the terms bishop and presbyter are still being used interchangeably. Nevertheless change is being made. The office of bishop as chief presbyter over all the others is growing ... (Although) we can sense an apologetic transitional note as the author of the didache tries to sell the bishop and deacon: 'Accordingly elect you yourselves bishops and deacons ... for they too render you the service of prophets and teachers. Do not despise them; after all they are your dignitaries together with the prophets and teachers.' [19]

Summary

In this thumb-nail sketch of the apostolic Church we get a sense of the nature and mission of the Church. At least, I did! I also got a sense of the responsibility of the newly baptised in each new Church to provide their own ministries and take full responsibility for the Church, i.e. for themselves. But I would say that the variety of ministries is the most striking thing about the apostolic Church. The contrast between that Church and the Church that I grew up in, pre-Vatican II, is most striking.

In order to clarify the meaning of the ministerial priesthood for the future, one has to focus again on:
(i) the meaning of Church;
(ii) how it was organised at the beginning;
(iii) how ministry and priesthood functioned in the early Church;
(iv) how the ministerial priesthood took over or replaced many of the other ministries.

We have to resurrect that apostolic model of Church with all its gifts and ministries! Not exactly as it was – that would be to see the Church as a museum – but in forms and structures suitable for today. The Vatican Council of John XXIII has begun that process. Its definition of the Church as the People of God, not just the clerics, was the paradigm shift that catapults us back to the apostolic Church and prepares us to be the full Church of Christ in the third millennium. We have the theology, we have the Holy Spirit. What we need is the commitment and the courage to review and to renew, to clarify and work out the roles, relationships and patterns needed for tomorrow.

Two Millennia of Ministries

1. Apostolic Church

12 Apostles

72 Disciples

Prophets, Teachers, Evangelists, Healers, Deacons, Presbyters,
Bishops, Travelling Apostles, Pastors
Interpreters, Administrators, Community leaders, Counsellors

2. 1500 Years

Bishop, Priest
(Ministerial Priesthood)

3. Vatican II

Emerging roles and ministries

Deacons, Pastoral Administrators, Parish Sisters
Catechists, Ministers of the Eucharist, etc.

(See chapters 13 & 14)

172

PART III: THE PRIESTHOOD IN TWO MILLENNIA

An historical overview

Doing an overview of the historical development of the priesthood has been literally a revelation for me! It shows the influence of human factors and of historical contexts, more than doctrinal or theological influences. It also shows that priesthood cannot be, and never was, defined separately from 'reality' or 'context'.

Finally, awareness of the existence of different 'models' of priesthood at different times, for centuries even, and pendulum swings in the theology and practice of priesthood over the centuries, throws light on the changing theology and role of the priest today. As Seamus Ryan says in *The Furrow*, May 1988: 'To know a little history is to be a prisoner of history. In the course of the Church's history it is possible to pinpoint at least four significant shifts in the evolving pattern of priestly ministry. All of these have profound implications for our contemporary understanding of the priesthood, and reveal that some of the tensions which many priests are experiencing in their ministry today have deep roots in unresolved issues in past history.' [20]

Evolution of priestly ministry through the ages

I will now outline five stages in the evolution of the Christian Catholic priesthood, based on Seamus Ryan's research.

1. The priesthood in the Old Testament

The priest of the Old Testament was primarily involved with sacrifice or cult, especially after the emergence of the rabbi who was not a cultic figure or priest, but an interpreter of the law and a minister of learning and good works who lived among the people and ministered to them in their everyday situation.

Of the Tribe of Levi ... an elite caste ... admission by birth or ancestry ... primarily a man of the sanctuary ... priesthood primarily conduct of cult.

Description: cultic / elitist.

2. Priestly ministry in the New Testament

Jesus not of the tribe of Levi ... a 'layman' in Jewish terms ... the One and Eternal High Priest ... His ministry performed among the people, the marketplace and the 'holy places' of Christianity, not the sanctuary; ... the people 'a holy people, a royal priesthood', a community of disciples with a variety of gifts and ministries; apostles, prophets, teachers, evangelists, pastors (Eph 4:11-14). He left a Church, a gospel, eucharist and ministry.

Description:
people-centred, life-centred, bible-centred, eucharistic

3. Priesthood from the third century

During this period there is a shift from a New Testament theology of priesthood to a clerical and hierarchical model. This process began with the advent of persecution and heresies and therefore the need for strong, centralised authority in the Church. With the evolution of the strong, monarchical bishops around the time of Irenaeus of Lyons (d.202), the varied ministries in the New Testament tended to disappear. The gifts of many became the domain and competence of one. Ordination supersedes baptism as the source of ministry, and gives jurisdictional and administrative powers as well as status. The clerical elite of bishop and his assistants, the deacons and elder-presbyters, are gradually becoming 'the Church'.

Then a major historical secular event changed the role of the priest in the fourth century: 'Over the centuries, especially with the Church's changed political status under Constantine in the fourth century, the ministry of leadership in the Church came to be patterned more and more on the style of the levitical priesthood. The ministry took on a distinctive 'clerical' dimension. With the collapse of the Roman Empire the clergy took over secular roles of importance (hence the title 'secular priest') and this further accelerated the transformation of the clergy from a service 'elite' to a power 'elite'. There is little awareness that all the baptised share in the priesthood of Christ, or that the Holy Spirit enriches the

Christian community with various ministries. There is an inevitable decline in the significance of non-ordained ministries. It is no longer baptism but orders which give real status in the Church ministry.'[21]

Priesthood is separated from community, theoretically at least. It becomes clericalised and professionalised. Power and status and secular pursuits 'invade' the priesthood. The 'cultic' notion of priesthood comes to the fore. 'As Yves Congar says: the first priestly act is the ministry of the word. We have become a bit forgetful of that fact. The middle ages understood our priesthood as founded on Aaron and therefore linked it to the cultic-ritualistic priesthood of the Old Testament; then it defined this very priesthood by the power to celebrate the eucharist.' [22]

Description: clerical, secular.

4. The priesthood in Reformation times

This was an evolution from the medieval understanding of priesthood to the 'anti-Protestant' definitions and emphasis of the Reformation. As Ryan says: 'Luther and Calvin laid down the main lines for a Protestant understanding of ministry. They denied the sacrificial character of the eucharist and played down the difference between the priesthood of the ordained and that of the baptised. The preaching of the gospel was at the heart of the ministry (they said).'[23]

Ryan continues: 'The council of Trent did not embark on a theology of the priesthood. If it sought to reform it also sought to defend. The difference between the ministry of the ordained and that of the baptised was strongly affirmed.'[24]

If in the anti-Catholic teaching of Luther and Calvin the meal aspect of eucharist was emphasised, then the Council of Trent emphasised the sacrificial aspect; if they played up the ministry of the people, they were seen as playing down the ministerial priesthood. This had to be countered. If preaching the gospel was given more emphasis than the offering of the sacrifice of the Mass then the cultic aspect of priesthood had to be re-emphasised by the Catholic Church. Context and reality and history once again played a big part in the development of priesthood as it always does.

Trent and beyond

'Clericalisation' of ministry ... gifts and ministries centralised ... laity passive, fossilised? ... ordination supersedes baptism as the sacrament of the Church ... the clergy become the Church ... priests put on pedestals ... emphasis on the eucharist as sacrifice rather than meal ... cultic and 'devotional' priesthood to the fore, the role of the priest is very clear and well defined ... so is the role of the lay-faithful, though it is passive.

Description: clerical, cultic, devotional.

5. The priesthood today

In the 1900's the development of biblical scholarship, ecumenism, and the liturgical and catechetical movements, all open up the bible and questions on Christology, Church, ministry.

The Holy Spirit was moving. Who would pick up the vibes? A newspaper? A young upwardly mobile cleric? Or an old, easy going fat Italian priest who was close to retirement but who had been reading scripture, history and the 'signs of the times' all his life? John XXIII and Vatican II would open up new questions and new horizons about ministry in the Church. Ryan says: 'We see a shift from a polemical theology of priesthood ('a theology against Protestants') to a broader ecumenical understanding of priesthood at Vatican II.'[25] The Vatican Council, with its abundance of biblical scholars, theologians and the practical and pastoral experience of thousands of bishops and priests, opened up the Bible and the treasury to the Church's experience and history, to look anew at ministry and priesthood. In, first of all, defining what a Christian was before it decided on different ways of being Christian, e.g. clerical and lay, the Council made a master stroke. A Christian is a baptised person, a full member of the Church, the

People of God. Christians or members of the Church are divided into clerics and laity. The clergy or ordained ministers are servants of the People of God.

Baptism was once again declared the primary sacrament. All the members of the Church have gifts and ministries through the power of the Holy Spirit. The priesthood of the laity or the common priesthood is highlighted once again. The ministerial priesthood or 'priestly' priesthood is located within the Christian community and for its up-building. Ordination builds on baptism and enhances it. A priest is a person first, with great dignity before God; he is a Christian next, with its dignity and, finally, he is a priest. Priesthood is a partnership of gifts and ministries and functions within the Church and is divided into the priesthood of all the baptised and the priesthood of the ordained.

The role of the priest

At Vatican II '... the proclamation of the gospel is unambiguously stated to be the first and primary responsibility of priests, and the sacramental ministry is situated within the context of a ministry of proclamation, thus rediscovering a fundamental insight of St Paul: 'As often as you eat this bread and drink this wine, you proclaim the death of the Lord'.[26]

The eucharist is the summit and source of the whole Christian life and so it is the high point of the Christian life, of priesthood, of proclamation and of the Christian ministry. Ryan continues: 'The Council situates the ministry not above the Church but within it ... The late patristic age and the early middle ages had bent towards portraying priests and bishops as a kind of Christian version of the Old Testament priesthood (cultic/ritualistic model) and this is not entirely absent in Trent's interpretation of the priestly ministry.'[27]

Description: Bible-centred, cultic, life-centred.

Priesthood of the ordained and of the baptised

Vatican II, in defending the unique priesthood of the ordained, tried to clarify its nature and meaning and relate it to the priesthood of the baptised. It didn't succeed very well. 30,000 priests left the Church in the following ten years. The special synods on the ministerial priesthood in 1971 and on the laity in 1987 tried to make further clarification regarding ministry and priesthood. The synod of 1990 on training and formation of priests brought the theology and understanding further. But there are still muddy waters, as one would expect in an era of transition. The lack of clarity or lack of definition of the role of the priest and the role of the laity in the Church is a reality in the Church today.

Perhaps it is a good, though painful reminder of the emergence of a new and more powerful Church. Perhaps it is a reminder of the awakening of the 'sleeping giant' referred to at Vatican II as the 98% or the passive lay faithful. Perhaps, finally, it is a reminder that ministry and priesthood are the gift and responsibility of the 100%, the whole People of God.

Notes
1. William J Bausch, *Ministry*, XXIIIrd Publications, CT 1984.
2. Edward Schillebeeckx, *The Church with a Human Face*, SCM, London 1985.
3. Bausch, op. cit., p. 15.
4. Ibid.
5. Ibid., p. 16.
6. Ibid., p. 19.
7. Thomas Franklin O'Meara OP, *Theology of Ministry*, Paulist Press, New York 1983, p. 142.
8. Schillebeeckx, op. cit., p. 47.
9. See Bausch, op. cit., p. 19.
10. Max Thurian, *Priesthood & Ministry*, Mowbray, London 1983, p. 50.
11. Bausch, op. cit., p. 19.

12. Ibid., p. 20.
13. Ibid.
14. Ibid., p. 21.
15. Ibid., pp. 22-23.
16. Ibid., p. 23.
17. Ibid., p. 24.
18. Ibid., p. 27.
19. Ibid., pp. 27-29.
20. Séamus Ryan, 'Priesthood and the Seminary', *The Furrow*, May 1988, p. 297.
21. Ibid., p. 298.
22. Bausch, op. cit., p.41.
23. Ryan, op. cit., p. 298.
24. Ibid.
25. Ibid.
26. Ibid.
27. Ibid.

CHAPTER 11

The Role of the Priest in Theory and Practice

PART I: FROM THEORY TO PRACTICE

Seven years training: a vision of priesthood

The week before I was ordained, in May 1965, I remember well being interviewed for TV on the role of the priest. I was crystal clear about what it meant. I had just completed seven years study to take up that role in Dublin. My teaching had been very clear on the role of the priest. At least so I thought! My ordination card encapsulated my understanding of that role. On it was the prayer to Christ the King:

'O Christ Jesus, I acknowledge thee as King of all, whatever has been made has been made for Thee ... I pledge myself to promote the triumph of God's rights and those of Thy Church. Divine Heart of Jesus, I offer thee my feeble help to make all hearts recognise thy sacred Kingship and thus to establish the reign of thy peace throughout the world. Amen.' [1]

On the back of the card was:

Hail Christ Victorious
Michael Casey,
ordained to Christ's priesthood,
30th May 1965.
Pray that I may show Christ to the world always

That was my role – to show Christ to the world. The interview for *Radharc*, which was then in its infancy, was carried out by a very perceptive young priest, Fr Peter Lemass. My summary sentence, which telescoped seven years training and reflection, was that the role of the priest was 'to show the face of Christ to the world'.

That sentence will always, for me, be the core and will never change. It contains a number of basic ideas and realities:

a. The priest is simply and always an *alter Christus*.

b. He must bring Christ's values, teaching, practice and person to the world.

c. The priest must try, as a weak and imperfect person, to be like Christ in thought, word, action and spirit.

d. The priest will suffer, as Christ did, because gospel values are contrary to human greed, individualism, the consumer society, luxury, injustice – which will always be part of society.

Those were my thoughts in ordination week as I waited like a greyhound wound up in the starting traps at Shelbourne Park! I couldn't wait to get out. I would change the world. Let me get out! I can't wait! I was full of zeal and goodwill and youthful naïvety. My starting point and point of reference was the empty tomb, the hope that Christ could bring to the world. But I hadn't walked the road to Calvary. I hadn't suffered. I had a lot to learn.

The Ordination Rite [2]
The Ordination Rite confirmed and clarified the teaching on my role as a priest. The ordination rite is the official commissioning and ordaining by the Church of the new candidate for the priesthood. On his ordination day, he hears the mind of the Church on what his role as a priest is meant to be in the world.

The *Entrance Antiphon* says:
'The spirit of the Lord is upon me;
He has anointed me.
He sent me to bring good news to the poor,
and to heal the broken hearted.' Lk 4:18

The *Collect* says:
'Father, you have appointed your son Jesus Christ eternal High Priest. Guide those he has chosen to be ministers of word and sacrament.'

The bishops' instruction says: 'It is true that God has made his entire people a royal priesthood in Christ. But our High Priest, Jesus

Christ, also chose some of his followers to carry out publicly in the Church a priestly ministry in his name on behalf of mankind. He was sent by the Father, and he in turn sent the apostles into the world. Through them and their successors, the bishops, he continues his work as Teacher, Priest, and Shepherd. Priests are co-workers of the order of bishops. They are joined to the bishops in the priestly office and are called to serve God's people.'

The first sentence above is a powerful statement about the ministry of all the baptised ('the priesthood of all the baptised'). All the baptised have responsibility for the Church, not just the bishops and priests. But Christ chose some to be fulltime public ministers in the Church ('the ministerial priesthood'), to serve the rest of the Church.

The bishop goes on: 'They are to serve Christ the Teacher, Priest, and Shepherd in his ministry which is to make his own body, the Church, grow into the People of God, a holy temple. They are ... to be moulded into the likeness of Christ, the supreme and eternal priest. By consecration they will be made true priests of the New Testament, to preach the Gospel, sustain God's people, and celebrate the liturgy, above all, the Lord's sacrifice.'

The Ordination Rite clearly states that the role of the priest is:
a. to represent Christ, the one eternal priest, in the world.
b. to be his public minister in the Church for the service of the people.
c. to continue the work of Christ as Teacher, Priest and Shepherd.
d. to make the Church grow more into a living, caring Christian community, a holy temple in the world, the Kingdom of God on earth.
e. to be fulfilled in the Christian community, in partnership with the other ministries of the People of God.

That is the role of the priest which is officially communicated to every priest at ordination. That is the official mandate from the Church given through the bishop. That is the basic, or core, role which the Church wants all its priests to fulfil.

May 1990

As I look back after twenty-five years experience of 'priesting,' I see a huge gap between the role of the priest in theory and the role of the priest in practice. What the diocese told me to do in theory, at ordination, and what it tells me to do in practice, as an ordinary priest in the parish, is as different as chalk and cheese. The two are a thousand miles apart. One is North pole and the other is South Pole. Images that come up include: They send me out to play football as part of the team, but they have me digging drains in the pitch! I thought I was playing but I'm carrying the jerseys! I was meant to be a Minister of Community, a Minister of Values, a Minister of Sacrament and a Minister of the New Testament but I have been fixing school drains, signing passports or have been a waiter at table for the rich!

These images are exaggerated and negative but they contain a good deal of truth. They contain seeds of the 'crisis of priesthood' so often referred to in Church literature on the priesthood. People became priests to serve Christ, to be Good Shepherds in the world, to preach the gospel. People who are priests want to fulfil this ministry. They get their meaning from that and their motivation. There must be some congruity between the primary role of the priest as stated in the ordination rite and the practice in reality. If there isn't, then there is automatic crisis for priesthood. Dioceses and religious orders have a duty to examine the theoretical and practical role of their priests. My gut feeling is that most of the 100,000 men who left the priesthood since the 1960s did so because of a crisis of meaning in ministry – the gap between the espoused theory and the theory in practice of priesthood. Without a doubt, celibacy was a major issue as well, but I would say that meaning was the major reason.

Minister or Manager?
Fr John Marshland's description of his role fits:

'Parish accountant and administrator,
typist and banker, news duplicator,

183

reference composer and pencil-end biter,
passport endorser, certificate writer.

Digger of garden, inspector of drains,
checking the roof each time that it rains.
Re-designer of churches, re-arranger of pews,
closer of windows, repairer of loos.

Visitor, caller in, knocker on doors,
target of tale-spinners, cadgers and bores.
Something to everyone as I'm passing by,
occasionally wondering, 'Just who am I?'.' [3]

Seamus Ryan comments : 'I am quite sure that were the question put to priests in Ireland today (and more especially to parish priests), 'Where do you experience the greatest sense of frustration in your priestly ministry?', many would reply along these lines: 'Most of my energy gets drained on matters which have little to do with being a priest and where frequently I have little skill and competence. As a result I find myself cutting corners on the more central work of leading people to God.'

The funnel
It has become a very popular image in the United States for parish priests to describe themselves as being at the bottom of a huge funnel. 'Almost everyone in the Church pours their own project down the funnel: a Marian year from the Pope, a vigil for peace from the cardinal, endless paper work from the bishop, some new initiatives from the Commission for Vocations or the Commission on Liturgy, while local organisations (The Legion, the Vincent de Paul, the Prayer Group, etc) all add their own demands, not to mention the idiosyncrasies and occasional inspirations of the individual parishioners.'[4]

Also, having varying, contradictory and excessive expectations from people does not help. Carrying out a complex and confused role in an era of transition adds to the problem.

The experience of 'priesting' in Ireland

Here is Fr Ray Brady's summary of the varying expectations of the priest after his consultation of priests in the provinces about priesting in Ireland:

'Priest, why don't you spend more time at prayer?

Priest, why don't you spend more time with youth?

Priest, why don't you spend more time visiting people in their homes?

Priest, why don't you spend more time at study and reflection?

Priest, why don't you manage the football and hurling teams?

Priest, why don't you put on the musicals and produce our dramas?

Priest, what are you doing about social injustice?

Priest, what are you doing about adult education?

Priest, what are you doing about liturgy?

Priest, what are you doing about our school and the appointment of teachers and the heating?

Priest, what are you doing about ecology issues ... and the nuclear threat ... and women's groups ... and third world consciousness ... and unemployment?

Priest, what are you doing about yourself and your growth as a person and the new skills you need?'[5]

And Brady concludes with a very perceptive remark to the National Conference of Priests of Ireland: 'It is easy to caricature. It is not easy to see the way forward.'[6]

In the excerpt above, Brady mentions between fifteen and twenty areas that are perceived as part of the role of the priest in Ireland today. I will add at least one hundred and one more in alphabetical order:

A to Z: The role of the priest

Priest, what are you doing about

    alcoholics, adolescents, adoration, amalgamation, altar girls, altar rails,

    baptisms, budgets, bingo, blessing of houses, pets, boats, babies?

Priest, what are you doing about
    choirs, confessions, computers, culture, conscientisation,
        collections outside the church door;
    devotions, development plans, devaluation of church
        property,
    extradition, the elderly, education, ecumenism, economics,
        electricity bills, evangelising skills?
Priest, what are you doing about
    funerals, fund-raising, fostering, folk group materials;
    GOAL, Gorta, Gamblers Anonymous, guidelines for
        ministries;
    hospitals, halloween, the Hospice, help for the poor;
    itinerants, incense, inequality, insurance on the parish plant?
Priest, what are you doing about
    justice, junior infants, juvenile delinquency;
    liturgy, litigation in school, liaison with parents'
        committee;
    music, ministries, the missions, meals on wheels,
        moving statues;
    no-name club, notifications of baptisms and marriages,
        nominations for school board?
Priest, what are you doing about
    oils, the organ, organisations;
    passports, prisons, pioneers, pilgrimages, parish magazine,
        pilfering from shrines;
    qualifications of teachers, quantity surveyors?
Priest what are you doing about
    roles, ritual, rights, reality in the church today;
    spirituality, sodalities, scapulars, street traders;
  touchers, teachers, technology, tax evaders;
  unity, unions, unisex liturgies, universality in the Church;
  vandalism, vestments, Vatican Two;
  wills, weddings, women's rights,
  X-rated films;
  'Your man on the organ', your tax, your housekeeper,
    your retreat, your curate, your role;
and a zillion other things?

I have been involved in most or all of the above in my role as priest over the past twenty-five years. I know I could double the list if pressed. Is there any role more scattered, more diffuse and in need of clarifying and re-defining?

Brady says that there is: '... quite a bit of frustration and anger among priests in Ireland, even among those who say they are generally happy, and this frustration and anger is linked closely with the urgent need to spell out priorities for priests.'[7]

And he adds a second serious issue among priests, which is related to the former and to the confused state of the role of the priest in Ireland today: 'There is some annoyance, occasionally intense annoyance, with the Church as institution: the structures of this institution are often perceived as outdated, tedious, ineffective.'[8]

PART II: MY OWN EXPERIENCE

Killester
I was appointed full-time parish chaplain to Killester Vocational School in August 1965. This was a school of approximately 250 boys. There were two of us full-time priest/teacher/chaplains. I was also appointed chaplain to the Holy Faith nuns, which involved saying Mass, and part-time chaplain to Killester Parish for weekends. This involved Mass and confessions, with my voluntary involvement with youth in the parish as time went by. As a priest, I was very happy and very fulfilled during those years in Killester. My role was very clear. I was full-time chaplain to youth. My ministry was directly with about 500 young people in the school and parish. I taught them, dialogued with them, listened to them, walked the road of life with them, and they taught me.

This was a learning time for me. I was learning evangelising skills and pastoral skills and survival skills. In the 'Tech' or Vocational School, I had the support of a senior or experienced priest the whole time. I had the usual problems that inexperienced teachers have: lack of control in class, always feeling I had to be a nice guy because I was a priest and a teacher of religion; being fooled by city lads as a green 'culchie' from Kerry. So cultural adaptation was a difficult part of my role since all of my life experiences and images were rural. During this period in Killester, seven years in all, I spent a lot of time adapting the Bible's teaching and values to the lives and vision of the young people.

On reflection, I was working directly with the Bible and the young people themselves. My role was very directly evangelisation and pastoral care. Secondly, my 'parish' was clearly identified and clearly demarcated – 500 youth approximately.

My main pastoral care area outside of the school was setting up youth clubs in the area or linking up with existing ones, such as St Brendan's Club in Artane and Fr Denis Laverty's Youth Club in Donnycarney. My main memory of the latter club, a very active youth club, was the amount of fights that could break out and be quelled in the three-hour session in the hall! No wonder there was so much 'action' when the chief bouncer was 'Bomber', who was the Vocational School's super heavyweight boxing champion of Dublin. Bomber would never pass up the opportunity of a brawl or of making an omelette out of two eggheads! Bomber usually ended every battle by starting a war.

Out of school my involvement with young people was continuous and close through Killester Basketball Club which I set up with a group of local teenagers in the parish in 1967. We had 779 members and 53 teams playing out of a church carpark. It was a mixed club. We deliberately started the basketball club rather than football to cater for girls as well as boys. The club is now run by the children of the sixties and seventies. It has been a very good social and friendship club and works at coaching with many local primary and second level schools. My role in the club was the pastoral care of youth, developing youth participation and linking them with Church.

Overall conclusion

My experience in Killester would tell me that the role of the priest as full-time chaplain to a school or to a particular group, e.g. youth, is a very clear one, in sociological and evangelising terms. The target group is clear and well defined. It is homogenous. There is direct and immediate contact with the groups. These facts do not necessarily guarantee success but the role is clear. In my ministry to the Vocational School and the youth of the area in Killester there was congruity between the theory and the practice of my role as the priest because:

a) It was a small community – school and club;

b) There was direct contact between priest and community;

c) There were no other structures coming in the way of ministry and evangelisation.

Bayside

At the end of my seven years in Killester, I was exhausted and close to burnout. We didn't have that word in those days! I had been up everyday for the seven years at 6.30 am except Saturday, Sunday and holidays. I taught all day and did youth work in the evenings, and stayed up chatting in family homes till midnight and later many nights. I had endless energy – or so I thought. But of course many young priests don't know how to pace themselves, as I didn't.

I had been very happy and very fulfilled in Killester. But then the bubble burst. All of a sudden I realised that I hadn't had a clue! That I had been ministering out of a very simple and simplistic philosophy of life. That I had come from a cosy, comfortable and fairly cocooned rural background. That I hadn't really suffered in life. That mine was a ministry of easy answers. I exaggerate slightly because I did have the normal suffering of a teenager growing up, of life at boarding school and my father, to whom I was very close, had died in 1969. He had been critically ill on the day of my ordination – a happy-sad day therefore. But I could not have understood brokenness, broken homes, broken lives, broken dreams. I became very hard on myself for the next four or five years. I demanded perfection. I punished myself. I questioned everything.

The next four years in Bayside, 1972-76, were a mixture of frustration and happiness. Happiness, because of the warmth of the people and a wonderful parish priest, Chris Mangan, with a very supportive fellow curate Mick Lambe. Frustration, because I was very confused during that period. My theology had been a theology of easy answers, I felt. I saw life now as very complex and outside our control, almost. I was searching for meaning, meaning in rites and roles and in my life, and not finding much. I was going through a crisis but was unable to minister out of my weakness and brokenness because, in my experience up to then, the one thing one was not allowed to do was to fail. The role I was asked to fulfil as a priest was really one of services, to do all sorts of things for people. To fill papers, sign forms, cards, organise youth, run the altar boys group, visit someone in hospital – always one more than one was able to – to say Masses, run schools, count money. Of course many of these things and others were enjoyable and fulfilling, but the overall feeling was lack of meaning, cut-offness from the deeper realities of priesting and ministering. In those years I experienced a lot of the problems about the role of the priest that I have verbalised in the earlier chapters here, but I couldn't put them into concepts or words then. For example:

a. A priest immersed in administration instead of evangelisation is like a fish out of water.

b. A priest involved eternally in services instead of *communio* and real ministry feels like a dispensing machine.

c. Being labelled a 'social worker' rather than a 'priest' by some older priests. That hurt a lot because I was so insecure. Translated positively, it reads to me now, 'You were a Vatican II priest involved in community and life issues and dealing with the whole person rather than 'saving souls' and being a sanctuary or sacristy priest – the Trent or pre-Vatican II model. In those early days after Vatican II the more 'churchy' priest model was seen to be more 'holy' and therefore more priestly, and therefore its proponents held the higher ground.

Frustration

My frustration, I am also now clear, was with the role of the priest. This frustration had to do with the context, the theology and the changing role of the priest. Some examples of these would be:
1. the structures of parish which are so diffuse and varied;
2. the lack of focus of parish as structure;
3. so many and differing expectations from different people, the diocese and fellow priests;
4. confusion between my role and the emerging role of the laity (ministerial priesthood versus priesthood of the laity);
5. the fact that Vatican II diminished the role and importance of the priest (not deliberately, of course).

Role of the priest and Vatican II

With regard to the latter, I loved most of Vatican II. My personality, temperament and idea of ministry suits collaborative ministry, partnership, community, empowering people, making policy together. So I am all for these. But there is no doubt that Vatican II, which dealt primarily with two groups and two roles in the Church – the laity and the bishops (the first Vatican Council had dealt with the Pope and papacy) – left many priests feeling unloved and undervalued; the taken for granted cart-horses. Why have so many priests left the ministry since 1965? I have no doubt that Vatican II did a wonderful job for the Church in general and for the world, which is benefiting from the new definitions of Church, spirituality, sacramentality, mission, and the re-defined role of the laity. But the role of the priest was left in a bit of a mess and still is, despite the 1987 Synod on the Laity and letters of Pope John Paul II to priests, 1989-90. The crisis in the priesthood persists. There is still a lack of clarity about the role of the priest at the theoretical level in the theology of the Church and hence also at the practical level. I will say more about this later.

Finding myself in Toronto

Because I had become very involved with community development and community groups in Bayside, I did the diploma in
Social Science at UCD in 1975 on the advice of Professor Conor
Ward, a priest in the diocese, and Mary Whelan, a local person
who was involved with the parish and who also lectured in community development in UCD. The development of community,
an understanding of community, and building Christian community were becoming an important part of my ministry. In 1976 I
was sent by Archbishop Dermot Ryan to the university of Toronto
for two years to study community. Those two years saved my life.
They gave me a chance:

a. to find myself in the middle of my tasks and roles;

b. to reflect and make space in my life;

c. to look at models of ministry, of Church and community development.

Freire and McLuhan

I did a master's degree on community and wrote a thesis on the
'person and community'.[9] The latter was a useful clarifying experience about the values, ideologies, policies, underlying my pastoral work. During this time I also came in contact with two people
who would have a large influence on my pastoral work since
then, Paulo Freire and Marshal McLuhan. Freire's analysis and
psycho-social method are powerful tools for community development and pastoral development. McLuhan's understanding of
the power of image and symbol, and of the electronic age, are
crucial to the work of the Church and to anyone working in media
and communications today. McLuhan was the most brilliant
human being I ever met. On a personal level, I was thrilled when
the great guru of the media spent two of his classes discussing my
work, community and community building, and the issues involved in today's society which are pro- and anti-community.
McLuhan, a very thoughtful Catholic, helped me to see greater
meaning in my ministry.

McLuhan's main thesis about Church was that the Church had

192

just come into the vernacular and written age (at Vatican II) when the world had moved on to the electronic age and the age of image. Image, ritual, symbol would be vital for the Church in the seventies, eighties and nineties plus. I took that message very seriously in Sean McDermott Street – the power of the media, press, radio, TV, and used them all; the outdoor Stations of the Cross, the visual Church on the streets; use of imagery in the liturgy, even slide/tape or video as a way of looking at the people's image of themselves and others' images of them. All in all, I believe McLuhan's and Freire's teachings and approaches could make a major contribution to the development of parish and communities.

While in Toronto I took time to study more deeply the third great influence on my work outside the theologians, Saul Alinsky, the great Chicago community activist who had so much influence on the poor and the Church there. He married the Church structure of parish and the Church's social teaching to his skills of community action and development to great affect and thus empowered poorer people in Chicago. Aliskey showed me again the power of the gospel when brought to bear on unjust social situations and realities.

Sean McDermott Street

Though I was very fulfilled as a person while working in Sean McDermott Street, my frustration increased about the role of the priest and the role of parish and other Church structures. The issues identified in Bayside continued:

a. diffuseness of parish structure;
b. lack of focus of it;
c. diverse, varied and contradictory expectations of the priest;
d. confusion after Vatican II between the role of priest and the role of laity.

Added to these in Sean McDermott Street were:
e. the contradiction of blinding poverty in the middle of a well-off Irish society;
f. the ambivalence of an Irish Church caring but not seeming to

193

care enough, in a city of Dublin categorised as 'two cities',[10] and in a Dublin Church that could be categorised as 'two churches';

g. a parish structure geared to only 15-20% of the people – the 'practising', generally those who went to Mass.

h. the lack of planning, policy and priorities by the diocese – the 'sponsoring' body of parish and of my work.

i. the gap between the theory and practice of the role of the priest.

PART III: MY PRIESTHOOD IN CONTEXT

I will now try to put my priesthood in context by relating my priesthood and priesthood today to the stages or models of priesthood as proclaimed in different eras of the Church's history (see chapter 10). As Seamus Ryan said, the role today is influenced by different theologies, traditions and models of priesthood from the past history of the Church.

Researching the history of priesthood was really enlightening for me. I studied the history of priesthood during my training but it left no lasting impression. This is to cast no aspersion on the professor. It is just that I had not experienced the practice of priesthood myself and it would have been just theory. But now that I have experienced the practice of priesthood for twenty-five years, the different stages and models of priesthood through history jumped out of the pages at me.

1. Trent

The priesthood which I was ordained into was quite clearly the priesthood of the Council of Trent. It was the model of priesthood as envisaged and practiced by the universal Church worldwide for four hundred years. It was the priesthood of every Catholic parish. This model of priesthood was embedded in every culture and especially in the Irish culture. It was part of the solid and then seeming unchanging tradition and culture of the Church.

Trent, which was a product of the history of its own time, and one of defence against attack and excesses, gave us its model of priesthood. This model was primarily sacramental, cultic and hierarchical or clerical, with a greater emphasis on sacraments and eucharist than gospel, and on orders than on baptism. That was the pre-Vatican II or Trent model of priesthood that I was ordained into and that still lives on very strongly today.

2. The secular priest

The second historical model of priesthood that was most influential on my priesthood was that of the 'secular' priest in Constantine's time in the fourth century. We are still the secular priests with all the baggage that that entails and, therefore, the encumbrances that come in the way of being servants of the gospel and of the Church. One night I was chatting with Fr Gerry Griffin in Ballymun and he said, 'Being a parish priest is the most secularising job you could be in.' I really felt there was a lot of truth in that statement. The priest, of course, must work in the world and fulfil his role there, but his role is not to be the servant of secular powers or to be so immersed in secular tasks and pursuits that his primary role as minister of the gospel and the People of God gets lost.

The first apostles were aware of that danger and resisted it. Their primary role was ministry (mediation between God and people) and evangelisation, and they would never depart from that. As leaders of the Christian community, they would have taken responsibility for all aspects of the life of the Christian community. In doing this, they distinguished between different tasks and roles, i.e. proclamation, evangelisation, pastoring, leadership of local Churches, social service and care (deaconate, almsgiving), prophecy, healing, discernment, speaking in tongues. The apostles were involved in management, but only in so far as it facilitated ministry and the building up of the Christian community. In recognising their primary role of evangelisation and leadership in the Christian Community, the apostles did two things:
(1) they fulfilled their own primary role effectively;
(2) they encouraged and expedited the fulfilment by all the People

of God of their roles and responsibilities as gifted members of the Body of Christ.

3. Vatican II
A third influence on the role of the priest today is Vatican II. With the hindsight of history, the coming together of the Christian churches through the growth of ecumenism, and a renewed understanding of ministry through biblical scholarship, Vatican II has given us a new, enriched and more rounded teaching on ministry (chapter 10).

Vatican II, in returning to a wider New Testament understanding of ministry and priesthood,
1. re-defined the Church as the People of God;
2. re-defined the role of the laity and therefore also,
3. changed the role of the priest.

For the past twenty-five years, the Church has been trying to work out these new roles in practice. And of course there has been role conflict and role confusion as well as role development and clarification.

The role of the priest
At Vatican II the proclamation of the gospel is declared to be the first and primary responsibility of the priest, and his sacramental ministry is situated within the context of this ministry of proclamation of the gospel. The eucharist is declared to be the summit and the source of the whole Christian life and so is the high point of priesthood and proclamation. But evangelisation is prior to sacramentalisation and both are for the building up of the People of God into the kingdom of God.

My priesthood in practice, and my role as priest, has been influenced by the 'Trent model', the 'Constantine model' and the 'Vatican II model' which said that evangelisation was the core and sacramentalisation the cream of 'priesting'.

I would think that the pre-Vatican II or Trent model of priesthood is still the primary model in the thinking patterns and cultural expectations of the majority of the faithful, certainly in Ireland. Of course that is to be expected since it got a four-hundred-year headstart on the Vatican II model which is only twenty-five years old. Cultural and traditional models die slowly.

4. Christ as model

The fourth, and I would say the biggest influence on my priesthood and role as priest in Sean McDermott Street especially, was Christ as model and image in the New Testament. To try to serve him is the core reason why I became a priest. He and his way of life have been my chief inspiration, hope and role model at the deepest level. I have not been able to live up to his practice often, but when the diocese said one thing and some priests said another, when some people made this demand and others made that, when I was down and out or feeling great, Christ was always the bench mark or core criterion of what I should do. I hope this does not sound too holy or righteous! (Why do I hope that?) When I was really down or very confused in Sean McDermott Street, there were two things I held on to – Christ and community. When there was a clash, or seeming clash, between Christ and institutional Church, I always chose what I saw as Christ's position – or, as the bishop might say, 'He did it his own way!' The grace and power of Christ is working very strongly, I have no doubt, in anyone who is trying to struggle to establish his kingdom, no matter how inadequately or feebly.

Summary

There are four models, (at least) of priesthood impinging on and influencing my role as priest and the role of other priests. These are the Trent model, the Constantine 'secular' model, the Vatican II model, and the Christ model. So the models or theology of priesthood are an important influence on the role of the priest and ministry in practice.

Another major influence is the context of ministry – the people with whom one works, the area, and also the larger society, and, of course, the diocese and the local and universal Church. A third influence is the personal – one's background, family, personality, life experiences, relationships, health and attitudes to life.

So the role of the priest is not a simple one. In theory it may be, but not in practice. The role of the priest is influenced by tradition, by theology, by context and the 'personal' and is continuously evolving and changing.

Notes

1. Quoted from my Ordination Card, Clonliffe College, Dublin, May 1965.
2. *The Rite of Ordination of Priests*, Veritas, Dublin 1978. *I have used the Post-Vatican ordination rite because that was the theology of priesthood that I was taught during my last three years in the seminary.*
3. Séamus Ryan, 'The Priesthood and the Seminary', *The Furrow*, May 1988, p. 300.
4. Ibid., pp. 300-302.
5. Ray Brady, 'What Priests Say' in *Being a Priest in Ireland Today*, Dominican Publications, Dublin 1988, p.51.
6. Ibid.
7. Ibid., p.50.
8. Ibid.
9. Michael L Casey, *Community Building: A Personal Statement*, University of Toronto, 1983, unpublished MA thesis.
10. See 'A Tale of Two Cities' in *Hard Facts, Future Hopes*, CSSC, Dublin 1988.

CHAPTER 12

The Primary Role of the Priest

During my research trip to the USA in the Summer of 1989, I stayed with family friends, Martin and Trish Fleming. It was John Denver country, near the Blue Ridge Mountains and the Shenandoah river in Virginia. Beautiful country! One could contemplate the role of the priest forever there! Their son, Geoffrey, picked me up at Washington Airport but I didn't meet their bright Irish-American, fifteen-year-old daughter Tara the first night as she was working late in the local MacDonalds restaurant. When she came home, she asked her Mom what I was researching and her Mom said, 'Mike is writing a book on the role of the priest today.' 'That'll be a short book,' says she snappily!

Later, when I went on to San Francisco, I met a lot of Irish people at the Irish Centre. One man from Listowel in Kerry asked me what I was doing and when I told him, he scratched his head and said, 'The role of the priest? I know the role of a lawn mower and a combine harvester, but the role of the priest today – that's beyond me!' Who am I to contradict an intelligent Kerryman?

The primary role of the priest
Vatican II stated unambiguously that proclamation of the gospel was the first and primary role of the priest. And Christ, when he instituted the ministerial priesthood, said to his apostles, 'Go, therefore, teach all nations' and 'Baptise them' (make them members of the Church, the People of God). The primary role of the priest, who represents Christ the Eternal Priest in the world, is to preach the gospel of Christ through the ages. This gospel of Christ is to transform the world and to build up the kingdom of God in

the world, a kingdom of justice, peace and love. The primary role of the priest is to be a minister of Christ. And that means:

'Serving Christ the teacher, priest and shepherd in his ministry, which is to make his own body, the Church, grow into the People of God, a holy temple ... By consecration, he will be made a true priest of the New Testament to preach the gospel, celebrate the liturgy, above all, the Lord's sacrifice, and sustain God's people'.[1]

The US Bishops' Committee on Priestly Life and Ministry state that, 'The fundamental role and function of the pastor (priest) ... leadership, teaching and pastoral care ... were the same in 1967 and 1987. Indeed they have their roots in the mandate of Christ to his disciples and in the earliest understanding of the Christian community. What has changed, however, is the manner in which these functions are carried out, as well as the needs of the people of the Catholic community.'[2]

Teacher, Sanctifier, Shepherd

The primary role of the ministerial priesthood since Christ would seem to be to represent Christ the teacher, priest and shepherd in the world. Was this role the same in 90, 590, 1090, 1590, 1990? Is it still the same? This is an important question. Did the primary role of the ministerial priest get lost, or recede, when other roles loomed large or took over? What is the relationship of the primary role to secondary and tertiary, or ancillary roles? Ward, Fichter and others have done some valuable research into the role of the priest in the parish from a sociological point of view, so hopefully we will clarify some of these questions as we go along. I am confused about them now! So let us plough on and maybe gain clarification!

Cardinal Emmanuel Suchard, quoted in Fichter, says,'The sacerdotal function, always in essence the same, can take, and has in fact taken in the course of the ages, different forms and functions, in which stress is laid in turn on its royal, prophetic or sacrificial character. Thus it is that a priest, and more particularly a bishop, has become at different times *pater familias*, ruler, defender of a city, regent, judge and so on.'

And Fichter comments, 'This indicates a historical pliability in the sacerdotal role, not limiting it to the sacraments, the sanctuary and the sacristy.' The same interpretation, from a wider historical perspective, is given by Wach.[6] 'Through his regular dealings with a group of people or individuals who come to him, rely on him, and depend on him for the performance of necessary cultic acts, the priest becomes a guide, adviser, comforter, 'pastor', and 'confessor'. Through this immediate and intimate contact, the priest exerts tremendous influence to which the history of civilisation bears witness. This influence was originally primarily religious but extended soon to the moral, social, cultural and political spheres.'[3]

The role of the priest through the ages

Obviously context, need, culture, tradition, expectations and the 'personal' influence the form, expression, and particular emphasis of the role of the priest at different times. At the historical level, we saw different emphases in the five stages of the history of priesthood. (See chapter 10)

Christ as model

Christ was the origin and the perfect role model for priesthood in the New Testament era. His priesthood was performed among the people. He came to bring the Good News, especially to the poor, and to 'establish the kingdom of God on earth'. He was teacher, priest and shepherd. He was 'about the things of God' among people, the perfect mediator and witness. Christ modelled himself less on the Old Testament priest – the person in charge of cult – than on the rabbi, the itinerant teacher of religion.

The priest of the New Testament in the person of Christ would play a different role from the Old Testament priest:

a. He would perform his ministry among the people, in society, in the marketplace as well as in the Church.

b. He would be a preacher of the Good News - an evangelist.

c. He would be shepherd – the Good Shepherd – forever concerned for the spiritual and temporal needs of the flock (not just spiritual life, but also their temporal life, and needs, e.g. feeding 5,000, making the poor his priority, preaching for justice, peace, the kingdom of God on earth – 'Thy kingdom come, on earth as it is in heaven.')

d. Finally, Christ was a sacramental priest, the High Priest and mediator of the New Covenant. He would ask his disciples to celebrate the eucharist in memory of him, to baptise in the name of the Trinity, and to forgive sins. So he commissioned and ordained new ministers of word and sacrament and pastoral care to be servants of the Church, the People of God. As we saw in chapter 6, the role of the New Testament priest in the apostolic Church was very much a partnership one, a minister among many other major ministries.

The primary and secondary roles of the priest
Let us now examine the 'fundamental role and functions of the priest' as expressed in the Roman Pontifical when the person being ordained is told what he is to do: 'Serve Christ the Teacher, Priest and Shepherd in his ministry.'[4]

Other titles for these functions or roles through the ages are the prophetic, sacrificial and royal functions of Christ or, as they are also known in the Church, the ministry of word, sacrament and pastoral care.

The primary role of the priest through the ages has been to represent Christ, the One and Eternal High Priest as teacher, priest and shepherd. As I have said earlier, each of the different aspects of this role has been emphasised at different times, sometimes the cultic or sacrificial or priestly role, (Trent or pre-Vatican period), sometimes the evangelical or teaching role (early Christian community and Vatican II), sometimes the pastoral or shepherd's role. The important thing to emphasise here is that, in Christ, all three were part of an integrated ministry. They formed a unity in ministry. They complemented each other; they were never separated. Nor must they be today. All three are necessary for building up authentic Christian communities.

One role, three functions

I will now examine the three primary functions to which the priest is called by Christ and the Church. In his excellent, and aptly titled little booklet, *Called to Serve, Called to Lead,* (subtitled *Reflections on the Ministerial Priesthood*), Cardinal Joseph Benardin gives very clear teaching on the three primary functions of serving Christ in the ministerial priesthood. They are as teacher, priest and shepherd.

1. Teacher/Evangeliser

'Go, therefore, teach all nations.' (Mt 16:16) These words of Christ, spoken to the apostles, his first disciples and priests, have rung out through the ages, in the minds and hearts of all priests. These words proclaim his primary function – proclamation of the gospel. The priest is, first of all, a preacher of the word of God, a minister of the gospel, an evangeliser. As Paul says, 'Everyone who calls on the name of the Lord shall be saved. But how shall they call on him in whom they have not believed? And how can they believe unless they have heard of him? And how can they hear unless there is someone to preach? And how can men preach unless they are sent?' (Rom 10:13-15)

As Bernardin says, 'We receive that commission at ordination. Teaching ministry is essential to the ministerial priesthood.'[5]

The Second Vatican Council's injuction, declaring that the proclamation of the gospel is the first and primary role of the priest, has, in my view, to be taken much more seriously today in the training of priests and in the practice of priesthood. Vatican II, was in fact, re-asserting the priorities of Christ.

Vatican II re-asserted the role of evangelisation before sacramentalisation and administration in the life of the Church and the priest. In the pre-Vatican II, or Trent model of Church and priesthood, sacramentalisation had taken priority over evangelisation, often producing the over-sacramentalised and under-evangelised Church – the extreme of which was the conveyor-belt baptising and creation of nominal Catholics, especially in Latin America.

The Holy Spirit, through Vatican II, is proclaiming again the message of Jesus, Peter and Paul and the New Testament, that evangelisation, is the first and primary responsibility of the Church and of the priest. The needs of the world and of the Church today proclaim the same message. Pope John Paul II and many cardinals and bishops of the Church have proclaimed the 1990s the decade of evangelisation and the third millenium the millenium of evangelisation.

The priest as evangeliser
If the priest is to be an evangeliser, a good evangeliser, an effective and imaginative evangeliser, how is he to do that unless he is re-immersed in the Bible, re-biblicised himself? My major question for myself and other priests and diocesan authorities is: how can we become again ministers of the Bible, people of The Book? How can we be re-trained and re-oriented from being ministers of administration to becoming ministers of evangelisation? Priests cannot be both. One cannot be a full-time civil servant and at the same time, a full-time servant of the gospel. Ask the apostles. 'It is not right for us to neglect the preaching of God's word in order to handle finances (administration). So then, brothers, choose seven men among yourselves who are known to be full of the Holy Spirit and wisdom. We ourselves, then, will give our full time to prayer and the work of preaching.' (Acts 6:2-5) There is need for a megashift in the Church from administration to evangelisation, with sacramentalisation put in the context of evangelisation, as Vatican II and Christ did.

The pastor as teacher: The new Code of Canon Law
Canon 528, 1, is very specific about the role of the priest (pastor) as teacher.

'The pastor is obliged to see to it that the word of God in its entirety is announced to those living in the parish: for this reason he is to see to it that the lay Christian faithful are instructed in the truths of the faith especially through the homily which is to be given on Sundays and holydays of obligation and through the catechetical formation which he is to give; he is to foster works by which the spirit of the gospel, including issues involving social justice, is provided; he is to take special care for the Catholic education of children and young adults; he is to make every effort, with the aid of the Christian faithful, to bring the gospel message also to those who have ceased practising their religion or who do not profess the true faith.'[6]

If evangelisation is made the priority in the Church, this canon must be studied very carefully. It contains a huge agenda for the Church and the life of the priest. It is the Church's reflection on the role of the Bible today and the role of the priest put in a concise manner in the context of parish only.

It contains six elements, distinct but related. The role of the priest as teacher or evangeliser is:

1. to see that the gospel is proclaimed to all in the parish. How does he do this?
2. to see that the faithful are instructed;
3. to oversee catechetical and religious formation;
4. to ensure that the gospel is practised at the social and macro level in the parish and community;
5. to emphasise the catechesis of children and youth;
6. to evangelise the 'unchurched', non-practising, and the alienated, with the help of the laity.

The role of the priest as evangeliser is a full-time job, as Christ meant it to be.

Conclusions
Some important conclusions follow from the fact that proclamation of the gospel and evangelisation is the first and primary role of the Church and the priest.

1. The priest must be steeped in the Bible, especially the New Testament.

2. Evangelisation must be made the top priority of the Church today. It is not now.

3. If evangelisation is to become a priority, then other present priorities, like administration, must be set aside and given to other ministers in the Church such as full-time lay parish administrators; or do as the apostles did – create new ministries. The Church or the priest cannot have two or three sets of priorities. For something to become a priority, first of all a decision must be made for it to be so, and secondly, the other previous priorities must be relegated to second or third place or discarded.

4. The priest and people must learn many new and creative evangelising skills, e.g. use of the media, of popular culture, of like to like; learn from the Church in other countries (See chapters 8, 9, 14).

5. The priest must not only be an evangelist or teacher. He must train and facilitate others to be the same. He must be a facilitator of ministries of evangelisation and be trained for this.

6. In the pastoral Church of the future, Bible scholars and lay evangelists will be as necessary as catechists and social workers and teachers are now. How do we gear our training institutions for this changeover?

7. Preaching: There must be even greater emphasis on preaching. I am reminded again of Greeley's comment that preaching is the greatest need of the American Church today.

2. Sanctifier

Canon 528,2, outlines the role of priest (pastor) as sanctifier or minister of sacraments.

'The pastor is to see to it that the most Holy Eucharist is the centre of the parish assembly of the faithful; he is to work to see to it that the Christian faithful are nourished through a devout celebration of the sacraments and especially that they frequently approach the sacrament of the most Holy Eucharist and sacrament of penance; he is likewise to endeavour that they are brought to the practice of family prayer as well as to a knowing and active participation in the sacred liturgy, which the pastor must supervise under the authority of the bishop.'[7]

So, as well as being a minister of the word, the priest is also a minster of sacrament.

'Every high priest is taken from among men and made their representative before God, to offer gifts and sacrifices for sins.' (Heb 5:1) The ministerial priests, bishops and priests, are the ministers of sacraments in the Church and for the Church. They have a unique role and special identity as ministers of sacraments in the Church. The priests of the new covenant, 'the ordained ministers of Christ, perpetuate his eternal sacrifice (the eucharist) when, obeying his command at the Last Supper, they 'do this in memory' of him. In his priestly role, then, the ordained minister is the source of sacramental contact with Christ.'[8]

The ordained priest represents Christ the Eternal Priest at the heart of his Church. He helps to actualise and bring to fullness the Church as the sacrament of Christ in the world. His specific task is to build up the Body of Christ, the Church, as a minister of ministries.

As a minister of sacrament the priest is always a minister or servant of Christ and of the Church. He has no meaning apart from them. He is ordained for service to Christ and the Church, the People of God. The priest as sanctifier is a mediator between God and people. As the spiritual leader of the people in the parish, he is to preside at the eucharist, leading the parish in worship, in receiving the bread of life, and then scattering in service to the whole human community.

The role of the priest as sanctifier and minister of sacrament is expressed in a very deep and meaningful way through the sacrament of the Church itself, and the sacraments, especially baptism, eucharist and penance. Indeed all the sacraments, if understood in the context of the gospel and life, and related more closely to these, will have a lot of meaning in the life of the priest and the Christian community.

Sanctifier and leader

As well as being a minister of sacrament and sacraments, the 'priestly' role of the priest is to be fulfilled today as:
(a) Christian Leader.
(b) Liturgical Leader.
(c) Spiritual Leader.

(a) Christian leader

The priestly role is to be fulfilled as a Christian leader of a community in an often secularised society, and in a capitalistic and material society. This is a role of great challenge and meaning. It is a deeply gospel and prophetic role, which is often a crucifying and demanding or even alienating role. As comforter of the afflicted and afflicter of the comfortable, he will often find himself in conflictual roles if he is faithful to the dictates of the gospel. As a Christian leader, the priest is called to lead the People of God towards the values and ways of the kingdom and to build a caring Christian community. In this sense he is a sanctifier of community.

(b) Liturgical Leader

Secondly, the priestly role is to be fulfilled as liturgical leader of the people in the eucharistic assembly, as a minister of ministries within the Church, and, in the broader context of the parish, to link worship and service, liturgy and life. Encouraging and coordinating ministries within the Church and developing meaningful liturgies with the help of the lay faithful could form a large and very significant part of the priest's daily and weekly ministry.

(c) Spiritual Leader

Thirdly the priestly role is to be fulfilled as spiritual leader or *animateur spirituale,* of the People of God in the Christian community. This role can vary from individual spiritual direction, an art and practice almost lost by the modern administratively-oriented and over-worked priest in the parish, to providing spirituality and renewal courses in the parish, to making rites and rituals and sacraments more meaningful, and to making the parish a more spiritual, Bible-centred, God-centred and people-centred community. 'The pastor's task is not limited to individual care of the faithful. It extends by right also to the formation of a genuine Christian community.'[9]

So the role of spiritual leader has both individual and communal aspects. Prior to Vatican II, this spiritual leadership role would have been seen as provision of the sacraments and guardian of morals and of the faith. Community-building would not have been seen as an important part of the role. Today, the sacramental, moral and community roles should be seen as equally important and totally interconnected.

Amateur therapy messiah?
Nobody has written more pungently about the religious and spiritual role of the priest today than Fr Andrew Greeley:

'It is not easy, gracious Lord, to be a young priest today. Many of the foolish certainties of the past are gone. But a man cannot live without some certainties, without some kind of faith; and it has become hard for a young priest to have faith. Some tell him that there is no more need for religion; others insist that the priesthood is irrelevant; still others say that if he wants to be a celibate he is probably a homosexual. The sacred, he hears, is being replaced by the secular; the Church is a dying organisation without a future. Those that are 'really with it' are getting out. The relevant clergyman is the protestor, the self-righteous moralist with easy magic answers for social problems and no answer for religious problems, the amateur therapy messiah, the political revolutionary, or the hysteric who speaks with tongues.' [10]

And Greeley, firing a few arrows at the type of priesthood he does not accept, says:

'Some of his (the young priest's) contemporaries think it fashionable to have no convictions at all; they argue that they are not interested in substance but only in process. Alas, good Lord, as you well know, they have only the most superficial knowledge of what process is. I think that they are afraid of conviction and commitment, afraid to lead, afraid to take a stand, afraid to preach your word, afraid to be anything but superficial.

Small wonder that your servants, the lay People of God, have so little respect for them.

But this young priest is different, Lord, from many others. He does have faith. He does have the conviction necessary to preach your word. He does believe that if the priest is not a religious leader he is nothing.' [11]

Greeley concludes his *Complaint on Behalf of a Young Priest* with a prayer:

'Help this young priest to know how important he is, how many people look to him for guidance, how many want to share his convictions, how many stand ready to love him if he is strong enough to share his faith with them. If he wants to be an amateur therapist – or even a professional one – that's all right, but let him see that's no substitute for being a priest, for preaching the Good News of life that you came to bring us.

Grant him, O Lord, the wisdom to see that, while the language and the style may change, the Good News is both as Good and as New as it ever was.' [12]

Clarifications needed

Clarifications will have to be made about the sanctifying role of the priest in the future. How he can best exercise this sanctifying role in the Christian community will have to be carefully examined. A few preliminary thoughts strike me based on my experience in Sean McDermott Street:

1. The appointment of a lay manager on parish administration would make the role of the pastor much more effective and meaningful.

2. The role must be community-based and community-oriented. In other words, the priest must fulfil his priestly, sanctifying, and sacramental role not in isolation from community and peoples' needs, but immersed in them. The priesthood must be put back into the heart of the People of God, the Christian community. The 'sanctuary priest' or the 'sacristy priest' is not the answer. The 'community-based priest' is, although the priest must move from administration to Christ's sacramental and evangelical functions.

3. Shepherd

As I was writing this chapter Ireland lost it's Cardinal. Our Cardinal, Tomás Ó Fiaich, died suddenly and the nation was literally in mourning, to such a huge degree that it has surprised the national media and even many Church people. Tomás Ó Fiaich was a very fine priest, a very good teacher of the faith, an able articulator of national ideals, but that is not what has moved the people. It is Tomás Ó Fiaich, the shepherd of the flock, the beloved *pastor bonus*, the simple man of the people who laughed with them, cried with them, suffered with them. The heart is more moving than the mind. Love is greater than ideas. The priest is called above all to be a good shepherd. It is after all the image by which Christ, the great and eternal High Priest, used to describe himself. The title 'pastor,' which is that used for the parish priest in the USA, and is now also used in the New Code of Canon Law, is a very apt one.

In Canons 519 and 529, the New Code articulate the Church's vision of the role of priest as pastor or shepherd, in today's Church.

Canon 519

'The pastor is the proper shepherd of the parish entrusted to him, exercising pastoral care in the community entrusted to him, under the authority of the diocesan bishop in whose ministry of Christ he has been called to share; in accord with the norm of law he carries out for his community the duties of teaching, sanctifying and governing, with the co-operation of other presbyters or deacons and the assistance of lay members of the Christian faithful.'[13]

This canon is pregnant with meaning in terms of good theology of Church, ministry and the role of the priest today.

1. The parish priest is juridically and canonically appointed by the universal Church and its chief shepherd on earth, the Pope, to be a shepherd of a smaller flock – the People of God in a parish, be that territorial or a community of interest or needs. The priest's primary role as pastor is particularly stressed. The priestly teaching and leadership role is to be exercised within the context and vision of pastoring. So pastoral leadership is not just management. It is about care and caring in essence.

2. Pastoring is a primary role of the priesthood in the Church. The Pope, bishops and priests are all called to be pastors of their flocks in the Universal Church, the diocese and the parish respectively. But this is meant to be in a holistic, unified way as the one priesthood of Christ, the Good Shepherd. Pastoring is a collegial ministry which will be best achieved by a collegial mentality, with collegial structures, among all the priests in the pastorate. Enunciation of the principle of collegiality between Pope and bishops, and encouragement of pastoral councils and priests' councils at local level, were all attempts by Vatican II to implement the unity of the priesthood and the sense of brotherhood and service rather than power, status, hierarchy and division.

3. Within the parish and the Church of today, pastoring and pastoral care is the responsibility not just of the ministerial priesthood but also the priesthood of the baptised. All Christians who all share in the priesthood of Christ are called to be good shepherds. Hence the emphasis on collegial structures in the parish and collaboration in pastoral care. All the baptised have responsibility for developing caring communities and caring structures. In this context, the role of the priest as pastoral leader is a partnership role.

The pastor's obligations
Canon 529, 1
'In order to fulfil his office in earnest, the pastor should strive to come to know the faithful who have been entrusted to his care; therefore he is to visit families, sharing the cares, worries and especially the griefs of the faithful, strengthening them in the Lord, and correcting them prudently if they are wanting in certain areas; with a generous love he is to help the sick, particularly those close to death, refreshing them solicitously with the sacraments and commending their souls to God; he is to make a special effort to seek out the poor, the afflicted, the lonely, those exiled from their own land and similarly those weighed down with special difficulties; he is also to labour diligently so that spouses and parents are supported in fulfilling their proper duties and he is to foster growth in the Christian life within the family.'[14]

The authors of the Code are of necessity selective in naming areas of work under the role of priest as pastor. But they do specify the areas that they see as most important. They have prioritised. The list would be about one fifth of the duties and responsibilities that I was called to fulfil as pastor in Sean McDermott Street and Bonnybrook!

Every pastor and pastoral team must prioritise. How the priorities are arrived at and what the priorities are is important. If there is to be a unity between the presbyterate at parish and diocesan level, there must be some level of prioritising together and of mutual goal-setting – long and short term. In this context, a diocesan vision statement, a Diocesan Pastoral Plan are not luxuries but necessities today.

Co-responsibility
Canon 529, 2.
This canon begins: 'The pastor is to acknowledge and promote a proper role which the lay members of the Christian faithful have in the Church's mission by fostering their associations for religious purposes.' And it concludes: 'The pastor is to co-operate with

the bishops and presbyterate of the diocese to foster real *communio* among the people in the parish, diocese and universal Church.'[15]

From practice it is obvious to me that the priests alone cannot fulfil the total role of pastoring the Church today. The needs are too big and too various. The priests haven't enough skills and gifts and energy. The 2% cannot do what the 100% are called to do. Christ, the early Church and Vatican II all have called the People of God to use their gifts and ministries to represent the Good Shepherd in their Church and in the world today, as Church.

The Good Shepherd model.
'Jesus went around visiting all the towns and villages. He taught in the synagogues, preached the Good News about the kingdom, and healed people with every kind of disease and sickness. As he saw the crowds, his heart was filled with pity for them, because they were worried and helpless; like sheep without a shepherd. So he said to his disciples, 'The harvest is great but the labourers are few. Pray to the owner of the harvest that he will send out workers to gather in the harvest." (Mt 9:35-38)

The role of the pastor, and the feelings of a pastor, are all well expressed in this passage by the Chief Pastor. The role of the priest is primarily about the 'Father's business', about teaching and promoting the kingdom of God on earth. It is about articulating God's vision of creation and life and uniting God and his people through sacrament. It is also about the equality and the dignity of each person before God, each as made in his image. It is, therefore, about access to the fruits of creation in practice – a life, a job, and other basic human needs. The priest, after the example of the Good Shepherd, is a pastor of God's people in their spiritual and basic human needs.

The role of the priest is about promoting the life and values of the kingdom of God on earth. So the role can and must operate at different levels; some may operate at the macro, some at the micro or individual. The unity of the priesthood in Christ suggests a unity of the ministerial priesthood, bishop, priest, deacon. It also postulates the unity of this ministerial priesthood with the priesthood of the laity.

Shepherding with and for Christ cannot be achieved by a divided Church or a divided priesthood. Neither can it be achieved by dividing soul from body, heart from mind, heavenly from earthly aspirations.

Conclusion

In this chapter I have tried to clarify the primary role of the priest. I have concluded that it is to re-present Christ as Teacher, Sanctifier and Shepherd. I have briefly sketched what this might mean, at least theoretically, and hopefully given some pointers towards a renewal of the role of the priest in practice. The role of the priest as Teacher, Sanctifier and Shepherd, outlined especially in the New Code of Canon Law, is clearly a full-time job.

Notes

1. *The Roman Pontifical*, 1978, pp. 207-208.
2. *A Shepherd's Care: Reflections on the Changing Role of Pastor*, USCC, Washington, December 1987, p. 6.
3. Joseph H Fichter SJ, *Social Relations in the Urban Parish*, Chicago UP, 1954, pp. 124-125. See also Emmanuel Cardinal Suhard, 'Priests among Men, in *The Church Today*, Fides, Chicago 1953, p. 282, and Joachim Wach, *Sociology of Religion*, Chicago UP, 1944, p. 366.
4. *The Roman Pontifical*, 1978, p. 207.
5. Joseph L Bernardin, *Called to Serve, Called to Lead*, St Anthony Messenger Press, Cinncinnati 1981, p. 10.
6. *Code of Canon Law* (1983), Canon 528:1, America edition.
7. Ibid., Canon 528:2.
8. See Bernardin, op. cit., pp. 16-17

9. 'Decree on the Ministry and Life of the Priest' in *Documents of Vatican II*, Geoffrey Chapman, London 1966, p. 545.
10. Andrew Greeley, *Complaints against God*, Thomas More Press, Chicago 1989, p. 67.
11. Ibid., p. 68.
12. Ibid., pp. 69-70.
13. *Code of Canon Law* (1983), Canon 519, American edition.
14. Ibid., Canon 529:1.
15. Ibid., Canon 529:2.

SECTION IV

Towards the future

CHAPTER 13

Ministry:
New Roles and Models

In this chapter I will do three things:
Firstly, I will draw out a list of ministries, some new and some re-models from my own experience of ministry and priesthood over the past twenty-five years.
Secondly, I will give some of Pope Paul VI's seminal thoughts on ministry today, concluding with his 'for example' list of ministries.
Thirdly, I will look at the apostolic Church as a model for ministry and priesthood today and give a representative list of New Testament ministries.

PART I: MICK CASEY: TWENTY-FIVE YEARS EXPERIENCE

Based on my twenty-five years experience as a priest, and on the primary criterion of evangelisation and of ministry, i.e. faithfulness to the gospel and faithfulness to people, I will now propose some new models of ministry and priesthood for today and the future. 'New' means new for the Church in my own diocese, and probably elsewhere in the Church. Some may have been used in the apostolic Church, some may be renewed models of a present ministry, e.g. the priesthood. Some may be amalgamations of different ministries. New ministries, like the New Testament, will always contain major elements of the old!

1. (i) New priest

Ministerial versus managerial role
New priest is firstly the priest without management or administrative responsibilities. Priesthood, as I have practised it, has been

primarily a management or administrative model with all that that entails: management of the parish plant, management of finances, management of schools, management of many organisations and groups, not necessarily related to evangelisation or pastoral care. All of the above have accumulated into the role of the priest, and buried or obstructed his primary role of evangeliser, sanctifier and pastor.

New priest would be primarily an evangeliser and pastor of the Christian community. He would return to the role of the first apostles which was primarily that of evangelisation. 'It is not right for us to neglect the preaching of God's word in order to handle finances.' (Acts 6: 2-3) The first Christian communities had a basic need, which was the preaching of the gospel, and this was the basis on which they were set up. Every Christian community today has the same primary need – the preaching of the gospel.

Christ as model
Christ appointed his first apostles to 'Go teach all nations', to preach the gospel, set up Christian communities and help those communities grow through word, sacrament and pastoral care. 'Teach all nations', 'Feed my lambs', 'Feed my sheep', and 'Do this in memory of me' are three primary 'words' of Jesus to his first ministers that have echoed through all the ages of the Church. Evangelisation, sanctification and pastoring were primary roles that Jesus fulfilled as mediator between God and people, heaven and earth, and he wanted his ministers and priests to be the same.

Theory to practice
New priest's role would be quite different from 'old priest's role. It would be as different as that of the New Testament from the Old Testament – the latter elitist, cultic, the former people-centred, life-centred and gospel-centred. It would be a more slimmed-down, streamlined, more focused model of priesthood. It would express the primary vocation and ministry of the priest to be an *alter Christus* as minister of word, sacrament and pastoral care.

The new role of the priest would take a number of decades to work out in practice. It would take experimentation to learn how best it could be implemented. It would take time for priests who are used to the present model to make the transition. Some never would probably! That would be OK, just as teachers who are teaching for thirty or forty years could not be expected to make the transition from a subject-centred curriculum to a child-centred one.

'Sure, the 'new priest' would have nothing to do if you took away all his management and administrative role?' It would seem like that at first. But were the apostles idle? Is a good catechist ever idle? Would a priest be idle if he could be a full-time pastor (without management)? Pastor for the sick, the dying, the poor, the rich, the unemployed, the worried, the depressed, prisoners, families, youth, professionals, intellectuals, workers, schools (as distinct from manager)?

I won't try to develop fully the role of new priest but I know in my head and in my bones that there is more work in the primary role than any priest would be able to accomplish. I also know that it would be a move in the right direction, a more ministerial type role and a much more fulfilling one. It is also the gospel model and the one delineated in the New Code of Canon Law.

As I develop some other ministries which I know would be necessary for maintaining and developing a Christian community, the role of 'new priest' will become clearer, hopefully. To maintain and develop any community or organisation one needs a number of ministries or roles, all working in relationship with each other. The needs of the Christian community are no different. Management, governance or leadership; preaching, teaching, formation in the gospel; development of community, of services, ministries and organisations; worship, liturgy, sacramental and pastoral care; all of these are part of the foundation, maintenance and development of a Christian community. All must function as a unity, in relationship. All of these would form the working agenda for new priest in conjunction with the laity.

Evangeliser

The role of new priest as evangeliser and pastor must be worked out in the context of each community or parish of the future: the growth of evangelisation; making the Bible the central book in the life of the priest and the parish; developing evangelising skills and teams; a new emphasis on preaching; outreach and re-evangelisation of the alienated and of culture or macro forces – all of these would form the core of new priest's evangelising role. (See also chapters 11, 12)

Sanctifier

As the designated Church leader of the Christian community, new priest would also be a unifier and a symbolic sign of unity, community and care. He would be a network-convenor as well as a leader in the liturgical field. In this Christian community leadership role, he would be a minister of community, a minister of service, as well as a minister of sacrament and a minister of ministries in the liturgy. This more holistic model of priesting would help make real again the link between evangelisation and sacramentalisation, worship and service, liturgy and life. In this more unified and integrated role, he will be a leader in the sanctuary, sacrament and society but in a different way from that of a priest who was manager and administrator of parish plant. He will retrieve a primary role of *anamchara* or spiritual director of individuals and groups.

I remember well the comment made to me by Fr Joe Carroll SJ, pastoral assistant to the bishop in the diocese of Oakland, California, on this role of spiritual director: 'When someone comes to a priest in the parish today, looking for spiritual direction, he usually goes looking for a Jesuit.' How true! Unused gifts die. Many, many groups today, some who have left the Church, are searching for spirituality, and often without the priest. Not that they always need a priest; nonetheless the priest is not always seen as one who is into spirituality in a big way. I would see the new priest as an *animateur spirituale* of individuals (spiritual director), of communities and of society, and I will deal with this in 1 (vi) below.

222

Pastor

In his role as pastor, new priest will have more time for pastoring. Relieved of the heavy management and administrative role, he will more easily fulfill the role that Christ so often emphasised as a primary one for himself, i.e. Good Shepherd. The concept of Good Shepherd conjures up ideas of looking after the weak, feeding all, not just on bread alone but fulfilling peoples' basic needs, both spiritual and social. As a minister of pastoral and community care, new priest will have to emphasise and witness the values of compassion, caring, sharing and so be a counter-witness to any anti-human or anti-community societal values. At the group or community level, the new priest's primary pastoral role will be to create a caring Christian community. (See also chapter 12)

One primary role

In my view, a person can only fulfill one primary role properly. In the case of the priest, that role must be management and administration *or* evangelisation, pastoring and sacramentalising. If the primary role is evangelising, then pastoring and sacramentalising can fulfil a very strong secondary but integrated function in that role. In the apostolic Church we see a very clear distinction of roles along these lines in Jerusalem, the mother Church of Christianity.

Peter and the apostles kept their primary role as apostles or evangelisers of the Universal Church and James and the presbyters were the pastors of the local Church at Jerusalem. It is clear that Peter and the apostles were part of the Church at Jerusalem but more like returned missioners would be or the Pope in the Church at Rome. Different tasks and different roles as part of one Church were very clearly being adhered to, and worked out in the apostolic Church.

The role of the bishop

The same principle about primary and secondary roles would apply to the role of bishop as to that of priest. He must decide what his primary role is: evangeliser, manager, pastor, or financial controller. Lots of parish priests and bishops are trying to fulfil four or five primary roles at the one time, but of course the answer is that they cannot. It is not possible. All become secondary roles and roles become confused and are likely to be ineffective. Just like other people in leadership positions, a parish priest or bishop must choose one clear primary role and get other people to fulfil the other roles as their primary roles.

New parish team

What would the new parish team look like? The parish priest could fulfil the primary role as pastor, and only it, with that of evangelist fulfilled by the curate or deacon or full-time lay evangeliser. He could have a lay person whose primary role would be parish managing director, i.e. a full-time parish manager who would manage parish plant, schools, finances, organisations and link with pastoral and community development. And so on with other ministries as the parish community would need them or be able to cultivate them and afford them. This scenario can also be developed at deanery or cluster-parish level as parish lines blur for certain reasons, e.g. three parishes co-operate or cluster with one episcopal vicar or pastor. The same model could apply to a deanery or larger number of parishes. This approach allows for more specialist ministries, more resources, back up and more variety, all pluses, than one parish could generate. The research on *The Parish Project* in the USA showed that big parishes or area pastoral development could be the best in terms of the aims of evangelisation and Christian community development: more gifts, a variety of services, more choice, more community.

1. (ii) Parish Manager: a full-time job

To manage the parish and its affairs

This role must be separated from that of parish priest or pastor. This will take time. It is not the same role as that of pastoral administrator which has been developed in the USA over the past ten years. The role of Pastoral Administrator is that of the person who has replaced the pastor or parish priest in priestless parishes. This is usually done by a sister or a deacon or a lay person. The role of lay Pastoral Administrator in the USA is the same as that of the present parish priest in Ireland except for saying Mass and administering some of the sacraments. The evangelising, pastoring and managerial roles are all together still in the role of a pastoral administrator. They need to be separated, as in the role of the priest as pastor, I would think. There has to be role fatigue, role diffusion, and role confusion, in the practical functioning of the parish administrator, just as there is in the present role of the pastor or parish priest!

The role of Parish Manager can certainly be clarified and made more effective through a study of the experience of the non-priest Pastoral Administrators in the USA, and evaluation of that role. It is clear that management plays a vital role in the task of evangelisation, just as it does in any task like winning a World Cup, running a parish, or a successful business. Management of resources, of time, of people, or structures, of information, all play a vital role in the running of an organisation. The same applies to the parish, to diocese and to Church. But the question is, who does the management and administration?

Working out the relationship of management to pastoral care and evangelisation will be important in clarifying the role of the Parish Manager.

Finally, the employment of people with proven managerial skills can only be a plus for the development of the Church and the promotion of evangelisation within the new continent which has emerged today. What a difference it would make to a diocese if a senior top level manager were to manage the diocese and allow the bishop the freedom to be full-time pastor and evangeliser. The same principle applies to deanery, cluster of parishes or the parish itself.

Pastoral Managing Director

A manager or pastoral managing director could also be employed at cluster parish level, deanery or diocesan level. So there are different levels of choice in terms of area and type of job/function at the managerial level:

a. Parish Manager;

b. Pastoral Administrator (in a priestless parish).

c. Pastoral Managing Director (at cluster, deanery, diocesan level).

The parish manager or pastoral managing director would manage the parish resources primarily in terms of plant, finance, organisation, schools and personnel.

1. (iii) Local priest

In 1983, when I was at the heart of my ministry in Sean McDermott Street, marching with the street traders, looking for justice, fasting with the Youth Employment Action Group, looking for a factory and jobs, celebrating the continued development of a locally-administered Youth and Community Services, and seeing a clear link developing between evangelisation, local people, and community development, I decided that the real long-term answer for priesthood would be to ordain local people. I felt that some of the local people were really 'priesting' and ministering, in the deepest gospel and community sense, without being ordained. Some of these local community leaders were from and of the people, knowing their needs not only in their heads and in surveys, but in their hearts and bones and marrows. They knew they were acting as local community and local Church. Priesthood would be one again with Church/community in them, if they were ordained, and the fracture between priesthood and the local community would be healed. Priests would be no longer outsiders but would be of the people, of the community. That would change the attitude to priesthood and vocations and would bring home once again to the community its responsibility to 'produce' vocations and ministers. The Holy Spirit would supply the gifts and ministries, as he always did in the Church. A local priesthood, from the Christian community, is the future of the Church, of ministry, and of priesthood, in my view. A corollary to that is that Christian community must be built up before there are more 'vocations' to any ministry. A Christian community is needed to produce vocations. A Christian community involved in its own governance, development, mission, is a pre-requisite to taking responsibility for ministries and vocations in its own service.

A locally selected candidate for ministry and priesthood, ratified or ordained by the bishop, should be the ideal priest pastor for the future. That was the model in Jerusalem with James and the local presbyterate. That was the model in many eras of the Church's history. It is likely to be the model in many parts of the world Church of the future. The local priest would perfectly articulate the Christian community's life, concerns and issues in the light of the gospel and the needs of the people. Chosen from the people, by the people, for the people and about the things of God – word, sacrament, community – local priest would reflect the tradition of the Church in ordaining ministers from local Christian communities, and also meet many of the needs of the Church today. Will it happen? If local leaders were ordained priests, then the present, celibate, seminary-trained priest could assume the role of mobile evangelist cum Christian community development person, like the apostles and travelling apostles such as Paul in the early Church. One would not want two priesthoods but different roles for different functions of priesthood.

1. (iv) Christian community development worker

This role is for a full-time community development person specially trained for the development of the parish and the local community. In other words, a professionally trained community development worker who also has theological and pastoral or evangelising skills. Some sisters and some lay people are fulfilling that role already but the training and the role need to be explicitly thought out and clarified as part of team ministry for the future. Some are working now in parish or as adjuncts to parish work but, if they were appointed by the parish, they would be part of the parish team with equal input into policy, governance, planning and the life of the parish. The worker would be a minister in the parish for the parish community. He or she could also be employed at the deanery or cluster parish level.

If there is a great erosion of community today, as there is, if there is a great need of community today, as there is, and if small communities are the future of the Church, as they seem to be, then Christian community development workers are a necessity to the Church today.

The role of the parish or Christian community development worker would be:
to foster a caring Christian community;
to give form to the vision of Church as communio;
to impart community development skills to staff, community leaders and parishioners.
to have input into parish policy, planning and the overall responses of the community to its needs.

1. (v) New apostle/new evangelist

This would be a full-time minister of the Bible. It is not the role of catechist, therefore, who is a teacher of the faith and a former of people in the faith.

New apostle would have the primary role of proclamation, of being a person of the Bible. This role could be filled by a lay person, a sister, a brother or a priest. The role is best exemplified today by some full-time scripture scholars who have chosen to live and work in parishes rather than seminaries. They bring the Bible alive for people and society; they train people as individuals and groups to come to love the Bible, to read it, to apply it to their lives. Some leaders of Basic Christian Communities perform a like role in that they help people know the Bible, reflect on it and apply it in the individual and central context. The Young Christian Workers leader or full-time worker is another role model, as is the catechist in some developing Churches. Not all need be Bible

228

scholars but would have training, a minimum of two years, in Scripture – its origins, nature, its basic teachings, its spirituality, its role in Church and life and society. They would also need practice or immersion as new apostles/evangelists.

A study of role models and training models, and experimentation, would be necessary to 'blood test' this model. This ministry is still at the half-caterpillar half-butterfly stage in my mind, but I can imagine the butterfly and see the great need for such a ministry in parishes and the Church today.

1. (vi) Animateur Spirituale

This is a ministry dealing with spirituality in all its aspects. Spiritual direction of individuals and groups, spiritual renewal programmes and processes for individuals like home retreats, guided spiritual reading and direction; renewal courses, programmes. This person would also deal with issues like spirituality and secularisation, spirituality and community development, spirituality in business, spirituality for parish staff and ministers, family spirituality; youth and spirituality; the alienated and spirituality.

I feel that parishes are like barren deserts with regard to this whole area. There are some exceptions but very few. The focus of parish life and the role of the priest towards management, maintenance and survival has shifted the focus. But the gospels, Vatican II, people and their needs, are calling the Church, parishes and priests back to the core aspects of ministry and gospel today.

I have come across many role models of this ministry which is *anamchara* or spiritual director but more than those. It has individual, communal and societal aspects as the title suggests. Fr Bill Bausch is fulfilling this role as the pastor of his parish in Colts Neck, New Jersey. He is a head ahead of the rest of us priests as the name of the area suggests! Sr Christine Legley fulfils the role as 'spiritual minister' in my cousin Neilie Casey's parish of St Philip the Apostle in Clifton, New Jersey. Sr Christine wrote to me describing her new role:

'As a spiritual minister, the main bulk of my time is spent in spiritual direction. I presently have thirty-seven people, men and women, ranging in age from 30 to 60 years, who come to me for spiritual direction. Most of those who come, pray for half an hour to one hour per day. I try to help them see the impact their prayer has on the marketplace. I only wish you could witness the change in these people and those in the prayer group.

I also conduct a prayer group of about fifteen people twice a month. This I do with a lay person who has been trained in spiritual direction. We use scripture reading and send the people off for twenty minutes' prayer. Another job is to set up the annual parish retreat for which everything is cancelled, even the Bingo! I try to vary the presenters to expose our people to all different types of prayer experiences.

A new part of my job which is just beginning is to work with the four lay deacons of our parish. Where this will go I'm not sure ...'

This is a very interesting parish-based model of spirituality.

There are many centres of spirituality run by the Jesuits and other religious orders that could throw light on this ministry of *animateur spirituale*. I'm sure there are parishes and small communities with role models as well. We need to do some research to unearth them.

Summary

These are some ministries that I propose as a result of my experience as a priest for twenty-five years:
1. New priest.
2. Parish Manager.
3. Pastoral Managing Director (diocese, deanery, parish cluster).
4. Pastoral Administrator.
5. Local priest.
6. Christian community development worker.
7. New apostle/new evangelist.
8. *Animateur spirituale*.

PART II: POPE PAUL VI AND MINISTRIES

In this chapter I have started with my own experience, then I have gone to sources, making comparisons with others' experiences and, finally, I have drawn conclusions. This resembles the approach of experiential learning, i.e. experience, reflection, conclusions. It is also, roughly, the model of my overall study, and, as I pointed out earlier, the model of Vatican II in *The Church in the Modern World*, and CELAM at Medellin and Puebla. I was delighted, therefore, when I found Pope Paul VI taking the same approach to ministry and priesthood today in his magnificent apostolic letter *Evangelisation Today*. This letter, which must surely be the Magna Carta for the Church in the world and for ministry in the Third Millenium, starts from the present – the reality of the Church and the world (in 1975). He begins the letter by referring to the context of evangelisation and ministry:

'There is no doubt that the effort to proclaim the gospel to the people of today, who are buoyed up by hope but at the same time often oppressed by fear and distress...'[1]

And:

'This is what we wish to do – to make the Church of the twentieth century ever better fitted for proclaiming the gospel to the people of the twentieth century – the single objective of the Second Vatican Council.'[2]

Back to the sources

Then, having set the scene and the context, Pope Paul goes back to the sources, Christ the Evangeliser, the Holy Spirit and the apostolic Church (EN 6-16), making the point that it is the task of the whole Church to evangelise and that ministries are an expression of the gifts of the Holy Spirit to all the members of the Church. Under the heading 'Diversified Ministries', Pope Paul goes on:

'We cannot but experince a great inner joy when we see so many pastors (Pope, bishops, priests, deacons – ordained ministers), religious and lay people, fired with their mission to evangelise, seeking suitable ways of proclaiming the gospel effectively. We encourage the openness which the Church is showing today in this direction. It is an openness to meditation,(reflection on the nature of the Church, of ministry, priesthood, evangelisation, and the needs of people and the world today) first of all, and then to ecclesial ministries capable of renewing and strengthening the evangelising vigour of the Church. ... A glance at the origins of the Church is very illuminating, and gives the benefit of an early experience in the matter of ministries. It was an experience which was all the more valuable in that it enabled the Church to consolidate herself and to grow and spread.'[3]

Pope Paul draws our attention to the apostolic Church for a model of evangelisation and ministry for today. It was a Church that worked as well.

Needs of today

Then Paul VI says very wisely: 'Attention to the sources, however, has to be complemented by attention to the present needs of mankind and of the Church. To drink at these ever-inspiring sources and at the same time to know how to adapt oneself to the demands and needs of today – these are the criteria which will make it possible to seek wisely and to discover the ministries which the Church needs and which many of her members will gladly embrace for the sake of ensuring greater vitality in the ecclesial community.'[4]

Faithfulness to the gospel, and faithfulness to people, are the two criteria for ministry (EN 4), and these criteria must inform the Church today in its search for new ministries.

In 1972, in the apostolic constitution, *Ministeria Quaedam*, Pope Paul carefully reformed the ancient minor orders. This reform recognised only the ministries of lector and of acolyte, but it also allowed the Bishops' Conferences to establish other ministries in response to local needs. Then, in his apostolic exhortation, *Evangelisation Today* (December 1975), Pope Paul VI urged the Church to adapt to the demands and the needs of the times and to search wisely for the ministries which it needed.

Pope Paul VI then gives a list of six ministries which are examples of old and new ministries: 'these ministries, apparently new, but closely tied up with the Church's lived experience down the centuries.'5

1. Evangelists/apostles – Christians devoted to service of the word.
2. Catechists.
3. Directors of prayer and chant.
4. Helpers/social workers – 'Christians devoted to helping brethren in need'.
5. Leaders of small communities.
6. Founders/directors of apostolic movements.

PART III: NEW TESTAMENT MINISTRIES

I will now simply outline lists of ministries as I find them in the New Testament.

(a) 1 Cor 12:4-12:
'There is a variety of gifts but always the same spirit; there are all sorts of service to be done, but always to the same Lord; working in all sorts of different ways in people, it is the same God who is working in all of them. The particular way in which the spirit is given to each person is for a good purpose. One may have the gift of preaching with wisdom given him by the Spirit, another may have the gift of preaching instruction (catechist?) given him by the same Spirit; and another the gift of faith given with the same Spirit; another again the gift of healing through the same Spirit; one the power of miracles; another prophecy; another the gift of recognising spirits; another the gift of tongues and another the ability to interpret them. All these are the work of the one Spirit who distributes different gifts to different people just as he chooses.'

St Paul mentions nine gifts in this passage. Nine gifts equals nine ministries? It appears that, in the apostolic Church, gifts were sought out and were confirmed in public for the service of the community. St Paul also emphasises that everybody and anybody could have this gift or vocation. The vocation would be fulfilled by the bearer of the gift being willing and the community calling him or her to exercise it (ordaining them).

(b) 1 Cor 12:12-30:

'Just as the human body, though it is made up of many parts, is a single body, so it is with Christ (the Church). Nor is the body to be identified with any one of its many parts (clerical or lay, preaching, teaching, handing on the faith, or social services, etc). Instead of that God put all the separate parts into the body on purpose. If all the parts were the same how could it be a body? (Or a Church?) As it is, the parts are many but the body is one. Now you together are Christ's body; but each of you is a different part of it. In the Church, God has given the first place to apostles, the second to prophets, the third to teachers; after them, miracles, and after them the gift of healing; helpers, good leaders, those with many languages. Are all of them apostles, or are all of them prophets, or are all of them teachers? Do they all have the gifts of miracles, or healing. Do all speak strange languages, or all interpret them?'

Paul has a beautiful understanding of Church, and of people, and community development. There is a great sense of Christian community building and living as a partnership of many, with many people involved in taking responsibility for the life of the community. Paul emphasises unity a lot – one body, one spirit, one Lord, one community or Church. He equally emphasises the need to avoid uniformity. Many gifts, many parts, each for a different purpose, each needed for the good of the whole, unity but not uniformity.

A community of ministries

Paul mentions nine ministries in this latter list in Corinth. So that is eighteen ministries in all in this passage to the people of Corinth. Some may overlap but that is not our concern at this point. Note in the latter list that Paul seems to be giving a hierarchy of ministries. He does the same in his epistle to the Ephesians, quoting the list of ministries instituted by God himself in the Church.

Enda Lyons comments:

'One point which comes across is the great sense of involvement which existed in the parish of Corinth. Clearly it was not just a few priests who were involved in the life of the parish and who felt responsible for its well-being. Indeed it would be difficult to identify in his passage a person who exercised the role which we now know as the priest's. All sorts of people were active – apostles, prophets, teachers, good leaders, different kinds of preachers, helpers, people whose service had to do with miracles, people who had a healing ministry, people who served the community by recognising spirits, and so on. I might mention that we find that a similar situation existed in the communities in Rome and Ephesus. Thus Paul reminds the Christians in Rome that there are some whose gift is teaching, others who are preachers, others almsgivers, and others who do works of mercy (Rom 12:4-8; cf also Eph 4:11- 2). It is clear that in neither of these letters does the author set out to give a complete list. So, if today people experience their local Church as a community in which one person, the ordained priest, is called and empowered to serve, while all others have a passive role, then their experience is very different from that of the early Christians in Corinth and indeed in Rome and Ephesus as well. As Thomas F O'Meara says of the New Testament Churches:

The ministry of co-ordination and leadership was not the whole ministry, but one important ministry among others, with responsibilities and limits (*Theology of Ministry*, page 85).

The atmosphere in the parish of Corinth is very much that of 'a ministering community and a community of ministers'.'[6]

(c) Eph 4:11-13:
'It was he who 'gave gifts to mankind'; he appointed some to be

apostles, others to be prophets, others to be evangelists, others to be pastors and teachers. He did this to prepare all God's people for the work of Christian service, in order to build up the body of Christ.'

So Paul gives us five ministries here, all instituted by God for the Church. Max Thurian, Brother of Taizé, and a great theologian of ecumenism and ministry, comments as follows:

'There is an order in this enumeration: apostles and evangelists share a ministry of an itinerant nature, of mission and foundation; prophets and pastors and teachers have ministry of a stable nature, of building and continuation. Moreover the apostles and prophets belong to the first generation of the Church: they are the first founders and builders of the Church. 'You are fellow citizens with the saints and members of the household of God,' writes St Paul, 'built upon the foundation of the apostles and prophets' (Eph 2:19-20); the apostles are the first missionaries-founders, the prophets are the first preachers-builders. The evangelists appear as the first apostles' helpers in mission and in founding Churches; the pastors-teachers are successors to the prophets in preaching and teaching and in building up local Churches. 'Do the work of an evangelist', writes Paul to Timothy (2 Tim 4:5); the latter had been associated with Paul in an apostleship of mission and foundation.

Thus we see the initial apostolic college develop; for the ministry of mission, of foundation and of supervision was necessarily extended according to the demands of the growing Church.'[8]

(d) Rom 12:4-9:
'We have many parts in the one body and all these parts have different functions. So we are to use our different gifts in accordance with the grace that God has given us. If our gift is to speak God's message (preach), we should do it according to the faith that we have; if it is to serve (social ministry), we should serve; if it is to teach, we should teach; if it is to encourage others (counselling?), we should do so. Whoever shares with others should do so gener-

236

ously (almsgivers); whoever has authority (leadership) should work hard; whoever shows kindness to others (works of mercy) should do so cheerfully.'

Paul here mentions seven ministries and one is again aware that this is not an exhaustive list. The ministries are, roughly: preacher, teacher, social worker, counsellor, almsgiver, administrator, leader; and some of the ministries have a likeness to each other. Yet they are different. There is a likeness between serving others, (social service, social work) and sharing with others (almsgiving), yet they are quite different. One is giving things, the other is giving self. One is passive, the other is active and developmental. One is 'giving people fish', the other is teaching them how to fish. There is need for both in any community, parish or diocese.

The point I want to make here is that many of the ministries that seem alike could be quite different. One would need to know the exact circumstances, needs and context to understand the differences. For instance there is a big difference between pastor (parish priest), parish manager and parish administrator as I have described them earlier, but they are all in the field of management and so could be seen as having almost no difference. So some of the ministries described in the New Testament above are in the area of mission/evangelisation, foundation of communities; others are in the area of maintenance of a community; some in the doctrinal, teaching area, others in the social and caring area; some are pastoral, others are developmental; some are around the needy and marginalised, others around leadership, governance, management. All are in the service of the gospel or the kingdom of God. All are part of evangelisation. All are gifts and ministries given by the Holy Spirit in the service of the People of God.

New Testament ministries
In summarising the ministries mentioned in the three texts of St Paul (1 Cor 12, Eph 4 and Rom 12), and some New Testament texts mentioned earlier with regard to ministerial priesthood, I have drawn up a list of thirty ministries. From this list of thirty,

we can extrapolate seventeen ministries which do not seem to overlap. They are some of the ministries of the New Testament. These ministries were devised by Christ and the apostolic Church to meet the needs of the Church at its beginning. They are ministries of mission, foundation, development, maintenance and growth. All different gifts with the different skills required at the different stages of setting up, maintaining and developing parishes and Christian communities. The Church of the twentieth and twenty-first centuries must develop its own list of ministries in answer to the needs of its times and the promptings of the Holy Spirit.

The list of New Testament ministries that do not seem to overlap are:

1. Apostles.
2. Prophets.
3. Evangelists.
4. Pastors.
5. Teachers.
6. Administrators.
7. Healers.
8. Overseer/bishop.
9. Elder-Presbyter.
10. Deacon.
11. Almsgivers.
12. Counsellors.
13. Community leaders.
14. Social Workers.
15. Linguists.
16. Discerners/Interpreters.
17. Miracle Workers.

New Testament Church as model for the third millennium

The Church of the New Testament is the gospel model of Church for us today in the diocese and parishes. Ministry in the New Testament is the gospel model of ministry, for all ministry and priesthood today and tomorrow to be modelled on. The Church of the apostolic times gives us the mind and practice of Jesus with regard to Church, ministry and priesthood.

As Pope Paul VI said, it is a vital and inspiring model but, nevertheless only a model. It is the Church of the first century, in the world of the first century, meeting the aspirations and needs of the Church/People of God of that time.

The Church of the twentieth and twenty-first centuries is a Church which must make the gospel its own in our time. It is the Church which must 'first of all be evangelised herself before she can evangelise others.' It is a Church which must live in the world of the twentieth and twenty-first century, meeting the challenges, the transitions and the possibilities of the People of God and of the world in the twenty-first century. With the one Father, the one Foundation Stone, Christ, the one Spirit, and still being the One Body of Christ, can we fail? Never, if we try to make Christ live in our lives and in our world today.

Notes

1. Pope Paul VI, *Evangelisation Today*, No. 1, p. 5.
2. Ibid., No. 2, p. 6.
3. Ibid., No. 73, p. 97.
4. Ibid., No. 73, pp. 97-98.
5. Ibid., No. 73, p. 98.
6. Enda Lyons, *Partnership in Parish*, pp. 68-69.
7. Max Thurian, *Priesthood & Ministry*, p. 47.

CHAPTER 14

Ministry:
The Practice of the Church Today

Standing at the end of the second millenium of Christianity and at the beginning of the third, one cannot but be aware of the rich heritage of Christianity and its potential for good in society. One is equally struck by the potential of the renewal undertaken at Vatican II, the potential of the Church of the 100% as against the clerical model or the Church of the 2% with the 98% as passive on-lookers.

In this chapter we will look at emerging models of pastoring and ministry and the theology underpinning them. This review will show us the new richness of the post-Vatican II Church, but it will also highlight the shortage of priests, the full-time professionals and leaders in the Church. Will this continue? Will the shortage accelerate as it is doing at the moment? If it does, who will be the priests of the future? Who will decide? What will the circumstances be? Let us look at the statistics on priests worldwide and reflect on some of the issues that arise.

Priesthood and parish worldwide
The November 1989 issue of *Pro Mundi Vita Studies*, which is given totally to the study of priestless parishes, will be my source for most of this chapter. In a short introduction it says:

'The starting point for the present study is the established fact that more or less everywhere there is a decrease in the number of priests in relation to the number of believers. This is a universal situation (see charts pp 253-4). The aim of the study is not so much to examine the causes of this situation; rather we should like to take an objective look at what is being done in order to cope with this situation. Throughout the world pragmatic responses are being sought and implemented. A survey of these responses could well provide inspiration for the decisions which require to be taken for the future.'[1]

The author, E. Michel, then goes on to say: 'From these responses, we can see a type of ecclesiology which certainly calls into question the traditional manner in which ministries have been organised within the Church.'[2]

Pro Mundi Vita then prints two comments relating to this situation, the first with regard to Africa:

'The task of the priest is becoming heavier year by year. Logically, therefore, we must either multiply the number of priests tenfold (we should then have one priest for 1,000 baptised) or we should stop baptising people, because the Church continues to beget the faith of her children whom she has not the means to feed; this is the very denial of her most venerable tradition'[3]

Ernest Michel concludes the introduction by quoting Jan Kerkhof's article from *Concilium*, No. 153, 1980: 'It is clear that large parts of the Church find themselves in an impasse in this area of the numerical proportion between priests and communities. For whole countries, this is a situation which has existed for several generations and even for centuries. We should remember that, in the early years of the Church, and for centuries thereafter, the 'normal' ratio of priest president to believers was 1 to between 50-300.'[4]

Michel concludes his commentary: 'So far, the only solution the Church has been able to offer for this serious problem is the ordination of men (not women), married or not, to the diaconal ministry, allowing them, among other things, to celebrate baptisms and marriages, or the institution of men (and not women) for the service of the Word (lectors) and for the service of community prayerand the eucharist (acolytes). In addition we have seen the birth of celebrations led by members of priestless communities, and

CHART 1: Present Parishes and Quasi-Parishes Worldwide[5]

COUNTRY	NUMBER OF PARISHES						NUMBER OF PRIESTS (secular and religious)	
	with a resident secular priest		with resident religious priest		served by a priest from another parish			
	1976*	1987**	1976	1987	1976	1987	1976	1987
Austria	2,053	1,915	592	571	394	591	6,099	5,533
Belgium	3,281	2,685	352	475	284	805	13,432	11,065
Czechoslovakia	2,642	2,310	224	167	1,259	1,810	4,054	3,386
France	15,597	12,384	832	899	20,851	22,916	41,163	34,261
FRG	9,002	7,998	873	877	1,812	3,073	22,576	21,609
GDR	732	662	47	33	117	138	1,525	1,363
Italy	23,041	21,396	2,071	3,237	3,337	2,262	61,784	60,196
Netherlands	1,333	1,012	427	637	39	127	6,083	5,799
Poland	6,590	7,897	465	588	46	88	18,529	21,386
Portugal	2,612	2,273	117	159	1,593	1,882	5,035	4,596
Spain	12,133	10,490	696	947	8,543	10,017	33,369	31,124
Switzerland	1,338	1,141	149	202	191	343	4,308	3,974
Yugoslavia	1,831	1,972	372	384	475	444	4,097	4,245
Other countries (except USSR and Albania)	6,655	7,353	522	643	301	907	21,932	19,974
TOTAL EUROPE	88,840	81,488	7,682	8,653	39,242	45,403	241,379	228,511

* *Annuarium Statisticum Ecclesiae* 1976, Vatican City, 1978.
** *Annuarium Statisticum Ecclesiae* 1987, Vatican City, 1989.

CHART 2: Parishes and Quasi Parishes served by:[6]

| | 1976* | 1987** | 1987 PER CONTINENT | | | | |
			Africa	America	Asia	Europe	Oceania
Diocesan Priests	129.810	129.942	3.521	34.619	8.692	81.488	1.622
Religious Priests	24.247	26.335	3.620	10.142	3.272	8.653	548
Non-Resident Priests	44.157	53.108	891	4.851	1.823	45.403	140
Permanent Deacons	84	230	27	124	4	68	7
Non-ordained religious	60	82	9	33	18	9	3
Women Religious	332	883	54	655	40	130	4
Lay People	342	950	268	196	70	372	44
Vacant	1.474	979	191	263	51	449	25
TOTAL	200.506	212.409	8.591	50.883	13.970	136.572	2.393

* *Annuarium Statisticum Ecclesiae 1976*, Vatican City, 1978.
** *Annuarium Statisticum Ecclesiae 1987*, Vatican City, 1989

known as Sunday Celebrations in the Absence of a Priest. At the time when the Congregation for Divine Worship publishes a 'Directory' for such celebrations, signed in Rome on 2 June 1988 and addressed to the Church as a whole, it is extremely interesting to be able to measure the extent to which this phenomenon has developed in various parts of the world and to evaluate all that is involved, in order to discern some perspectives for the future.'[7]

There are many issues involved in the present reality of the growth of priestless Christian communities. There is the question of the continuous growth of the Church. There is the decision by many more young people in the first world not to become priests. There is also the reality of present Church policy which perpetuates the present situation. This policy seems to give celibacy a higher priority than availability of eucharist for Christian communities. Only time and the work of the Holy Spirit will show us the way for the future.

TEN EMERGING MODELS OF PASTORING

I will now discuss ten models of Christian community leadership as examples of the response to the pastoral needs of the Church today and the shortage of priests. I will also try to locate these models each in their particular context, theology and model of Church. Each model, as each ministry, comes out of a history, a theology, a culture and context, and probably the most striking thing of all about all the models is the similarity of thinking, theology, and the patterns of evolution or development behind them all. Many of them relate to my experiences of ministry in Sean McDermott Street and to my reflections on the role of the priest and ministry. Indeed, in my research for this section, and in my reflection on it, I have been very struck by the similarity of thinking and practice with regard to ministry and priesthood worldwide. It is so obvious that it is the response of people working with the same gospel, with the guidance of the same Spirit, dealing with the same issues and needs worldwide. It is most interesting and, indeed, encouraging to encounter the same thinking in

Ireland, in Latin America, in Asia and Africa and North America. The one Spirit must be at work in the Church and in the world!

1. The Catechist as emergent pastor[8]

Context: Zaire, Africa
Under the heading 'Assemblies without the celebration of the eucharist: A Sign of Hope or a Sign of Crisis in the Ministry?' Paul Rutayisire (PMV) says:

'Today, the Catholic Church in Africa has some 75 million members (13% of the total population of the continent). By the year 2,000, Africa will be the second Catholic continent (with 100 million believers) immediately after Latin America. These excellent results, which are partly explained by rapid population growth and by intensive pastoral activity in various spheres of Church life, should not lead us to forget the darker side of the picture, and urgent challenges. Among these challenges is the fact that although the Church in Africa continues to grow, it has fewer and fewer priests. Even in a country like Zaire, where people speak of a 'boom in vocations to the priesthood', not all dioceses have been equally successful in 'Africanising' staff. This gulf between the numbers of ordained ministers and Christians appears inevitable, at least as long as access to the sacrament continues to be linked to the ordained celibate ministry, and as long as the present formula of seminaries, which are very costly both from the financial point of view and in staff, is maintained. Moreover the Church cannot count on a renewal of missionary support given the fact that the missionary institutes can no longer find recruits in their usual catchment areas. From the point of view of ministry, the present position of the Church in Africa, as a result, can be considered one of crisis.'

The author then goes on to give some examples of attempts to respond to the crisis, which is partly the result of the 'structural and ecclesiological model inherited from the missionary era.'

Zaire: The mission station
'While the Second Vatican Council and Pope John Paul II have, on several occasions, stressed the right of Christians to receive the sacraments, and even more the central place of the eucharist in Christian life, in Africa, the ratio of priest to Christian believers has never been worse. As a result, because of a lack of priests, a great number of Christians are prevented from receiving the eucharist for much of the year. This 'sacramental penury' creates confusion in the minds of Christians and above all among catechists who, since they are not aware of the theological discussions around ministry, ask themselves why they cannot preside over the eucharist when they are allowed to do everything else.'

The role of 'new catechist'
'How do these priestless communities, in dioceses in 'the bush', live and function? At the head of the Christian community of a village there is a *mulami* (a catechist) who directs more or less the whole of Christian life. It is he who leads the daily prayer. Every Sunday, he brings together the faithful and presides over the liturgical celebration without the 'eucharistic part' as such. He preaches and he leads the choir if there is no one else to do it. It is he who, with colleagues, prepares people for the various sacraments (baptism, eucharist, confirmation, anointing of the sick). Where priests are able to visit the community but rarely, it is he who baptises the children and the catechumens. His role even extends to the spiritual direction of the members of the community: he gives guidance and, when necessary, plays the role of judge for Christians who are in disagreement, or in the case of couples in difficulty. Again it is he, together with the committee of the community, who pays regular visits to sick members, they pray with them and if necessary provide material support. He provides spiritual comfort for the dying by praying with them. He directs the prayers during funerals, and it is he who indicates when mourning may come to an end either partially or definitively. This is how many Christian communities without a priest function.'

The author goes on to say that many of these outlying communities were dynamic but that their centre of gravity and authority lay elsewhere, i.e. 'in the mission', 'with the father'. The catechist remained 'the man of the missionary fathers'. He was their stand-in or substitute in the community. He was not the 'minister' of the local community, chosen by the community for the community, but chosen by the missionary to fulfil his mission and carry out his orders.

Would this model of Church without a priest have developed in the apostolic Church, a Church without the eucharist? It would have been unthinkable, I imagine. It would have been seen as a contradiction in terms. The apostles and their delegates, the travelling apostles, set up self-sufficient local Churches. The Christian community produced its own ministries to meet its needs, centred on the eucharist. That was the norm.

The author makes the point that a new model of Church is, in fact, being invented in Africa. The new catechist is the product of a newly emerging ecclesiology which emphasises the co-responsibility of all the members of the Christian community and the diversity of gifts in the community.

He concludes with the following observation: 'The movement of pastoral renewal in Africa is also characterised by a much wider lay participation in the sharing and exercise of pastoral responsibilities. It is this new state of mind which has led to the re-definition of the role of the catechist. From the role of 'priest's deputy', the catechist who has been trained in one of the growing number of specialised training centres has become the 'minister' of the community ... This has meant some change in the catechist's identity, 'to such an extent that to continue to use the term 'catechist' to designate the role these men play in the Church becomes a misnomer.'

2. The assembly presidents[9]

Context: The Dominican Republic, Latin America
This experiment came into being quite unexpectedly one Sunday

evening in December 1967 in the Sierra Central, in San Jose de las Matas (Jicome), one of the remotest areas. The priest had no choice but to close the Church for at least a month, until his next visit.

'But the new bishop of the area had an idea: why not choose lay people to be responsible for the different sectors of the scattered villages; to bring the people out of their 'Mass Catholicism' and help them to form communities. Since he only had two or three priests, what, practically, could he do? Were the towns to be the only places to enjoy Sunday worship led by a priest, as they had done down through the centuries since independence? Why should the peasants, who make up 70% of the population and who had always remained faithful in their own way, have to make do with a visit from a priest once a month?'

The author goes on to tell us that: 'It was this reflection which resulted in the experiments of the assembly presidents (1967) who are charged with a mission by the bishop to preside over the liturgy of the word, or to distribute communion, and to lead the community under the guidance of the priest. These people are not sacristans or catechists, still less are they there to fill a gap; they are lay people who exercise a specific function within the local Church.'

'By 1970 there was already a team of professors, a programme and a flexible training course covering three years, as well as a week of spiritual exercises each year for the presidents.'

The role of the assembly president

It is interesting to see the evolution of the role of the assembly president in such a short time. One of the goals of the assembly presidents is to convert these 'Mass Catholics' into 'community-centred Christians'. A true ecclesial community means that the members are aware that they share a common faith which they must live out and make fruitful. The model for such a community is found in Acts 2:42-47.

Unlike the role of catechist in Africa, that of assembly president is new. The reason for its expansion is interesting: 'One might imagine that the idea of assembly presidents was born of a bishop's reflection or the discussion of theologians. Not at all. Rather it was people's lives which led to the discovery of this way evangelisation. The people's religious situation, their thirst for God, led catechists to greater activity. In doing so, they discovered people who were capable of giving themselves to the community, and of sacrificing themselves for that community.

One day, seeing this kind of religious revival, the bishop said to himself: why should these people not be given responsibility for the community, as well as the responsibility for celebrating their worship? For this kind of work the bishop had no need of seminary-trained priests, intellectuals ... truth to tell, he had none! On the other hand, he did have the men he needed, given training. Why, then, not choose lay people and train them to take charge of the community? Thus the new ministry of assembly presidents came into being.'

The number of assembly presidents increased to 250 by 1973, 1,000 by 1983 and 3,000 by 1988, just twenty years after their inception.

President to priest?
The author touches on an issue surfacing worldwide: 'Here we cannot avoid the questions increasingly being raised by the leaders of the local Church, including the presidents: why can the latter not become priests, when it is they who bring life to the community and help it develop? Why can they not exercise their ministry fully? And why should there not be two types of priest: the one celibate and totally available, trained to support the bishop in his magisterial role, and the other who would be the emanation of the community, the visible sign that that community had reached maturity? The answer lies, not with the leaders of the particular Church, but with Rome.'

3. Celebrants of the word [10]

Context: Honduras, Latin America

The request for a priest who didn't exist led to a new pastoral development in Honduras:

'The diocese of Choluteca, in Honduras, is perhaps the last to organise its pastoral service around celebrants (*celebradores*) of the word. In 1966, Mgr Marcel Gerin (a Canadian) received a visit from peasants from the interior of his diocese who came to ask him to send a priest to their rural communities, in order, they said, that they could celebrate Holy Week with dignity. He was forced to consider the possibility of replacing the priest by catechists. It should be added that the people of the region in question have a very special devotion for the penitential ceremonies of the Lord's passion. Having no priest available, the bishop suggested that they should propose one of their own members so that he could be given appropriate training to fit him to celebrate the basic elements of Holy Week as they wished.'

Selection

The community selects and the bishop ordains or confirms that selection: 'The various communities put forward the names of men whom they considered fit to take up such a role, men who had the confidence of the community, meaning that they had given proof of a pious Christian life and unfailing devotion to their family and the community. After training them, the bishop gave them a kind of mandate.'

The role of the celebrants

First proposed for the celebration of the Holy Week ceremonies, the role of the celebrants of the word developed from 'in Church' leadership to leadership of the community. Given that these people already enjoyed a certain prestige in their community, and that they were trained for pastoral tasks and spiritual guidance, no matter how elementary this training might be, these celebrants of the word soon acquired a great influence over the members of their communities. They were considered as leaders and even took over the direction of the community in things material. As a result, they also exercised a role in encouraging social, economic and even political development within the community, something which was not foreseen at the outset.

A women's role?

We are told that 'in the beginning, celebrants were chosen from among the men only. Honduran males are very macho and do not readily allow women into sacramental functions. But they were taught to understand that women are fit not only to recite prayers. Very rapidly they realised that women are better, among other things, at helping and teaching other women and children. The women formed housewives' clubs or neighbourhood groups, led most effectively by other women. The women, too, were given appropriate training both with regard to their work in the home and with children and in leading the prayers of the community.'

A priestly function?

The celebrants are now performing many of the functions of a priest. How will their role develop in the future?

'In addition to their liturgical and catechetical role, there is the sacramental function. The celebrant is the *de facto* minister of the sacraments of baptism, and sometimes of extreme unction. He prepares couples for marriage, conducts funerals and is responsible for novenas, a practice which is widespread in the countryside. He administers the eucharist. The community considers that to live in the faith it must nourish itself through the eucharist. But it is not yet prepared to call for its catechist to be ordained priest.'

The author says that the life of the community has gained in quality to such an extent that vocations are growing. Often it is the sons of celebrators who request training for the priesthood. In 1982, there were eight seminarians in his diocese; in 1985, there were 95.

The author concludes: 'There is one constant factor in this birth of new structures in the Church of Honduras: the people's initiative. If the Church is able to open up paths towards greater participation by the laity, above all among the poorest strata of society, the latter will respond with such generosity that they will even be able to evangelise the leaders of the Church, who will feel obliged to create new structures of participation.'

4. Basic Christian Community Leaders

Community leaders, with various titles like *presidentes* (Dominican Republic), *co-ordinatores* (Brazil), *animadores* or *responables* or delegates (or ministers) of the word lead many new and vital small Christian communities in Latin American – 150,000 in Brazil alone. Sometimes the group is led by one leader who is specially trained and designated by the bishop; sometimes the position rotates during the year among two or three leaders chosen by the group.

These leaders facilitate the communities as a new way of being Church and of responding to their personal and community needs in the light of the gospel.

'Basic Christian Communities are like living cells in an organism newly coming to life. Generally, twelve to twenty persons make up a community. They usually come together in their neighbourhood or village once a week. They read sacred scripture, pray together, and sing hymns. They reflect on what the scriptures mean in their daily lives. That reflection frequently leads them to courses of political action to improve the living conditions in their *barrio*. Given the repressive political climate in many Latin American countries, such actions have sometimes resulted in jailings, deaths, and disappearances (persons are taken to a police station, for example, and are never seen again).

The impact of the Basic Christian Communities has been enormous on the Church and on other sectors of society. For the Church they have meant movement at the grass roots, something long overdue and largely unexpected.'[11]

The Basic Christian Community is
(i) giving a new sense of vitality to the Latin American Church;

(ii) empowering the laity;
(iii) linking gospel and life;
(iv) creating new forms of ministry;
(v) showing a new way of being Church in the future.

Basic Christian Community leaders are a new form of leadership in the Church. Are they emergent pastors and priests of the future?

5. The Pastoral Administrator.[12]

Context: North America
Many dioceses, right across the USA, have put parishes in the care of full-time lay pastoral administrators. They have become a welcome new addition to the Church. These pastoral administrators are employed to enhance and develop the spiritual and pastoral life of parish communities.

Priest shortage: diocesan planning
While mentioning that many dioceses in the USA are reviewing and restructuring, the author says: 'Thus, the archdiocese of Seattle in the State of Washington, which has a Planning and Research Department, was able to predict that by the year 2,000 there would be a decrease of 41% in the number of priests available for parishes, whereas there would be an increase of 19% in the Catholic population in the same period. The need for new ministers could not be clearer. In a report circulated widely in the Spring of 1989, entitled *Promoting Viable Faith Communities*, the archdiocese informed the faithful of the situation. The report (page 18) states that, 'There are certain courses of action which might appear to be solutions. But the Holy Father ... has clearly stated that the following courses of action are not going to be implemented. They are:
1. The use of resigned priests as sacramental ministers.
2. The ordination of married men to the priesthood.
3. The ordination of men for a limited term of service.
4. The ordination of women.

In these circumstances, the following courses of action are currently being actively pursued in the archdiocese of Seattle:

1. Expanding efforts to promote vocations to the priesthood.

2. Expanding and developing a variety of lay ministries.

3. Expanding and developing the permanent diaconate.

4. Studying how best to serve our existing parishes, with the understanding that in some cases amalgamation may take place, boundaries be redrawn or new parishes opened.'

The role of the lay Parish Administrator:

Diocese of Cincinnati

The role of the Parish Administrator, described here, is that of the pastor or parish priest except for celebrating the sacraments of the eucharist, penance and extreme unction.

1. Establish full-time Church/religious presence in the community.

2. Establish liturgy and spiritual life committee in the parish to work towards enhancing liturgical and sacramental life of the parish community; to support parish spiritual renewal; to improve quality of liturgical life so it becomes the source and focus of the Christian community.

3. Work with parish committee to conduct an evangelisation programme, outreach to parish community.

4. Conduct Communion services on a daily basis.

5. Conduct special para-liturgical services during Advent/Lent and other significant Church celebrations.

6. As part of the pastoral relationship with the people, and at the pastor's discretion, be invited to preach on occasions.

7. Work towards developing sacramental preparation for parishioners, youth and adults.

8. Provide consistent support to sick and shut-ins and grieving persons in the parish; e.g. bring eucharist/viaticum; preside at wake services; provide presence as parish administrator at funerals.

9. Attend, as parish co-ordinator, Parish Council meetings.

10. Be responsible for the maintenance of parish facilities.

11. Maintain financial records of the parish, e.g. writing cheques,

preparing and submitting financial reports. Be responsible for all expenditures of parish funds.'

Diocese: Colorado Springs
Another job description of the role of Parish Administrator is given here.

'Some dioceses go into greater detail. For example, in the diocese of Colorado Springs the pastoral administrator is asked to teach, to govern and to sanctify, but each case is set out in detail. Thus the teaching role is not limited to preaching but also involves developing, co-ordinating and implementing a total family religious education programme from kindergarten to adulthood; the governing role involves supervision of paid and volunteer staff, collaboration with other parishes in the diocese in pursuit of unified approaches to pastoral effectiveness, collaboration in ecumenical efforts of parish or diocese; the pursuit of social justice in parish planning and efforts. The sanctification role includes, in addition to eucharistic celebrations, the scheduling of the sacrament of reconciliation on a regular basis; providing for the sacrament of the sick on occasions when requested or required; seeing to preparation for marriage, baptism and confirmation, spiritual retreats, encouraging sacrificial giving as a way of personal and parish holiness. Other diocese are even more specific.'

Qualifications/salary
The Parish Administrator is a full-time job. It is an exciting pastoral ministry for our time. As the author says: 'Each diocese sets out the qualifications required, from the degrees (in particular, but not only, theology) to 'Evident life of faith and holiness ... ' which will enable him 'to speak in the name of the Church.' The salary corresponds to that of a middle-management position on diocesan scale and is within a range of US$20,000-30,000, plus individual health insurance and diocesan retirement plan, in other words, more than US$30,000. Salary for lay people is negotiable. In the diocese of Toledo, housing is provided by the parish, as is a car, petrol and insurance; one day off a week is permitted for con-

tinuing education (not on week-end); there are two weeks' paid holiday, and one retreat. Not much has been left to chance.'

The report concludes that there has been: 'No global evaluation of these initiatives or, in particular, of the work carried out by the pastoral administrators. No doubt it is still too early.'

6. Women as pastoral animators[13]

Context: Canada

The situation with regard to numbers of priests had also worsened in Canada over the last twenty years. 'In response to this shortage, pastoral policy was first of all to bring parishes together under one priest. Gradually, to facilitate the task of the priest in charge of two or three parishes, the bishop asked for the help of the men and women religious of the diocese. It was as a result of these linkings that the 'parish animators' came into being. The diocese of Amos played a pioneering role in the 'official' introduction of this pastoral service.'

Pastoral leadership closer to the people

The priest had become too far removed from the people. 'Because of the large number of parishes which he was obliged to serve, the priest was increasingly absent. Gradually the need was felt for a permanent form of pastoral leadership which would be closer to the people. The first parish animators were appointed on 9 September 1971. These animators are appointed by the bishop in co-operation with the major superiors of the communities and they are given a pastoral mandate, drawn up according to standard form.'

A new ecclesiology

Sister Bernadette Germain, in a workshop for the Canadian Canon Law Society during its 1987 congress in Montreal, made a very valuable contribution on the basis of her experiences in the diocese of Amos. 'She explained, among other things, that these initiatives are largely due to the driving force of Mgr Hains. He became bishop in 1967, and was deeply influenced by the ecclesiology of Vatican II. He was deeply convinced that everyone who was baptised should assume his or her responsibilities. In September 1973, he described the specific situation of his diocese in a pastoral letter entitled *Quarrivera-t-il demain?*

'Thus,' he wrote, 'the Christian leadership of parish communities, hospitals, and schools is threatened by the lack of new religious and priestly vocations ... Already some parishes are without a priest; others soon will be ... pastors and parish councils must try to determine if, within the parish, there is an adult lay person who, because of his or her personality, devotion, piety and judgement, could eventually take responsibility for leading the parish, either as a lay person receiving a mission from the bishop without ordination, or as a permanent deacon who will be ordained in the service of the diocese ... Rest assured,' he ends, 'the Holy Spirit has truly placed in each of the parish communities the dynamism necessary to provide the Christian people with a pastoral service which meets their needs.'

Ongoing development

As with the new catechists in Africa, the assembly presidents and celebrants in Latin America, and the parish administrators in the USA, these new ministries are in the process of continuous development.

'Training was offered to parish animators. It gradually developed and new pastoral structures came into being: the diocese was organised into regions, pastoral zones, to provide support to all those who committed themselves to this work and to provide a certain unity – but not uniformity – of action.These leadership services which at first were taken over by women religious, gradually, increasingly passed into the hands of lay people in response to pressing appeals.'

7. The emerging pastor

Context: USA

The day when there are more parishes than priests has arrived for many American dioceses. For some it arrived ten to fifteen years ago. In his fascinating book, *The Emerging Pastor*, Peter Gilmour has told in a most touching way the story of many of these 'priest-less parishes': 'The sadness of the parishioners, the 'dying experience' with its different stages as the pastor departed or died, and then the 'resurrection experience' where the new lay 'pastor' has been accepted and she, or he, has helped the local Christian community to take responsibility for itself, to thrive and to grow.'

Gilmour calls these new parish leaders emerging pastors because: 'The phrase 'emerging pastor' accurately reflects both the current state of this phenomenon and the current stage of its development. This phrase indicates that this particular reality is a movement which already has seen both widespread experimentation and acceptance in some American dioceses. It also avoids the use of negative and/or conflicting language in naming the reality – like 'non-ordained' which while descriptive, is not a positive definition, or parish administrator, which is sometimes used to describe the activity of a business manager for a large urban parish.'[14]

Not priest but pastor

This new figure who is emerging on the ecclesiastical landscape of the American Roman Catholic Church, is a non-ordained person who pastors a Catholic parish without a resident priest. He or she is not a priest but is a pastor.

This new leader of parishes, the emerging pastor, is common in much of the rural American Catholic Church, especially the south and the midwest and also right across Canada.

Challenge to clerical paradigm

The emerging pastor phenomenon in practice can be categorised as follows (Gilmour, pp 6-7): the non-ordained person is officially

258

appointed by the bishop:
1. to pastor an existing parish;
2. to pastor a new parish;
3. to pastor a non-geographical parish;
4. as part of team ministry.

In his book, Peter Gilmour chronicles the stories, the issues, the personalities, the struggles, the sorrows and the joys of these emerging pastors and the communities with which they emerge 'as challenges to the clerical paradigm of ministry and pastoral care.'

Gilmour also tells us that much work has been done in dioceses to clarify the role of the parish administrator, the emergent pastor, and the role of parish and diocese in the light of the new theology of Church ministry.

Gilmour, who has done a study of these priestless parishes in the USA, is very hopeful about the phenomenon of the emergent pastor:

'As these grassroot experiences become widespread, as the implications of these experiences become apparent, and as the Christian community correlates these experiences both with religious tradition and cultural assumptions intrinsic to this phenomenon (emerging pastor), new concepts of Church and new styles of ministry will continue to emerge. The actual process of Church growth and development has historically happened first through experience, and only subsequently through official definition and/or proclamation.'[15]

The role of emergent pastors
Gilmour says that many of these parishes, which had recent histories of poor pastoral leadership, have little or no foundation upon which to build a contemporary model of parish and ministry. So, the role of these non-ordained pastors is to embark on an educational programme introducing parishioners to a contemporary vision of çhurch, parish, and ministry.

Closures and transition
The author points out that many older people feel that without a priest there is no Church. But, 'the emerging pastor embarks on a programme of home visitation, and becomes an active member of the civic community. Usually within four to six months an attitudinal shift begins to develop. Many parishioners begin to sense new life in their parish, to feel a sense of parish participation and stewardship, and a sense of pride about their present and their non-ordained parish administrator.'[16]

Gilmour is insistent that new leaders and new ministries are needed in this age of death and resurrection in the Church. 'We need people who will minister to the breakdown (lack of priests, parish closures) and the breakthrough (new ministries, new Church).'[17]

8. Sunday Celebrants in Europe[18]

Context: France
We will now continue our journey with *Pro Mundi Vita* to Europe. 'All the countries of Europe, usually referred to as traditionally Christian, have been marked by a permanent decline in the number of priests, to a large extent due to the growing de-Christianisation and perhaps also the the difficulty which the Church has in responding to the challenges of modernity and secularisation.

Of European countries, France is certainly the one most affected by the lack of priests. It is therefore not surprising that for more than twenty years now we find celebrations led by members of these communities left priestless; these assemblies are known as Sunday celebrations in the absence of a priest, which some people interpret as 'in expectation of a priest'; others prefer to speak of celebrations led by lay people.'

A testimony
It is good to hear the authentic voice of first-hand experience:

'Fr Joseph Gelineau, 65, a Jesuit, and known above all for his musical compositions, has served as parish priest at Ecuelles, Sein-et-Marna, for some ten years. He guides efforts to make baptised lay people aware of their responsibilities and to form living communities. He tells us, 'One of the decisive reasons for coming to Ecuelles was the existence of Sunday celebrations led by local Christians. Increasingly, I was called on to help in training lay people to do this, and I failed to see how I could do this competently unless I was myself involved in this recent situation. Introduced shortly before by my predecessor, the celebrations by Christians without a priest represented a notable change in pastoral policy. Up until then, the tendency had been to bring the faithful from the small villages together in 'centres'. Firstly because there was a lack of priests; then because it seemed preferable to give an image of a more living Church in these centres rather than in almost empty churches. But this policy of grouping soon led to the Church 'deserting' the villages. It was those who were most deprived who suffered most: the poor, the children, the elderly, the marginalised. ... Once again preference was given to a Christian elite who were aware of their rights and enjoyed social autonomy. Another observation: coming together in urban centres is necessary for commerce, work, business, leisure activities. But for 'family matters', or 'religious matters', the opposite is true: people are looking for regional roots, places of 'memory'.'

Towards new ministries
Evangelisation and listening to the word was the beginning for Gelineau:

'When I arrived, I had one specific proposal, convinced as I was that everything begins with the Word of God: a weekly evening to 'read' the Bible passages for the coming week. Thus the kernel of committed members (twenty or so) was knit together in the gospel and in prayer. Moreover, they formed the 'pastoral council' of the five parishes.'

Gelineau goes on to tell us of his search for new ministries: 'The unavoidable decrease in priests in service over a relatively long

period, once it is re-situated in the wider framework of a profound change in the image of the Church in society, inevitably
calls – among other things – for a search for new ministries.'

To conclude, let us listen to Fr Gelineau's insight gained on the
anvil of experience: 'I should like to make three observations:
(i) The existence of Christian ministry is, by its nature, community-centred and collegial. Indeed, the lay leaders wish to be
responsible in solidarity before the bishop and the community.
They don't want to return to the 'monarchic' clerical image of
days past.
(ii) There is no longer any discrimination between the sexes in any
service, and we cannot re-introduce it (for example, a rejection of
the diaconate if there are not also deaconesses).
(iii) Prior theoretical training for the ministry in terms of theology
and the Bible are of little effect. Those concerned must exercise
these ministries if they are to understand what they are all about
and they must seek to train themselves.'

9. Woman priest: the pastoral assistant[19]

Context: Switzerland
The context in Switzerland, as in the USA, is that of priestless parishes. The emerging pastor can be part of a team in a cluster of
parishes or working on his or her own as a pastoral administrator.
'The number of priests in Switzerland has greatly diminished
over the last twenty years. Around 16% of parishes have no resident priest ... Moreover, the clergy is ageing. On the other hand,
parallel to this severe decrease in the clergy, a large number of lay
people now bear pastoral responsibility in the Church.'

The role of 'woman priest'
The pastoral district of Birrfeld, in the canton of Argau, forms part
of the parish of Windisch which covers five communes and brings
together some 2,000 Catholics out of a total population of 6,000.
Of these 2,000 Catholics, 1,500 are foreigners (75%), the highest

proportion of all of Switzerland. At the head of this pastoral district is a woman who has the title of pastoral assistant. Baptisms, first communions and confirmations are carried out at Windisch, but for almost everything else it is the Church of Birrfeld which serves as the parish, in particular for Sunday worship – in which at least eleven languages are used – and these services are conducted by the pastoral assistant, whom many people call *Pfarrerin*, which in English could best be translated as 'woman priest.'

10. Christian village animateurs [20]

Context: Luzon, The Phillipines
The magician on the motorbike
We finish our trip around the world in the Phillipines. 'It can safely be said that in the Phillipines, parishes and ecclesial communities are generally priest-centred. This is clearly the case in a local diocese where a priest says up to 15 Masses a day. How does he accomplish the trick? Proper timing and a motorcycle. He rushes from one chapel to another (who time their services fifteen minutes after the other). The priest makes it at the *Sanctus* and jumps on his motorbike at the *Pater Noster*. The magic works.'

This story seems almost unreal. How far removed this idea of priesthood is from priesthood in the early Church, where the community provided its own priests.

New concept of Church
We get a very interesting example of a transition from a priest-centred parish to a lay-centred one in the prelature of Infanta:

'Whereas, in general, liturgical celebrations and evangelisation in the communities are suspended for as long as no priest is assigned, many exceptions exist. In the prelature of Infanta, for example, the people, inspired by a particular concept of Church, responded creatively to the lack of priests. During the first Diocesan Pastoral Conference (1973) the priests, sisters and laity attending expressed their conviction that the responsibility for evangelisation rests primarily with the community for the baptised, with or without priest. Historically there were Christian communities before the presence of priests. The baptised had to be made aware again of their duty as evangelisers. The focus therefore was not on the lack of priests but on how to enable the faithful from Christian communities to evangelise those communities. The priority became the lay-leader-formation programme.'

The parish structure militated against pastoral care: 'A problem encountered in implementing this vision was the structure of the parishes, which were created for administrative purposes, regardless of whether there was a community alive to the faith or not. The shift was made from territorial parishes to existing Christian communities. A given territorial parish was divided into different subcentres which equalled a cluster of *barangays* (villages) contiguous to one another. With the help of trained lay leaders, people became organised around the Word of God and celebrated paraliturgies.'

How do Christian village *animateurs* operate? 'An example on the occasion of Easter might illustrate this. On Ash Wednesday there is a common celebration in the parish church with the blessing of the ashes. The lay ministers of the different sub-centres take these ashes to their centres and hold a para-liturgy with the imposition of the ashes. On Holy Thursday, the Mass of the Last Supper is held in the parish church, then the lay ministers take the Sacred Species to their own sub-centres and hold their para-liturgy with vigil before the eucharist. Lay ministers of the eucharist take care of the weekly, and even at times, daily communion of the sick. These ministers are mainly men, but women are not excluded. Baptism is generally administered by the priest, but an increasing number of lay ministers, after preparing couples for marriage, officiate at marriages. Some bishops have questioned this practice of designating lay persons to assist at marriages, despite the fact that Canon Law provides for it.'

The role of the priest

In the new ecclesial situation, the role of the priest becomes more that of minister to ministries, with a greater emphasis on his ministerial rather than managerial responsibilities: 'Unless there is a very strong and clear priority, the priest might even leave on Sundays, leaving it up to the laity to celebrate the Word of God and to distribute communion. Therefore, a continuing pastoral formation of priests is essential. Nor does this approach save the priest from a great deal of the priestly ministry, despite the fact that the laity take over some of his tasks. On the contrary, it multiplies his work in terms of a ministry which is not only something quantitative or haphazard, but a ministry which is programmed and prepared. Valuable time becomes available to conduct recollections and retreats.'

'In this process, catechists are not only important to teach the doctrines or to assist in pastoral activities. The emphasis is on them being models of Christian living. Hence the fact that some of them are engaged in the temporal sphere of organising farmers, fishermen and tribal communities.'

Christian community development

Lay ministries are being developed and the media used intelligently to evangelise and apply the gospel to everyday life. 'A significant contribution to the training of lay leaders and in organising Basic Christian Communities is the existence of a Church-owned local radio station. A Bible school has been on the air since 1975. This programme consists of co-ordinators who facilitate and of groups listening in the different sub-centres. The course is not geared towards individuals but towards listening communities and this has always been considered essential. The course itself has a simple dialogical format, usually between a priest and a lay person with the Word of God for the following Sunday as the subject matter. When the radio programme ends, the listening group takes over with the help of the co-ordinator, who makes sure that the message has been understood. Then the group relates this to their own situation, and if there is a need for action they make their own resolutions.'

Conclusion: new hope

Looking at ministry worldwide was a most hopeful and exhilarating experience for me. New and emerging ministries all over the world – many different and exciting but also very alike. Why? Because they are coming out of the same mentality – the mentality of Jesus. They are inspired by the same spirit – the Holy Spirit. They are in answer to the same needs – the human, social and spiritual needs of the People of God – sometimes survival needs! They are all part of a gospel response and most have been fashioned on the anvil of personal suffering, personal instincts and often personal survival!

Not everywhere, but in many areas, in what seemed like death and doom we see resurrection and new life and new hope. Out of 'dry bone' situations, new ministries are flourishing. This can be seen in Africa, Asia, America North and South, and, to a lesser extent, in Ireland.

Notes

1. 'Parishes without a resident priest', *Pro Mundi Vita Studies*, No 12, November 1989, Leuven, p. 2.
2. Ibid.
3. Ibid., p. 4.
4. Ibid., p. 5.
5. Ibid., p. 2.
6. Ibid., p. 3.
7. Ibid.
8. Ibid., see pp. 6-14.
9. Ibid., see pp. 14-19.

10. Ibid., see pp. 19-21.
11. Edward L Cleary, op. cit., p. 104.
12. 'Parish without a resident priest', pp. 22-25.
13. Ibid., see pp. 25-27.
14. Peter Gilmore, *The Emerging Pastor*, Sheed & Ward, Kansas City 1986, p. 4.
15. Ibid., p. 103.
16. Ibid., pp. 51, 54.
17. Ibid., p. 4.
18. 'Parish without a resident priest', pp. 28-32.
19. Ibid., p. 32.
20. Ibid., pp. 37-41.

CHAPTER 15

A New Beginning:
Themes and Recommendations

'... experience teaches that the only way to foresee the future is to prepare it in the present.'[1]

PART I: FACING REALITY

Over the past two years as a senior research fellow in the Department of Social Science at UCD, I have put together my reflections on the role of the priest and, by extension, the role of the Church and the role of the gospel in post-1960s Dublin and Ireland. I have done that reflection in the context of my experience as a priest in four different parishes over a twenty-five year period – Killester, Bayside, Sean McDermott Street, Bonnybrook. So my reflection is based on the realities of life in two middle-class suburbs, one large, mostly working-class suburb, and on the realities of life of inner city Dublin in a low income parish. This book is a reflection on practice.

It is also a reflection on the Ireland of today, the Ireland which the priest and the Church is called to serve and humanise. This is an Ireland of new challenges and contradictions, an Ireland where greed fights need, where might challenges right, and where in a population of three and a half million people, one million have slipped below the poverty line.

A corporate response
Having completed the reflection and put together its major themes and implications in the last chapter, I see my task as, in a sense, completed. From the start, I saw my research and reflection

as a beginning, a tool for others, a platform on which priests, pastoral workers, Church leaders, and hopefully, the People of God and other people of goodwill might build. My work is the work of one person and so is limited in terms of expertise, vision and possible outcome. What is needed to transform the Church and the Ireland of today is a corporate response by all the People of God and other people of goodwill. Hopefully, my research will add a new ripple to the stream of renewal which is already going on in the Church and in many parishes and religious communities. Hopefully also, it will make some small contribution towards making a better, more just and equitable society in Ireland.

A prophetic response

At its core, my study is about the role of Christ in the world. Why? Because the role of the priest, the role of the Church and the role of the gospel are, all three, about representing Christ, or being sacraments of Christ in the world. Christ instituted Church and priesthood to preach the gospel, to be his witnesses in the world, his Body and his 'words' through the ages. Hence my primary criterion for judging the role of the priest and the Church in this study is, in the words of Paul VI, 'faithfulness to the gospel and faithfulness to people.'[2] The priests and the Church through the ages, are called to preach the gospel, to be faithful to it, to be renewed by it and to make a gospel or prophetic response as Christ's representatives in the world.

The Church and the priests today, as they approach the end of the second millennium and the beginning of the third, are called to make a prophetic response to the needs of the people today, especially the less well off. Facing reality means facing reality as Christ would, though no priest or bishop or Church could do so as radically or as faithfully as Christ. The world and the Ireland of today badly need a gospel analysis and a gut gospel response from the Christian Churches and Christian people. Christ is calling the Churches of today to be promoters of justice, equality and human dignity in the midst of inequality, marginalisation and exclusion.

Pope John XXIII's response to the Church's needs in calling the Second Vatican Council was a prophetic response. So was that of the Latin American Bishops to the Latin American reality at Medellin and Pueblo. The response of John XXIII was an individual prophetic response but that of CELAM was a corporate one. Both are important. A prophetic response that I found very interesting was that of the 'Kairos' theologians in South Africa.[3] They saw three different 'theologies' in operation with regard to the problem of apartheid in South Africa:

(i) 'State Theology' (which) is simply the theological justification of the *status quo* with its racism, capitalism and totalitarianism. It blesses injustice, canonises the will of the powerful and reduces the poor to passivity, obedience and apathy.'[4]

(ii) 'Church theology' which expresses 'the official opinions of the Church, with their theological assumptions.'[5]

(iii) 'Prophetic theology' which 'speaks to the circumstances of this crisis and is clearly and unambiguously taking a stand.'[6]

In Ireland, as in other countries, all three 'theologies' are in operation. Christ and the needs of the marginalised and the poor are always calling for a prophetic response.

Difficulty of a prophetic gospel response

Will we get a gospel or prophetic response from the Church to the needs of today at the end of the second millennium? If we do, it will be difficult. It will hurt as it hurt Jesus. It will be resisted by vested interests, the powerful and the forces of evil. A prophetic response is more a conflictual than a consensus one, but it is one that leads to life and hope and resurrection.

A prophetic Church response: a paradox?

In a sense we are dealing with paradox here. How can Jesus the 'saint' be represented in the world by sinners? Or as Dalrymple[7] says:

'The sort of man that Jesus was, and what he was put to death for, poses a problem for the Church in every age. The problem is embedded in the fact that the Church is a two-thousand-year-old

270

institution whose task is to conserve the teaching of Christ down the centuries. How does a (large) conservative institution keep alive the message of a radical reformer? How does the establishment we call Church represent Jesus who was a critic of the Church establishment of his day and was actually put to death by that establishment?'[8]

Alliance of throne and altar?
Dalrymple heightens the paradox when he says that: 'The Church as a whole likes to work for the alliance of throne and altar ... (whereas) he was an outspoken prophet, an enemy of compromise. He clashed with religious authorities, because he did not like their compromising position. He was, it seems, in his style of life everything that the average Christian is not: itinerant, prophetic, risky, poor, uninterested in either his civil or religious status.'[9]

Dalrymple ends by saying that Christ knew he was building his kingdom through human beings, that the Church is often unfaithful to Christ, but that it is always called to renewal, to be a credible sign of Christ in the world.[10]

To face reality or not?
Facing reality is never easy but it is important. Consensus is often easier than conflict, but the needs of the people and the call of the gospel often demand more. I am challenged, other priests and all Christians are challenged, to face reality and to make it a better reality for all. That is the reality which this book is attempting to face up to.

What are we at?
What are we priests at in the name of God? Are we at management and control or ministry and community? Are we at maintainance or mission? Are we ministers of baptism or ministers of Bingo to fight inflation? Are we priests facing reality or facing extinction?

What are we priests and people at in Ireland? Will the Churches of Ireland in the Third Millenium be museums and heritage centres or will they have made a radical and successful transition to the Ireland of industrialisation, urbanisation, pluralism and choice? Will the youth of Ireland be athiestic or gospel-centred in the Third Millenium?

Whither Ireland in the Third Millenium? Will Christianity be swallowed up by capitalism and the economic model of society? Will local government disappear and will rural Ireland become a wildlife preserve? Will Church and State preside at the requiem of rural Ireland in the Third Millenium with M. Delors and Mr McSharry saying the prayers at the graveside? Will the growth of poverty, unemployment and emmigration go hand in hand with the growth of wealth as they did in the second half of the twentieth century? Or will the Irish people fight back?

PART II: SOME THEMES AND IMPLICATIONS

1. The gospel and society

This book is primarily about the relationship of the gospel and society. That is what the role of the Church is about and the role of the priest. Some implications of this theme for the gospel and the Church are the need for:

(1) in-depth analysis of the social reality;

(2) renewing and restructuring the Church at national, diocesan and parish levels to be a better instrument of the gospel and the promotion of justice, love and peace;

(3) moving from a 'wall-to-wall Catholicism' type Church to being Church in a pluralistic society;

(4) an examination of the implications of the clash of the capitalist economic model of society with the Christian model.

2. The Church

Another core theme is the meaning of Church and the re-definition of Church at Vatican II. This 'twentieth century revolution in the Church' has two major implications:

(i) The re-definition of goals and roles in the Church.

(ii) Restructuring of Church organisation to reflect a more colle-

(iv) A decision needs to be made as to who will be the priests of the future.

7. Irish society: the reality

This is the major theme of Chapters 1, 2, 3, 4, and 5. My experiences in Sean McDermott Street and the Ireland of the 1960s-90s. Many paradoxes or anomalies in Irish society. Great poverty alongside great wealth – twenty-sixth richest nation in the world (OECD); one third of population below the poverty line (ESRI).

Growth in wealth from 1960s to 1990 and growth in unemployment at the same time. Free education for all yet lack of access for the disadvantaged. A small population (three and a half million) and great resources of people, scenery, land, yet huge emigration.

Implications
(1) Growth of alienation among the 'have nots'.
(2) Good leadership in Church and State has the potential for solving major social problems and giving a life of dignity, relative prosperity and peace to all our people.
(3) The need for support of community development by Church and State.
(4) The need for integrated development.

8. Major social problems

Some of the larger, recurring social problems in the 1960s-90s: poverty and marginalisation, emigration, unemployment, centralisation and erosion of democracy, alienation, violence, growth of greed.

Implications
The need for:
(1) creative, courageous and prophetic leadership at national level;
(2) a minimum wage;
(3) the re-definition of work;
(4) local government reform;
(5) corporate and prophetic responses from within the Christian Churches at the macro and micro level.

PART III: RECOMMENDATIONS FOR THE IRISH CHURCH

1. A National Synod

That the Irish Hierarchy, in conjunction with the National Conference of Priests of Ireland (NCPI), organise a National Synod of the Irish Church in the 1990s to prepare the Irish Church for the third millennium.

Aims:
(1) Participation of the laity in the Church.
(2) Analysis and evaluation of the Irish social reality and of the Irish Church as an instrument of evangelisation and pastoral care in the third millennium.
(3) Corporate goal-setting and policy-making for the Irish Church in the third millennium.
(4) Renewal of the Church.

2. A National Pastoral Policy

That the Irish Hierarchy, as leaders of the People of God in Ireland, develop a National Pastoral Policy and Plan, in consultation and partnership with the People of God, which would give direction and inspiration to the Irish Church and people in the 1990s and third millennium.

3. Ministry and priesthood (National level)

That the National Conference of Priests of Ireland (NCPI) undertake a study of ministry and priesthood for today and tomorrow, based on the New Testament, and the needs and charisms of the Church today.

4. The Irish social reality

That the NCPI and the CMRS undertake a study and analysis of the Irish social reality in the 1990s, in the light of the gospel and the needs of Irish society, in order to focus the Irish Church on the basic needs of people, especially the less well off.

5. A prophetic theology

That the Irish Theological Association and the Irish Biblical Association reflect on the Irish social reality in the light of prophetic theology, as the Kairos theologians did in South Africa, and produce, on an intermittent or on-going basis, their reflections and proposals for a more Christian and gospel-based Irish Church and society.

6. Prophetic individuals and groups

That the Irish religious orders, male and female, continue to review their charisms, their role and their forms in Irish society, in the light of prophetic theology, and so give a renewed corporate and prophetic response to need, especially that of youth and the less well off.

7. Diocesan bishops

That diocesan bishops convene a diocesan synod or synods in the 1990s to prepare the local Church for the third millennium by making it a better instrument of evangelisation and pastoral care.

Aims: The same as for National Synod but in relation to individual dioceses.

8. Parish assemblies

That the bishops request all the parish priests of their dioceses to convene Parish Assemblies during the 1990s to look at the needs of the parish, and that the bishops provide appropriate diocesan support for such renewal where needed or requested.

9. Role of parish

That a study of the parish today be undertaken under the following headings:
The reality(ies);
The aims;
The problems;
The issues.

Aim: To critique parish, to improve parish and to develop alternative models (to parish) of evangelisation and pastoral care.

10. Ministry and priesthood (Diocesan level)
That a study of ministry and priesthood be undertaken by groups of clergy and laity in their diocese, as suggested in No 4 above at the national level.

11. The role of the priest
That priests in the diocese and in religious orders, of varying age and pastoral experience, be encouraged to respond to the findings of this book, e.g. by seminars, working papers, studies, study groups.

12. The role of the laity
That lay organisations like Pobal and the Commission for the Laity and other groups of lay people respond to this book and make an input into Church policy at national, diocesan and local level.

Notes
1. Pope John Paul II, *Address to Conference on Aids*, Rome 1989.
2. Pope Paul VI, *Evangelisation Today*, No. 5.
3. *A Challenge to the Church*, CIIR and BCC, London 1985.
4. Ibid., p. 6.
5. Ibid., p. 11.
6. Ibid., p. 18.
7. John Dalrymple, *The Cross a Pasture*, DLT, London 1983.
8. Ibid., p. 20.
9. Ibid., p. 20-22.
10. Ibid.